The Lawyer's Guide to Family Business Succession Planning

A Step-by-Step Approach for Lawyers, Business Owners, and Advisors

Gregory Monday

AMERICAN**BAR**ASSOCIATION

Business Law Section

Cover design by Catherine Zaccarine.

© 2020 American Bar Association. All rights reserved.

No part of this publication may be reproduced, stored in a retrieval system, or transmitted in any form or by any means, electronic, mechanical, photocopying, recording, or otherwise, without the prior written permission of the publisher. For permission contact the ABA Copyrights & Contracts Department, copyright@americanbar.org, or complete the online form at http://www.americanbar.org/utility/reprint.html.

Printed in the United States of America.

23 22   5 4 3 2

ISBN: 978-1-64105-691-5

Discounts are available for books ordered in bulk. Special consideration is given to state bars, CLE programs, and other bar-related organizations. Inquire at Book Publishing, ABA Publishing, American Bar Association, 321 N. Clark Street, Chicago, Illinois 60654-7598.

www.shopABA.org

To Stephanie Monday, MFA, JD, my spouse and
soul partner in life and all that lies beyond,
and
to our children, Alexander, Peri, and Nicholas,
my reasons why.

Contents

Acknowledgements

In writing this book, as in all my professional endeavors, I received great support and encouragement from my law firm, Reinhart Boerner Van Deuren s.c. In particular, I appreciate the support of members of firm management, including Jerome Janzer, J.D, Albert Orr, J.D., Lawrence Burnett, J.D., Lynn Stathas, J.D., and Jennifer D'Amato, J.D. Also, the content of this book reflects work for family businesses on which I regularly collaborate with my Reinhart colleagues, especially Christine Rew Barden, J.D., Wendy Rusch, J.D., David Sisson, J.D, and David Palay, J.D. I also received special assistance on the text and editing from Reinhart colleagues Jacqueline Held, Emily Gellings, Carol Schmitt, Karlee VanLaanen, and Alexandra Rechek (formerly with Reinhart). Thank you to Steve Pullara, CPA, for key advice on content. Thank you to the publisher, American Bar Association, and especially Richard Paszkiet, of the ABA, who had the idea for this book, asked me to write it, and has been with me at every stage of the project. Given this opportunity to publicly thank people, I also wish to acknowledge the invaluable, professional and personal, support, advice, and assistance I have received throughout my career as a family business lawyer from my mentors, David G. Walsh, J.D., Harvey Temkin., J.D., and Richard Langer, J.D. Thank you to my family business clients; I hope this book reflects how much I value their trust and appreciate the opportunity to work with them. Thank you to my parents, John and Judy Monday, for their DNA, their love, and their unabashedly biased faith in me. Most important, I thank my wife Stephanie Monday, M.F.A., J.D., and our children, Alexander, Peri, and Nicholas, for their love and encouragement and all the fun.

Introduction

This book is written for lawyers who represent family businesses and their owners, but this material can be read, understood, and used by family business owners and their other key advisors. The purpose of this book is to provide lawyers with a complete, thoughtful, step-by-step approach to family business succession planning. While the book is structured for family business succession planning, it is not just an organizational tool. Each part of the book also provides substantive guidance, insights, and resources that will help lawyers advise the owners, design the structures, and draft the documents to produce an effective, appropriate, and thorough succession plan for a family business.

The Case for a Family Business Succession Practice

A lawyer who practices in the areas of business law or estate planning and works with closely held companies or their owners can substantially enhance his or her practice (while making a positive impact on society) by developing the ability to assist family businesses with their succession planning needs.

The market for family business succession planning is vast. Some sources report that almost 90 percent of private companies in the United States are family owned,[1] and family businesses may be uniquely constituted to compete for market share going forward.[2] Even if the target client for family business succession planning is defined as a subset of family businesses, the number of potential clients is huge. Family businesses that are owned by the founder or a descendant of the founder with plans to pass ownership of the business to another family member may constitute up to half of all U.S. businesses.[3]

Family businesses are chronically underserved with respect to succession planning. According to a 2017 survey by PwC, 44 percent of family business respondents said that succession would be a major challenge over the next five years, and only 23 percent said that they had in place a robust, documented succession plan.[4] These numbers are consistent with what family business lawyers typically observe. Although family business owners are often blamed for this deficiency, their advisors also may be at fault. At least, in many cases, business owners cannot engage in quality succession planning unless their advisors lead them through the process. If the lawyer for a family business can offer a succession planning process that is well-organized, systematic, and presented in a way

---

1. Joseph H. Astrachan & Melissa Carey Shanker, *Family Businesses' Contribution to the U.S. Economy: A Closer Look*, Fam. Bus. Rev. 16.3 (2003) at 216.

2. *See, e.g.,* Josh Baron, *Will the 21st Century Belong to Family Business?*, Harv. Bus. Rev. (March 28, 2016), *available at* https://hbr.org/2016/03/why-the-21st-century-will-belong-to-family-businesses.

3. Astrachan & Shanker, *supra* note 1 at 216.

4. PwC, "The Missing Middle: Bridging the Strategy Gap in US Family Firms," (2017) at pg. 14. (A copy can be obtained at https://www.pwc.com/us/en/private-company-services/publications/assets/pwc-family-business-survey-us-2017.pdf).

that lay people can understand, most family business owners are appreciative and committed to engaging in thorough succession planning. This book will help enable lawyers to offer that kind of process.

Competition in this practice area is slight and often ineffective. The conventional opinion is that family business owners will not engage in succession planning because they are too busy, or they do not want to face their own mortality, or they want to remain indispensable, or it is too difficult. Many lawyers seem to accept these narratives and then create a self-fulfilling prophecy by ignoring the succession planning need in the market. In most cases, however, the only true impediment to family business succession planning is that it *is* too difficult for the owners to do it without the guidance of a proper advisor. Unfortunately, lawyers who have been discouraged from committing to a family business succession practice may not have the skills or experience to provide the necessary guidance. These lawyers may approach family business succession planning on an ad hoc basis, often providing services that are limited by a practice silo, such as estate tax planning or business organizations. This book will help lawyers provide guidance for succession planning that addresses all of the relevant legal practice areas and thus will help remove many of the difficulties that prevent family business owners from addressing their succession planning needs.

Family business succession planning can build a strong, broad, and lasting relationship between lawyers and clients. Family business succession planning, of necessity, allows a lawyer to engage with the highest levels of decision makers in a family business, often on a very personal level. Therefore, if the lawyer's firm provides other legal services for businesses, it is natural that a relationship built on these foundations would allow the family business lawyer to offer the assistance of his or her colleagues in other practice areas as the clients' other legal needs may arise. Family business succession planning also can create a relationship of trust between the lawyer and the next generation of owners and managers. As a result, a lawyer's relationship with a client built on family business succession planning may last the lawyer's entire career.

Representing family business clients and helping sustain their success is a worthy pursuit. By some measures, family businesses produce more than 60 percent of U.S. gross national product and employ more than 60 percent of the U.S. workforce.[5] The values and sense of mission with which family businesses are imbued can produce better products and services and can provide a more rewarding place for talented individuals to work.[6] Family businesses can be great citizens in their communities,[7] and many family business owners generate goodwill for their businesses and cohesion in their families through the use of private foundations and other charitable giving projects.[8]

---

5. ASTRACHAN & SHANKER at 217.

6. *See, e.g.,* Baron, *supra* note 2; according to the advocacy group Family Enterprise USA, family businesses generate 64 percent of U.S. GDP and account for 65 percent of domestic employment, and 78 percent of new job creation stems from family businesses (http://policyandtaxationgroup.com/estate-tax/family-businesses-jobs-economic-activity-and-charity/).

7. On a 2018 survey conducted by the Policy and Taxation Group of Family Enterprise USA, respondent family business owners on average made 79 percent of their charitable contributions to local charities, *available at* https://policyandtaxationgroup.com/estate-tax/2018-family-businesses-survey-reveals-commitments-challenges-concerns/.

8. *See, e.g.,* Charles Paikert, *Stepping Up at Family Firms,* N.Y. TIMES (Nov. 8, 2012).

In summary, a lawyer can establish a lifelong practice that is rewarding, both personally and professionally, by helping family businesses create, maintain, and implement a succession plan for ownership and management using an approach like the one described in this book.

How to Use This Book

This book is organized as an outline of a business succession project from beginning to completion, roughly in sequential order. Note, however, that many of the topics or tasks are interdependent, and therefore each section of the outline should be considered or anticipated throughout the project.

The book explains a particular, step-by-step process for family business succession planning. If a lawyer reads the book from start to finish, he or she should develop a very good understanding of how family business succession planning can be organized and accomplished. Each section explains key concepts, identifies issues that need attention, suggests one or more approaches, provides practice tips, and, when needed, refers the reader to other resources for further assistance on a particular task or substantive subject matter.

In addition, lawyers can refer to particular sections of the book to supplement their thoughts on a particular topic, provide instruction to colleagues or staff, or copy language that can be used to explain a concept to clients and their other advisors. The primary target for the process described in the book is a business that is owned by one or more family members who intend to pass ownership of the business to one or more of their descendants. However, many of the book's sections are relevant to business owners who may be considering an alternative disposition of their ownership interests. For example, many of the sections can help a lawyer assist business owners who plan to sell their interests to non-family insiders or who have not yet decided on a particular exit strategy.

This book provides a template for the lawyer. A family business lawyer may use the structure of this book as an outline for a family business succession project to help guide and organize the lawyer, the lawyer's staff, the business owners, and the business owners' other advisors. At the beginning of the representation, the lawyer may draft an outline of the project in the form of a memo, such as in a form similar to appendix A. Then, from time to time, the lawyer may update the memo as he or she and the business owners focus their thinking about the project, make key decisions, and complete particular tasks.

This will keep the project organized and will better coordinate the efforts of the various people working on the project. It will help the business owners understand the whole project and the importance of each element of the project in context. It also will help the business owners budget the time and financial resources needed to complete the project. Finally, it will help the owners appreciate the work that has been accomplished throughout the course of the project, particularly in proportion to the time and money spent.

As the family business succession project develops, the lawyer and his or her staff also can create a checklist, in a form similar to appendix B, to further enhance organization and efficiency. This tool translates the business succession planning outline into a specific list of tasks and documents for each part of the project, including the name of the party responsible for the task or document, the projected or effective date of the task or document, and the individuals who need to sign the documents to give them effect.

Sections 2.3.6 and 2.3.7 discuss in greater detail how to create the project outline and checklist, and subsequent chapters provide specific material for the outline and the checklist.

This book applies to a range of owner exits. This book will be most helpful with respect to businesses that are family owned and operated, particularly if the controlling owners intend to transfer ownership to successors within the family. However, even if the controlling owners have decided not to keep the business in the family, or if they are undecided about successor ownership, many of the tools and insights provided in this book will help the family business lawyer work with the controlling owners to plan their exits and the next stage of their family's economic collaboration. For example, if the business is to be sold to a buyer outside the family, this book contains material that will be helpful to sellers who intend to use the sales proceeds to transition to new family ventures, a collective family investment vehicle, or a family office. Similarly, this book will be helpful if the controlling owners are considering a transfer of ownership to a group of non-family insiders or even an employee stock ownership plan.

Key Concepts and Highlights

A few comments about key concepts and the foundations of the approach described in this book will help put the subsequent material in the proper context.

This approach to family business succession planning is based primarily on good business governance. The core of this book is about designing business governance structures that will apply to successor owners and managers, and then establishing contractual relationships and estate planning mechanisms that are consistent with those business governance structures. This book gives priority to governance, because governance can have a great impact on the immediate profitability of a business, as well as on stability in transition, success of future managers, and value for future owners.

This approach also emphasizes providing mechanisms for future owner exits that are fair and not disruptive. Some successor owners, particularly those in the minority, may wish to exit ownership and use the value of their interest for other purposes. A good family business succession plan will include a comprehensive buy-sell agreement with mechanisms and procedures for minority owner exits that are fair to the exiting owner but do not impair business operations or necessary growth.

This approach does not lead with estate tax planning, but it makes estate planning much more effective. After the lawyer has helped the client design governance structures and exit mechanisms that will apply to successor owners, it will be much easier for the present owners to decide how to allocate their ownership interests in their estate planning and to engage in strategies to manage estate taxes that do not create a cause of controversy among successor owners and other estate beneficiaries. This approach, however, also adopts a cautious attitude toward lifetime wealth transfers to avoid leaving current owners with a diminished quality of life as a result of overly aggressive estate tax management techniques.

This approach to family business succession emphasizes the use of rules, process, and structure, rather than trying to dictate substantive results. This means two things.

First, this approach attempts to create well-defined ownership and governance structures to enable owners and managers to make good business decisions, but it does not attempt to dictate what those business decisions might be in substance. Similarly, this approach is intended to create equitable governance structures and well-defined ownership rights that help avoid acrimony (or at least litigation) among successor owners who may have discordant personalities, incompatible value systems, or conflicting interests and objectives, but it does not involve a substantive exploration of family dynamics, family history, or individual psychology. Under this approach, if successor owners disagree about the business, regardless of the individual emotional or personal historical causes, they will have equitable means of resolving those disagreements and a structure for co-existing as owners, or they may exit ownership on terms that are fair to them and the other owners.

Chapter One:
Overview

This chapter provides a brief overview of the family business succession planning process as this book describes it. The overview summarizes, in roughly sequential order, each step in the succession planning process. This is intended to provide the reader with a quick reference and context for the substantive chapters that follow.

1.1 Commencing the Engagement

To begin the engagement, the lawyer meets with the family business owners and elicits information to determine the particular need for succession planning. The lawyer follows up with (a) engagement letters that identify the clients and allow the clients to consent to conflicts of interest that tend to be present when a lawyer represents family businesses and their owners, and (b) a request for additional information and documents needed in the business succession planning process. The lawyer drafts and provides to the clients an outline of the business succession project, and the lawyer and staff create a checklist of tasks to be performed and documents to be drafted as part of the project.

1.2 Valuation

Early in the succession planning process, the lawyer and the owners try to determine the subjective value of business ownership for each potential successor owner. This will help the lawyer and the owners produce a succession plan that is better tailored to the needs and expectations of the successors. Also, the owners should consider obtaining a reliable, formal opinion of the objective fair market value of the business (or the companies and properties that the business comprises). That formal opinion can provide guidance throughout the business succession planning process and can be utilized to structure transfers of ownership interests to successor owners.

1.3 Business Continuation Plan

The lawyer helps the owners develop a business continuation plan that consists of procedures and mechanisms designed to minimize disruption to business operations if leadership of a key owner-operator were suddenly terminated by disability or death before business succession could be accomplished. The business continuation plan is drafted in memo form, but it is supported and implemented by provisions added to the business's governing documents and the key owner's estate-planning documents.

1.4 Business Structure

The lawyer, in collaboration with the owners and their accountants and tax advisors, discusses whether to reorganize the business structure to better serve succession objectives and to capture opportunities to make ownership of the business more tax-efficient, at present and in the future. Restructuring the business also can improve governance and management processes, income and cash flow allocation, and protection of the owners' assets.

1.5 Governance Structures and Ownership Rights

The lawyer helps the owners amend governing documents to create governance structures that best serve the business and the owners, considering needs at present, during transition to successor ownership, and after succession is complete. At the same time, the lawyer and the owners create or update owner buy-sell agreements to appropriately restrict transfers of ownership but provide orderly exits for both present and successor owners, especially those who own a minority position. This is the proper time to decide on means of funding owner exits.

1.6 Key Contracts

The lawyer helps the owners negotiate and execute contracts with family members and other affiliated parties that clearly define their economic relationships, such as employment agreements, leases, loans, and contingent obligations, to avoid misunderstandings under successor ownership. The lawyer also helps the owners identify contracts between the business and third parties, such as loan facilities or manufacturers' agreements, that might be impaired or breached by ownership succession, and, if possible, helps the business renegotiate these contracts. If the contracts cannot be renegotiated or amended, then the lawyer helps the owners develop a plan to mitigate the potential adverse effects.

1.7 Senior Owners' Estate Plans

The lawyer helps senior owners update their estate planning documents with very specific provisions about who will succeed to ownership and how the ownership rights and benefits will be allocated and held when the senior owners die. Further, the lawyer helps the senior owners design trusts to protect family business interests as they pass to the successor owners and other estate beneficiaries.

1.8 Senior Owners' Exit and Retirement Planning

The lawyer collaborates with the senior owners' financial planners and advisors to develop appropriate retirement plans and other resources to satisfy the senior owners' economic needs and objectives, to supplement or backstop the return they will receive from their exit from the business. Some of this planning may involve retirement benefits offered through the business and some may be independent of the business. The lawyer then helps the senior owners structure a buyout at retirement that meets their remaining financial needs in retirement and that is properly secured and guaranteed to protect their ability to recover payment even if the business defaults under successor ownership.

1.9 Lifetime Wealth Transfers

The lawyer assists the senior owners with lifetime wealth transfers to their beneficiaries, as appropriate for purposes of business succession and (if applicable) to manage potential estate tax liability. Over time, the senior owners can transfer substantial amounts of wealth free of transfer tax liability. (Throughout this book, the term "transfer taxes" generally means gift taxes, estate taxes, and generation-skipping transfer taxes.)

Chapter Two:

Commencing the Engagement

This chapter describes how to begin a family business succession engagement. Although the chapter discusses the material in the context of a new client engagement, most of the material is also relevant to commencing a business succession project for a family business with which the lawyer already has a client relationship.

2.1 Ethical Rules Governing the Family Business Lawyer

Often, the primary lawyer for a family business is also the primary lawyer for the owners, a "trusted advisor" or "counselor" who provides legal services to the business, engages in estate planning with the owners, and sometimes serves as a fiduciary on a business board or as a trustee. It is important, however, to identify and address the ethical obligations and complications that arise when the lawyer represents the business, the owners, and other family members.

The trusted advisor or counselor model has advantages, because a lawyer for a family business also must be concerned with the family members' personal estate planning. Also, family business owners may get frustrated when lawyers insist on separate representation for family members involved in common transactions when no disagreements are apparent.

The following discussion relies on the ABA's Model Rules of Professional Conduct and the Comments to those rules. The lawyer for a family business should compare these rules to the corresponding state ethical rules that govern his or her practice and the relevant commentary to determine how they might warrant variance from the practices described in this section.

The ABA Model Rules accommodate the trusted advisor or counselor role, but they also identify times when the lawyer must narrow the representation and obtain informed conflict waivers or withdraw from involvement in a matter. In many cases, it may be most effective for the lawyer to represent the business, first and foremost, with an understanding that he or she can also represent owners and their family members, except when a conflict arises that cannot be waived.

2.1.1 The Lawyer as Trusted Advisor

The ABA Model Rules recognize that a lawyer's relationship with a client can reach beyond mere legal considerations and may involve representation of multiple related persons.

First, under the ABA Model Rules section "Counselor," Rule 2.1 (titled "Advisor") states the following: "In rendering advice, a lawyer may refer not only to law but to other considerations such as moral, economic, social and political factors, that may be relevant to the client's situation."[1]

The Comments to this Rule elaborate on this theme in a manner relevant to the family business lawyer. They observe:

> Advice couched in narrow legal terms may be of little value to a client, especially where practical considerations, such as cost or effects on other people, are predominant. . . . Purely technical legal advice, therefore, can sometimes be inadequate. It is proper for a lawyer to refer to relevant moral and ethical considerations in giving advice.[2]

Further,

> Matters that go beyond strictly legal questions may also be in the domain of another profession. Family matters can involve problems within the professional competence of psychiatry, clinical psychology or social work; business matters can involve problems within the competence of the accounting profession or of financial specialists. Where consultation with a professional in another field is itself something a competent lawyer would recommend, the lawyer should make such a recommendation. At the same time, a lawyer's advice at its best often consists of recommending a course of action in the face of conflicting recommendations of experts.[3]

These Comments reflect the reality that a lawyer's representation of a client may become an immersion in the client's business and personal affairs, rather than a simple commoditized transaction for the provision of legal services.

In addition, the ABA Model Rules provide specific permission for concurrent or dual representation of a business and its principals, subject to conflicts of interest rules and other ethical obligations. "A lawyer representing an organization may also represent any of its directors, officers, employees, members, shareholders or other constituents," subject to the rules governing conflicts of interest.[4]

2.1.2 Concurrent or Dual Representation

When a lawyer is retained to assist with family business succession planning, the primary client should be the business, because much of the legal work will involve business organization, governance, contracts, financing, and other matters that primarily serve the best interests of the business and its owners collectively. To engage in thorough succession planning, however, the lawyer may need to represent multiple affiliated companies that constitute the business, and may need to represent the business owners and their family members and fiduciaries to provide them with legal services, such as estate planning, assistance with trust administration, and tax advice.

On any particular part of a family business succession project, the lawyer's relationship with multiple clients among the business, ownership, fiduciaries, and family may

1. Model Rules of Prof'l Conduct R. 2.1 (2016).
2. *Id.* R. 2.1, cmt. 2.
3. *Id.* R. 2.1, cmt 4.
4. *Id.* R. 1.13(g).

constitute concurrent representation or dual representation. Concurrent representation occurs when the lawyer represents multiple clients in separate matters. In contrast, dual representation (also referred to as "joint" or "common" representation) occurs when the lawyer represents multiple clients in the same matter.

Concurrent or dual representation of affiliated clients, however, can lead to conflicts of interest. ABA Model Rule 1.7 sets forth the general rule regarding conflicts of interest. It states that "a lawyer shall not represent a client if the representation involves a concurrent conflict of interest," unless the conflict can be waived and the clients properly waive the conflict.[5] The Comment to this Rule provides a straightforward approach.

> Resolution of a conflict of interest problem under this Rule requires the lawyer to: 1) clearly identify the client or clients; 2) determine whether a conflict of interest exists; 3) decide whether the representation may be undertaken despite the existence of a conflict, i.e., whether the conflict is consentable; and 4) if so, consult with the clients affected . . . and obtain their informed consent, confirmed in writing.[6]

In short, a family business representation will require the lawyer to identify client conflicts and obtain informed written consents. The lawyer also should remain sensitive to the effect that changing circumstances have on the consequences of conflicts of interest.

2.1.2.a Identify the Client

Identifying the client in the context of family business planning can be complicated, because a business often consists of multiple companies, each company has a collection of individuals in ownership and management, and, obviously, a family is a group of individuals. The ABA Model Rules and Comments provide guidance on representing institutional clients and even representing a group of people with a common interest.

2.1.2.a.i Business Entity as the Client

According to the ABA Model Rules, "A lawyer employed or retained by an organization represents the organization acting through its duly authorized constituents."[7] The Comments explain, "An organizational client is a legal entity, but it cannot act except through its officers, directors, employees, shareholders and other constituents. Officers, directors, employees and shareholders are the constituents of the corporate organizational client."[8] To be clear, however, the Comments add, "A lawyer who represents a corporation or other organization does not, by virtue of that representation, necessarily represent any constituent or affiliated organization, such as a parent or subsidiary," except as the client and the lawyer might otherwise agree.[9]

Therefore, when a lawyer represents a family business, his or her engagement documents should specify which company or companies the lawyer is representing. Also,

---

5. *Id.* R. 1.7(a).
6. *Id.* R. 1.7, cmt 2.
7. *Id.* R. 1.13(a).
8. *Id.* R. 1.13, cmt. 1.
9. *Id.* R. 1.7, cmt. 34.

when interacting with constituents of an organizational client, the lawyer has a responsibility to communicate that the lawyer's representation of the organization does not extend to the constituent, particularly when the interests of the organization and the constituent may diverge.

> There are times when the organization's interest may be or become adverse to those of one or more of its constituents. In such circumstances the lawyer should advise any constituent, whose interest the lawyer finds adverse to that of the organization of the conflict or potential conflict of interest, that the lawyer cannot represent such constituent, and that such person may wish to obtain independent representation. Care must be taken to assure that the individual understands that, when there is such adversity of interest, the lawyer for the organization cannot provide legal representation for that constituent individual, and that discussions between the lawyer for the organization and the individual may not be privileged.[10]

The lawyer must be vigilant and exercise discretion on this point. "Whether such a warning should be given by the lawyer for the organization to any constituent individual may turn on the facts of each case."[11]

2.1.2.a.ii   Group of Persons as Clients

The Comments also recognize that a lawyer may be retained by a group of persons who wish to establish a business entity. In such a case, the lawyer cannot be retained by the entity, at least until it is created, and thus may represent some or all of the persons forming the entity as individual clients who have a common interest.

> [C]ommon representation is permissible where the clients are generally aligned in interest even though there is some difference in interest among them. Thus, a lawyer may seek to establish or adjust a relationship between clients on an amicable and mutually advantageous basis; for example, in helping to organize a business in which two or more clients are entrepreneurs, [or] working out the financial reorganization of an enterprise in which two or more clients have an interest. . . . The lawyer seeks to resolve potentially adverse interests by developing the parties' mutual interests. Otherwise, each party might have to obtain separate representation, with the possibility of incurring additional cost, complication or even litigation. Given these and other relevant factors, the clients may prefer that the lawyer act for all of them.[12]

To be clear, any representation in which the client is more than one person will require the lawyer to obtain each client's consent to conflicts of interest after consultation, even if the clients' interests are apparently wholly aligned in the matter at hand.

2.1.2.a.iii   Constituents of a Business Entity as Clients

Finally, the ABA Model Rules also recognize that, subject to conflict of interest rules, the lawyer for a company or business may also represent "any of its directors, officers,

---

10. *Id.* R. 1.13, cmt. 10.
11. *Id.* R. 1.13, cmt.11.
12. *Id.* R. 1.7, cmt 28.

employees, members, shareholders or other constituents."[13] Again, conflict waivers may be required.

2.1.2.b Determine Whether a Conflict Exists

When a lawyer represents more than one person in a family business succession project, a conflict of interest virtually always exists. However, it is important to understand the nature of the conflict to decide whether the clients can waive the conflict, to more effectively consult with the clients about consenting to the conflict, and to be alert for when circumstances change that might render the conflict no longer manageable even with consent.

The ABA Model Rules describe two types of conflict:

The first type of conflict is referred to in the Comments as "adverseness." It exists if "the representation of one client will be directly adverse to another client. . . ."[14] This type of conflict is fairly easy to recognize. The Comments explain:

> Directly adverse conflicts can . . . arise in transactional matters. For example, if a lawyer is asked to represent the seller of a business in negotiations with a buyer represented by the lawyer, not in the same transaction but in another, unrelated matter, the lawyer could not undertake the representation without the informed consent of each client.[15]

The example in the Comments arises often in the family business context when the family business redeems one of the owners, such as a retiring senior owner. In such instances, the lawyer representing the business as the buyer in the redemption might represent the seller with respect to estate planning and other personal matters not directly pertaining to the terms of the redemption. Other instances in which a conflict based on adverseness may arise may involve a lawyer representing the business with respect to employment agreements with family members, leases of family-owned real estate or equipment, and reimbursement agreements for family member guaranties of business debt.

The second type of conflict is more subtle. Even if there is no direct adverseness, a conflict may exist if "there is a significant risk that the representation of one or more clients will be materially limited by the lawyer's responsibilities to another client, a former client or a third person or by a personal interest of the lawyer."[16]

The Comments elaborate on this second type of conflict with respect to current clients.

> Even where there is no direct adverseness, a conflict of interest exists if there is a significant risk that a lawyer's ability to consider, recommend or carry out an appropriate course of action for the client will be materially limited as a result of the lawyer's other responsibilities or interests. For example, a lawyer asked to represent several individuals seeking to form a joint venture is likely to be materially limited in the lawyer's ability to recommend or advocate all possible positions that each might take because of the

---

13. *Id.* R. 1.13(g).
14. *Id.* R. 1.7(a)(1).
15. *Id.* R. 1.7, cmt. 7.
16. *Id.* R. 1.7(a)(2).

lawyer's duty of loyalty to the others. The conflict in effect forecloses alternatives that would otherwise be available to the client. The mere possibility of subsequent harm does not itself require disclosure and consent. The critical questions are the likelihood that a difference in interests will eventuate and, if it does, whether it will materially interfere with the lawyer's independent professional judgment in considering alternatives or foreclose courses of action that reasonably should be pursued on behalf of the client.[17]

The Comments also elaborate on conflicts arising out of a lawyer's duties unrelated to representation of a current client. "In addition to conflicts with other current clients, a lawyer's duties of loyalty and independence may be materially limited by responsibilities to former clients . . . or by the lawyer's responsibilities to other persons, such as fiduciary duties arising from a lawyer's service as a trustee, executor or corporate director."[18]

2.1.2.c Decide Whether the Conflict Is Consentable

The ABA Model Rules hold that some conflicts are "consentable," which means that the lawyer may proceed with concurrent or even dual representation, notwithstanding the conflict, if the clients consent. In contrast, some conflicts are not consentable and cannot be waived, such as when the clients' interests are "antagonistic" to one another.[19] "[T]he question of consentability must be resolved as to each client."[20]

"Consentability is typically determined by considering whether the interests of the clients will be adequately protected if the clients are permitted to give their informed consent to representation burdened by a conflict of interest."[21] In the transactional context, a conflict is generally consentable if "the lawyer reasonably believes that the lawyer will be able to provide competent and diligent representation to each affected client."[22] "Competent representation requires the legal knowledge, skill, thoroughness and preparation reasonably necessary for the representation."[23] With respect to diligence, the Comments say:

> A lawyer should . . . take whatever lawful and ethical measures are required to vindicate a client's cause or endeavor. A lawyer must also act with commitment and dedication to the interests of the client and with zeal in advocacy upon the client's behalf.[24]

Even if the lawyer decides that the conflict is consentable, based on the standard described above, the lawyer may not accept the representation unless "each affected client gives informed consent, confirmed in a writing signed by the client."[25]

---

17. *Id.* R. 1.7, cmt. 8.
18. *Id.* R. 1.7, cmt. 9.
19. *Id.* R. 1.7, cmt. 28.
20. *Id.* R. 1.7, cmt. 14.
21. *Id.* R. 1.7, cmt 15.
22. *Id.* R. 1.7(b)(1).
23. *Id.* R. 1.1.
24. *Id.* R. 1.3, cmt. 1.
25. *Id.* R. 1.7(b)(4).

2.1.2.d Consult with the Clients Affected

The ABA Model Rules suggest that when a lawyer asks the clients to consider whether to consent to concurrent or dual representation, notwithstanding a conflict, the lawyer should discuss the effect of the representation on the clients' expectations about the lawyer's role as an advocate.

> Informed consent requires that each affected client be aware of the relevant circumstances and of the material and reasonably foreseeable ways that the conflict could have adverse effects on the interests of that client. . . . The information required depends on the nature of the conflict and the nature of the risks involved.[26]

When asking clients for consent, it is prudent for the lawyer to advise them that they may wish to consult with separate counsel before consenting and when reviewing the written confirmation that the lawyer sends.

2.1.2.d.i Concurrent Representation

When the conflict arises out of a concurrent representation, such as when the interests of the lawyer's client in a transaction are directly adverse to the interests of someone whom the lawyer represents as a client in an unrelated matter,

> The client as to whom the representation is directly adverse is likely to feel betrayed, and the resulting damage to the client-lawyer relationship is likely to impair the lawyer's ability to represent the client effectively [in the other matter]. In addition, the client on whose behalf the adverse representation is undertaken reasonably may fear that the lawyer will pursue that client's case less effectively out of deference to the other client, i.e., that the representation may be materially limited by the lawyer's interest in retaining the current client.[27]

The lawyer should discuss and resolve these concerns with clients when seeking their written consent for the concurrent representation.

2.1.2.d.ii Dual Representation

Dual representation can be advantageous for an appropriate group of persons.

> In some cases the alternative to common representation can be that each party may have to obtain separate representation with the possibility of incurring additional costs. These costs, along with the benefits of securing separate representation, are factors that may be considered by the affected client in determining whether common representation is in the client's interests.[28]

Nevertheless, clients should also be apprised of the disadvantages of dual representation.

---

26. *Id.* R. 1.7, cmt. 18; *see also* the definition of "informed consent" at MODEL RULES OF PROF'L CONDUCT R. 1.0(e).

27. *Id.* R. 1.7, cmt.6.

28. *Id.* R. 1.7, cmt. 19.

The Comments summarize the concepts that clients must understand to provide informed consent to dual representation. "When representation of multiple clients in a single matter is undertaken, the information must include the implications of the common representation, including possible effects on loyalty, confidentiality and the attorney-client privilege and the advantages and risks involved."[29]

First, dual representation, more so than concurrent representation, creates the possibility that the lawyer's duties to any one client will be limited by duties to other clients in the dual representation. When conferring with the clients about dual representation, the lawyer should articulate this possibility.

> When seeking to establish or adjust a relationship between clients, the lawyer should make clear that the lawyer's role is not that of partisanship normally expected in other circumstances and, thus, that the clients may be required to assume greater responsibility for decisions than when each client is separately represented. Any limitations on the scope of the representation made necessary as a result of the common representation should be fully explained to the clients at the outset of the representation.[30]

Further, dual representation compromises attorney-client privilege.

> With regard to the attorney-client privilege, the prevailing rule is that, as between commonly represented clients, the privilege does not attach. Hence, it must be assumed that if litigation eventuates between the clients, the privilege will not protect any such communications, and the clients should be so advised.[31]

Similarly, dual representation compromises the lawyer's duty of confidentiality.

> As to the duty of confidentiality, continued common representation will almost certainly be inadequate if one client asks the lawyer not to disclose to the other client information relevant to the common representation. This is so because the lawyer has an equal duty of loyalty to each client, and each client has the right to be informed of anything bearing on the representation that might affect that client's interests and the right to expect that the lawyer will use that information to that client's benefit. . . . The lawyer should, at the outset of the common representation and as part of the process of obtaining each client's informed consent, advise each client that information will be shared and that the lawyer will have to withdraw if one client decides that some matter material to the representation should be kept from the other.[32]

Fortunately, the Comments recognize that keeping some information confidential between dual clients may not always require the lawyer to withdraw. The Comments concede that "[i]n limited circumstances, it may be appropriate for the lawyer to proceed with the representation when the clients have agreed, after being properly informed, that the lawyer will keep certain information confidential."[33]

---

29. *Id.* R. 1.7, cmt. 18.
30. *Id.* R. 1.7, cmt. 32.
31. *Id.* R. 1.7. cmt. 30.
32. *Id.* R. 1.7, cmt. 31.
33. *Id.* R. 1.7, cmt. 31.

2.1.2.e Confirm Consent in Writing

The Comments specify that consent must be in writing, but not necessarily signed by the client.

> Such a writing may consist of a document executed by the client or one that the lawyer promptly records and transmits to the client following an oral consent. . . . (Writing includes electronic transmission.) If it is not feasible to obtain or transmit the writing at the time the client gives informed consent, then the lawyer must obtain or transmit it within a reasonable time thereafter. . . . The requirement of a writing does not supplant the need in most cases for the lawyer to talk with the client, to explain the risks and advantages, if any, of representation burdened with a conflict of interest, as well as reasonably available alternatives, and to afford the client a reasonable opportunity to consider the risks and alternatives and to raise questions and concerns. Rather, the writing is required in order to impress upon clients the seriousness of the decision the client is being asked to make and to avoid disputes or ambiguities that might later occur in the absence of a writing.[34]

The best practice is to obtain consent signed by the clients involved, and, when one of the clients involved is a business organization, to obtain consent on behalf of the organization from someone other than one of the other clients involved in the conflict (or the consent of all the owners).

2.1.3 Payment of Owners' Lawyers' Fees by Business

When a lawyer for a family business provides personal estate planning advice and other legal services to owners and their family members, it may be appropriate for the business to pay the lawyers' fees, particularly when the services relate to business ownership, governance, or succession, such as managing personal liability for business-related obligations, marital property planning to protect ownership interests, and planning exits for owners that create a smooth transition of leadership and operations.

Payment of individual owners' lawyers' fees by the business, however, is a potential conflict of interest and thus requires informed consent. The ABA Model Rules state:

> A lawyer shall not accept compensation for representing a client from one other than the client unless: (1) the client gives informed consent; (2) there is no interference with the lawyer's independence of professional judgment or with the client-lawyer relationship; and information relating to representation of a client is protected as required by [confidentiality rules].[35]

The Comments explain that "[t]hird-party payers frequently have interests that differ from those of the client, including interests in minimizing the amount spent on the representation and in learning how the representation is progressing. . . ."[36]

---

34. *Id.* R. 1.7, cmt. 20.
35. *Id.* R. 1.8(f).
36. *Id.* R. 1.8, cmt. 11.

> If acceptance of . . . payment from any other source presents a significant risk that the lawyer's representation of the client will be materially limited by the lawyer's own interest in accommodating the person paying the lawyer's fee or by the lawyer's responsibilities to a payer who is also a co-client, then the lawyer must comply with [conflict of interest rules] including determining whether the conflict is consentable and, if so, that the client has adequate information about the material risks of the representation.[37]

Therefore, if a family business entity will be paying the fees for legal work that the lawyer does for its owners and other affiliated parties, especially if the business entity is also a client, the lawyer should do the following:

- Confer with the client to ensure that the lawyer and the client both believe that the arrangement will not undermine the lawyer's independent judgment about the client's interests.
- Confirm client consent in writing.
- As a matter of contract, obtain the business entity's agreement to be liable for payment of the fees, signed by an agent of the business entity other than the individual client.
- Set up a separate client file to keep the client's individual information confidential and apart from files of the payor entity and other affiliated clients.
- When billing work for the client, consider sending the service detail only to the client and a separate summary statement without the service detail to the payor entity, to further maintain the client's confidentiality.

2.1.4 Lawyer Serving on a Client Board or as a Trustee

When a lawyer representing a family business also serves on a governing board for one or more of the business's entities or serves as a trustee of a trust that holds family business interests, conflicts and other complications, such as confidentiality issues, can arise. Therefore, the lawyer should approach such service with caution.

The Comments discuss how to approach board service.

> A lawyer for a corporation or other organization who is also a member of its board of directors should determine whether the responsibilities of the two roles may conflict. The lawyer may be called on to advise the corporation in matters involving actions of the directors. Consideration should be given to the frequency with which such situations may arise, the potential intensity of the conflict, the effect of the lawyer's resignation from the board and the possibility of the corporation's obtaining legal advice from another lawyer in such situations. If there is material risk that the dual role will compromise the lawyer's independence of professional judgment, the lawyer should not serve as a director or should cease to act as the corporation's lawyer when conflicts of interest arise. The lawyer should advise the other members of the board that in some circumstances matters discussed at board meetings while the lawyer is present in the capacity of director might not be protected by the attorney-client privilege and that conflict of interest considerations might require the lawyer's recusal as a director or might require the lawyer and the lawyer's firm to decline representation of the corporation in a matter.[38]

---

37. *Id.* R. 1.7, cmt 13.
38. *Id.* R. 1.7, cmt. 35.

If the lawyer serves on a client business's board, it is the lawyer's duty to advise the board when the lawyer believes the conflict of interest caused by the lawyer's service on the board might require the lawyer to resign from the board or might require the business to retain independent counsel.

The lawyer should apply a similar analysis to conflict and confidentiality issues if the lawyer serves as a trustee of a trust that holds family business interests.

2.1.5 Future Conflicts of Interest

The ABA Model Rules allow a lawyer to ask a client to consent to a future conflict of interest, but the effectiveness of an advance waiver is based on facts and circumstances. Of course, the threshold question is whether the future conflict, if it arose, would be consentable. If it would be consentable, then the next question is whether the client provided informed consent, considering that it is more difficult for a client to understand the risks of a future conflict than a present conflict. The Comments explain:

> The effectiveness of [advance] waivers is generally determined by the extent to which the client reasonably understands the material risks that the waiver entails. The more comprehensive the explanation of the types of future representations that might arise and the actual and reasonably foreseeable adverse consequences of those representations, the greater the likelihood that the client will have the requisite understanding. Thus, if the client agrees to consent to a particular type of conflict with which the client is already familiar, then the consent ordinarily will be effective with regard to that type of conflict. If the consent is general and open-ended, then the consent ordinarily will be ineffective, because it is not reasonably likely that the client will have understood the material risks involved. On the other hand, if the client is an experienced user of the legal services involved and is reasonably informed regarding the risk that a conflict may arise, such consent is more likely to be effective, particularly if, e.g., the client is independently represented by other counsel in giving consent and the consent is limited to future conflicts unrelated to the subject of the representation.[39]

Finally, if a future conflict arises and it is not consentable, then an advance waiver is ineffective, regardless of the client's informed consent.

2.1.6 Network of Family Business Lawyers

In many instances described in this section 2.1, ethical rules or best practices would involve use of separate counsel by a client or its affiliates and constituents. Therefore, it is in the best interests of a lawyer's clients (and advantageous to the lawyer's family business law practice, generally) for the lawyer to identify other lawyers in the community who are particularly qualified to work with family businesses.

There are many, many family-owned businesses in the United States, and in many cases the legal needs of those businesses and their owners cannot be met by one law firm. In other words, there is plenty of work to go around. Developing a family business law practice is not likely to be a zero-sum competition with the other lawyers in a particular geographic market. In fact, many advisors to family businesses are likely to complain that

---

39. *Id.* R. 1.7, cmt. 22.

their clients' succession-planning legal needs are grossly underserved. Further, some lawyers have a greater capacity than others for the kind of patience, empathy, and sensitivity that serving family business clients can require, especially for an approach that minimizes disruption to family relationships.

For these reasons, it should improve, not threaten, a family business lawyer's practice to develop a network of qualified lawyers at other firms to whom the lawyer can refer family business clients or their owners when the lawyer has a conflict of interest.

2.1.7 Checklist of Engagement Letters with Conflict Consents

A lawyer's specific approach to engagement letters and conflict waivers will be governed by the ethical rules of the lawyer's jurisdiction. To the extent that those rules are consistent with the ABA Model Rules discussed above, the lawyer's engagement letters with a new family business client should include the following features:

• **Identity of the client or clients.** An engagement letter should be precise when identifying the client. If the client is a business organization, the letter should identify the organization and should address whether its affiliated organizations are included in the representation. If the lawyer wishes to include affiliated organizations, he or she should consider whether this raises issues of confidentiality or conflicts of interest, particularly if the affiliated organizations are not owned by the same owners in the same pro rata percentages.

• **Dual or concurrent representation.** If the lawyer is to represent more than one client among the family business and its owners, the engagement letter should be specific about whether the lawyer is representing them as part of a dual (joint) representation or representing them concurrently. For example, the lawyer might represent a corporation and its owners concurrently, but among the owners, the lawyer might represent spouses jointly. The lawyer should use separate engagement letters for each client, except those whom the lawyer is representing on a dual (joint) basis.

• **Privilege and confidentiality.** If the lawyer is representing multiple clients among the family business and the owners, the engagement letters should explicitly establish whether the lawyer is to keep one client's information confidential as against another client in the group. This is easier to do and more understandable with clients that the lawyer is representing concurrently, rather than jointly. As to clients that the lawyer is representing jointly, the engagement letter should warn them that if a dispute arises among them regarding the subject matter of the joint representation, the evidentiary attorney-client privilege may not apply to prevent the lawyer from disclosing their confidential information in litigation of the dispute.

• **Conflict of interest consent.** The engagement letters should identify conflicts of interest and obtain informed consent. In cases of dual representation or concurrent representation, each engagement letter should briefly explain why a conflict exists and identify the clients it involves, describe the risks that the conflict causes, but advise that the lawyer has concluded that the clients may consent to the conflict (i.e., it is a "consentable" conflict). The letter should suggest that the client may wish to seek the advice of independent counsel before consenting to the conflict. (If a business organization has in-house counsel, he or she can provide that independent review and advice for the organization as client.) The letter should state that the client's signature on the engagement letter will be confirmation of the client's consent to the conflict.

- **Future conflicts of interest consent.** If the lawyer believes that circumstances might arise in the future under which he or she might be asked to represent a person whose interests have become adverse to the client, then the engagement letter may include language providing advance consent to such conflicts. For example, if the lawyer represents the business and an owner concurrently, then at some point the business might ask the lawyer to represent it in negotiations for a redemption of the owner's interest. To obtain advance consent, the engagement letter should describe the types of conflicts that might arise and the clients that might be involved. The letter should try to provide some specificity to the types of future conflicts the consent is targeting. In particular, the letter should specify whether the advance consent is only for matters of transactional adversity or is intended to include adversarial proceedings. (See also section 2.1.5 for a discussion of the elements of an effective advance consent.) The letter should suggest that the client seek the advice of independent counsel before providing advance consent. The letter should state that the client's signature on the letter will be confirmation of the client's advance consent to future conflicts that are otherwise consentable.

- **Source of payment.** If a third party will be paying the client's legal fees, the engagement letter should seek to obtain the client's informed consent. For example, the parties may intend that one of the family's business organizations will be paying lawyers' fees incurred by family members for their estate planning or premarital planning or asset protection planning. In such cases, the engagement letter should treat the fee arrangement as a conflict of interest as described in the preceding paragraph. (See also section 2.1.3 for a discussion of the elements of an effective consent to this type of fee arrangement.)

- **Service in other fiduciary capacities.** Usually, at the time of the initial engagement, it will be too early to determine whether the lawyer will also serve the clients in other capacities, such as serving as a member of a governing board or as a trustee of family trusts, but if that is already contemplated, it may be prudent to address such potential conflicts of interest in the engagement letter or in correspondence delivered contemporaneous with the engagement letter.

- **Signatures.** The lawyer should obtain each client's signature on the applicable engagement letter. Although an individual who is a client may sign an engagement letter on behalf of a business organization, an authorized, independent agent of the organization should sign the letter to confirm any consents to conflicts of interest, including conflicts arising out of the organization's agreement to pay the individual client's lawyers' fees. If there is no such independent agent, then the lawyer should obtain the consent of all the owners—for example, by a written record of action signed by all the owners.

Although it is a best practice to obtain signed engagement letters and consents to conflicts, the ABA Model Rules, as noted above, allow some of these items, such as current conflict waivers, to be "confirmed in writing" without a client signature. For example, under the ABA Model Rules, a lawyer could have a thorough discussion of conflicts of interest at an initial meeting of the clients, obtain their spoken informed consent, and then confirm that consent in correspondence to the clients that also reiterates the substance of the discussion that satisfied the requirement that the clients be "informed" when providing consent. Such correspondence also should indicate that the lawyer advised them that they could consult with separate counsel before consenting to the conflict.

Engagement letters with conflict waivers are not the last word on conflicts of interest. The lawyer has a continuing duty to consider whether, due to a change in circumstances, a new conflict of interest has arisen warranting further informed consents, or a conflict of interest to which the clients have consented is no longer consentable.

2.2 Initial Client Meeting

Sometimes a family business client will contact a lawyer for assistance with family business succession, specifically. Sometimes, however, a family business succession project arises when the business owners are seeking assistance with estate planning or transfer tax planning. In the latter instance, the business owners (and the referral source) may not understand that proper estate planning for a family business owner usually requires attention to business succession planning.

Therefore, the initial meeting with the business owners is an opportunity to obtain information but also an opportunity for the lawyer to describe an approach to business succession planning and explain how it will enhance estate planning and improve the economic and practical effect of wealth transfers to the business owners' children or other beneficiaries. Even if the business owners intend to sell the business outside the family when they retire, it is important to address business continuation planning (see chapter 4) and retirement planning (see chapter 9). Further, the principles and structures used in business succession planning also can be used after the sale of a family business to govern the collective investment and ownership of the sales proceeds, perhaps as a family limited partnership or LLC or as part of a family office.

2.2.1 Establish Trust

In an initial meeting with owners of a family business, it is important for the lawyer to establish trust early on. When a lawyer is asking family business owners to retain him or her for multi-generational business succession planning, the lawyer is asking them for trust with their family relationships and, in many cases, a business that constitutes most of their wealth and their primary source of income. They are more likely to appreciate the lawyer's skills as an advisor if they first decide that they can trust the lawyer as a person.

In fact, research seems to indicate that trust (or warmth) is generally "the most important factor in how people evaluate you" upon first impression.[40] Competence comes second. This may be because people need to know that a person can be trusted to use his or her skill to help them, not to harm them.

Therefore, rather than rattling off credentials and launching into technical topics that demonstrate expertise, the lawyer should start the meeting by letting the clients tell the lawyer about their family and their business and respond to their comments on a personal level. It is okay if the meeting meanders at the beginning.

At the same time, the lawyer should be trying to determine whether the clients are a good fit for the lawyer. A family business client is generally a client for the lifetime of a

---

40. Jenna Goudreau, *A Harvard Psychologist Says That People Judge You Based On 2 Criteria When They First Meet You*, BUS. INSIDER (Jan. 16, 2016).

lawyer's practice, and the lawyer may be asked to serve the business and the family in fiduciary capacities apart from legal representation, such as serving as a member of a governing board or as trustee, directing party, or trust protector under the owners' estate plan. Therefore, it is important that the lawyer trusts and respects the clients and that their principles and objectives are not in opposition to the principles and standards that the lawyer may wish to maintain for his or her practice.

A further way for the lawyer to establish mutual trust is to make a site visit to the clients' primary facilities and, if possible, take a guided tour, without charging the clients for the time. This is usually a meaningful gesture to the clients, and it can provide the lawyer with valuable insights by making the business more specific and distinct in the lawyer's mind. It also gives the lawyer an early opportunity to meet key personnel and some of the other family members who work in the business. While the lawyer is on site, he or she can also review or pick up some of the business records needed for the representation. (See section 2.3.3.)

If the clients were referred to the lawyer by one of their other advisors, the advisor's participation in the initial meeting might also help to establish the clients' trust. Lawyer-client confidentiality is unique, however, and the presence of a third party might inhibit the clients' willingness to discuss sensitive matters. Also, if the clients perceive the referral source as someone who is trying to sell them a product, the referral source's presence at the meeting may impair the clients' faith in the lawyer's motives or the lawyer's allegiance to the clients.

2.2.2 Learn about the Business, the Owners, and the Family

The lawyer should not assume that the clients have properly assessed their needs with respect to business succession. If the initial meeting is too focused on a specific legal task that the clients believe to be the goal, the lawyer may fail to obtain information that will help him or her better assess the clients' needs and opportunities.

Therefore, the first part of the initial meeting should be a broad and somewhat free-form discussion touching on the following items:

- The substance of the business, its history, its current ownership, its estimated value, and its future;
- The owners' family members, those who are in the business and those who are not, and some sense of family dynamics both within the business and outside of that context;
- The senior owners' personal financial resources, currently and projected for after retirement;
- The general composition and substance of the senior owners' estate plans and any key or urgent changes that they would like to make;
- The owners' team of advisors, including those within the business; and
- The specific reasons why the clients are seeking the lawyer's help, and, in plain English, their goals and objectives for business succession and family wealth.

This discussion does not need to provide the lawyer with precise information. The lawyer will obtain more complete and more reliable information through a formal request for information and documents following the initial meeting. However, the discussion should enable the lawyer to propose a general outline for the business succession project and identify any issues that might need immediate or special attention.

2.2.3 Outline the Business Succession Process and Discuss Representation

After the discussion described above, the lawyer should have sufficient insight to outline the business succession process, tailored to fit the clients' circumstances, needs, and opportunities. The basis for this outline is the summary provided in chapter 1. The lawyer should review with the clients the items that the lawyer believes are applicable to them. The lawyer should provide a preliminary description of each item and why he or she thinks it will be important to the clients, whether it is a need or an opportunity or both.

In the preliminary outline, the lawyer should include a discussion of items that may need to be addressed by the clients' other advisors, or advisors that they have not yet retained. For example, business restructuring for tax efficiencies may need to be addressed by the clients' accountants, business valuation may need to be addressed by the clients' accountants or an independent service provider, and family dynamics may need to be addressed by a family business consultant.

With respect to family dynamics in particular, the lawyer should usually tread lightly. If the lawyer is not trained to provide family therapy, his or her approach to family dynamics should be guided by the motto, "Do no harm." In some cases, the lawyer's innate people skills, an understanding of human nature based on past experience, and dedication to a diplomatic approach may be sufficient, but the lawyer should focus primarily on establishing legal structures, contractual rights, and neutral processes that will protect the business, produce equitable results for the owners, and avoid formal adversarial proceedings, even when family dynamics are at their most volatile.

Reviewing a proposed outline of the succession-planning process also will help the lawyer and the business owners decide whom the lawyer should represent and will give the lawyer an opportunity to discuss the conflict issues, including source of fee payments, described in section 2.1.

2.3   Follow-up to the Initial Meeting

If the business owners have decided to retain the lawyer as counsel for one or more of the business entities and/or one or more of the owners, the lawyer should take the following actions to follow up promptly:

2.3.1 Engagement Letters and Conflict Consents

The lawyer should send engagement letters and seek client consent for conflicts, as described in section 2.1.7.

2.3.2 Request for Information and Documents

The lawyer should send the clients a request for specific information and documents needed to more precisely understand the clients' circumstances and to begin the work that he or she has agreed to do. The lawyer does not need original documents, but they should be reliable copies. For example, the lawyer generally should not rely on copies of legal documents that are not signed, not recorded, or do not otherwise have indicia of enforceable documents, unless he or she is intentionally seeking a draft document as a reference point. Receiving the documents in an electronic format may be the most efficient and cost-effective method.

The request will include relevant items from the list identified as Schedule A to appendix A at the end of this book.

2.3.3 Financial Disclosure Releases

The lawyer should send the clients financial disclosure forms addressed in blank. The lawyer's staff members can assist the clients in collecting the information and documents that the lawyer is seeking if the clients sign releases under which they direct their other advisors, service providers, and the custodians of their assets or financial records to provide the lawyer with information that he or she may request as the clients' legal counsel.

2.3.4 Contact with Other Advisors

With the clients' consent, the lawyer should make contact with the clients' other key advisors, particularly their accounting and tax advisors. Family business succession planning is a team effort, and clients will be able to pursue it most cost effectively and with best outcomes if the lawyer collaborates with their other advisors.

By working with the clients' other advisors and relying on them to do the work that they are better suited or better positioned to do, the lawyer can reduce the fees he or she will be charging the clients and thus reduce what might otherwise become an area of friction between the lawyer and the clients.

In fact, some of the clients' advisors or service providers, such as investment advisors or corporate fiduciaries, may be charging the clients a fixed fee for their services and therefore may be able to perform some tasks, such as collecting documents or retitling assets or even helping design retirement plans, without additional cost to the clients. By understanding and utilizing this feature of the clients' advisor team, the lawyer can demonstrate sensitivity to the economics of family business ownership and thus make it more likely that the clients will be willing to complete a thorough and comprehensive succession plan.

Also, establishing a positive relationship with the clients' other advisors and soliciting their advice and insights will improve the lawyer's work and might help him or her avoid critical mistakes, whether mistakes of fact or mistakes involving family dynamics, or even mistakes of law or tax. When one of the clients' other advisors disagrees with the lawyer, the lawyer should not be afraid to challenge his or her own assumptions and conclusions. It may be that the other advisor's suggestion is superior, or it may be that neither approach is best and that a more creative solution is needed. If the lawyer agrees to change course based on input from another advisor, the lawyer should take the opportunity to give the other advisor credit for the insight. It should strengthen the lawyer's relationship with the other advisor and demonstrate to the client that the collaboration is effective.

2.3.5 Business Succession Planning Outline

The lawyer should draft an outline of the step-by-step process that the lawyer is proposing for the clients' business succession planning needs. A template outline is included in appendix A of this book. The template outline includes at least one paragraph for the material covered in greater detail in chapters 3 through 10 of this book. The lawyer should tailor the outline for the clients' specific circumstances. Template topics that do not apply should be removed or, if a topic is relevant but has been previously addressed, the outline should include a few words to memorialize that information.

The lawyer also should tailor the outline to meet the clients' expectations for simplicity or detail. For some clients, a detailed ten-page outline might be appropriate, such as when the business's general counsel and independent board members might be involved in the planning process. For other clients, a much shorter outline relying on bullet points and sentence fragments might be preferred, especially if the client is the busy sole owner of a company that he or she operates as chief executive and sole director.

The succession planning outline can serve the following purposes:

- Drafting the outline will help the lawyer focus his or her review of the clients' information, circumstances, and objectives to formulate a preliminary approach to the clients' business succession planning.
- The outline will describe the project for the lawyer's staff and help the lawyer begin to allocate tasks among them. The outline will serve as the basis for the checklist (described in the next section of this book).
- The outline will communicate to the clients the scope and content of the project, as well as the proposed process and sequence of tasks. Further, the outline may include commentary that is intended to educate the clients regarding the importance and relevance of various topics, as well as some of the legal, financial, or practical considerations involved.
- The outline can be provided to the clients' other advisors to get their early input and to help collaborate and coordinate with them.
- The lawyer can update the outline and recirculate it when the plan changes or becomes better defined based on new information, input from other advisors, or decisions made by the clients, and each time a set of tasks has been completed. The outline can show the changes in redline or otherwise highlight the updates. This will help keep everyone organized, and it will help show the clients the progress and accomplishments that the lawyer has helped them achieve.

The lawyer should try not to overwhelm the clients with the outline. In some cases, it may be best to present the initial outline to the clients in a face-to-face meeting so that the lawyer can help explain it and answer their questions or address their concerns immediately. Also, some situations might warrant a much shorter, abbreviated outline. For example, if a small business will pass to an only child, the outline may not need to include some of the governance material, except as it may pertain to a period when the owners are winding down their involvement or are financing the child's acquisition of ownership.

2.3.6 Checklist for Tasks and Documents

A checklist for tasks and documents can provide an additional way for the lawyer and his or her staff to keep the project organized and track its progress. (See the template of a business succession planning checklist at appendix B at the end of this book.)

The checklist can be organized with a section for each topic of the business succession outline. If that is too unwieldy, the lawyer can prepare a master checklist, but carve out separate checklists for sections that are particularly lengthy and detailed.

One form of checklist that is effective separates each topic by a banner naming the topic, such as "Business Restructuring." Under the banner, the checklist can have the following columns:

- Tab reference and item number. For example, if the Business Restructuring banner is tab C and each document or task under that banner is numbered consecutively, then each document or task can be referred to by a tab reference and item number such as C.1, C.2, C.3, etc.
- Document name and a brief description of document or task. For example, "ESBT Election, designate Gregory Family Trust as electing small business trust."
- Document number, if the word processing or document storage system that the lawyer's firm uses assigns a document number that the lawyer and staff can use to retrieve the document.
- Person responsible. This may identify a staff member who is responsible for the task of drafting the document, or it may identify one of the other advisors or service providers, such as the firm that will provide an opinion of value.
- Comments or status, to indicate whether the document is in draft form, final form, or executed, and to provide other important commentary, such as "Corporate Secretary is looking for original stock certificates."
- Signatures needed, usually next to a box that can be checked when a signature is obtained. This column should also include boxes to be checked for witnesses and notary, if needed.
- Effective date. Sometimes tasks must happen in a particular sequential order or by a particular due date. For example, articles of amendment to articles of incorporation must be filed before a corporation can issue a class of stock that the original articles did not authorize. This column will help maintain the integrity of sequence and timing when it matters.

The checklist should be updated as needed, but completed items should not be deleted. The checklist is intended to document progress, as well as identifying unfinished business. It can be useful as a record long after the tasks are all completed, especially as it indicates document numbers and effective dates. Further, the checklist can be used to help identify documents that should be included in a transaction binder or added to company record books.

Chapter Three:
Business Value

This chapter discusses business value from two different perspectives, both of which are important to determine early in the succession planning process. The first perspective considers the value of the business for each individual owner or potential successor, defined in a broad and purely subjective sense. The second perspective considers the value of the business and its ownership units, defined in an objective, economic sense as the fair market value determined by a qualified business valuation professional.

3.1 Subjective Value of Business Ownership

The subjective value of business ownership for current owners and their potential successors is based on what each individual aspires to derive from the family business. There are four primary reasons to participate in ownership of a family business: cash flow, wealth accumulation, occupation/career, and family legacy. Different owners and potential successors may prioritize these considerations differently, and some potential successors may find no particular subjective value in some (or any) of these considerations.

If the owners can determine how each owner and potential successor prioritizes these four considerations, and which of the four considerations he or she might entirely disregard, then the owners and the lawyer can more effectively tailor the business succession plan and its specific elements, such as governance structures, buy-sell agreements, and senior owner estate planning.

3.1.1 Four Reasons to Participate in Family Business Ownership

The four reasons why an individual might choose to participate in ownership of a family business can best be understood in contrast to investing an equivalent amount of wealth in passive investments, such as a marketable securities portfolio. What can family business ownership provide that other investments or uses of capital cannot provide to the same degree or cannot provide at all?

3.1.1.a Cash Flow

Cash flow is one reason to participate in a family business, especially as an active owner (i.e., an owner who is employed in the business in some capacity). Although other investments, such as publicly traded bonds and stocks, can provide cash flow to the investor, the cash flow is quite limited in form and amount, and the investor has virtually no influence over cash flow decisions. In contrast, a family business can provide income or other cash flow to family members in a broad variety of ways and amounts, determined with the input of individual owners.

For example, a family business can provide cash flow as follows:

- **Dividends or distributions of profits.** A family business can provide cash flow through payment of dividends or distributions of profits to owners in pro rata shares.

    o   Usually, a flow-through entity, such as an S corporation, an LLC taxed as a partnership, or a limited partnership, can offer the most tax-efficient means of providing cash flow to owners through a distribution of profits. In contrast, payment of dividends from C corporations historically has been suppressed by the so-called "double taxation" of such income (i.e., C corporation income incurs a tax at the entity level and then the owners incur a tax on the dividends). When corporate-level income tax rates are low in comparison to individual income tax rates, however (such as under the Tax Cuts and Jobs Act of 2017), the impact of the double taxation is reduced and payment of C corporation dividends can be a more practical means of providing cash flow to owners. (For a more detailed discussion of the tax attributes of flow-through entities versus C corporations (or LLCs taxed as C corporations), see sections 5.7.1 and 5.7.2.)

    o   In some cases, a C corporation or an LLC taxed as a C corporation or a partnership can use different classes of stock or ownership units to provide unique dividend or distribution rights to different classes of owners. For example, owners of preferred stock could be granted the right to a limited dividend that has priority over payment of dividends to owners of common stock so that they have a more predictable cash flow from dividends. (Note, however, that the use of different economic classes of ownership units in family business entities can cause unintended transfer tax consequences— for example, under Section 2701 of the Internal Revenue Code.)

- **Compensation for owner-employees.** A family business can provide cash flow to owners in the form of compensation for services provided as a full-time or part-time employee or for participation in business governance, such as membership on an advisory or governing board or family council.
- **Compensation to family of owners.** A family business can provide cash flow to a spouse or children of owners in the form of compensation for services the spouse or children render to the business.
- **Deferred compensation and benefits.** A family business can provide cash flow in the form of deferred compensation or retirement plan benefits to owners after they retire from active employment in the business.
- **Compensation for other services.** A family business can provide cash flow to non-employee owners or their family members for services provided in support of the business. For example, the family business can use the services of a non-employee owner or family member who is an accountant, attorney, real estate broker, or other service provider. Also, if a family member provides a personal guaranty of family business debt, the business can pay the family member a guaranty fee.
- **Lease payments in support of the business.** A family business can provide cash flow to family members who own real estate or equipment that the family business leases from them.

• **Loan payments, asset purchases, or redemption proceeds.** A family business can provide cash flow in return for a family member loan to the business or by purchasing assets from a family member, or in exchange for a redemption of ownership interests. In such cases, there is a safe harbor for the minimum interest rate that must be paid to avoid transfer tax consequences, but the family business may pay a higher rate that is commercially reasonable if the goal is to provide greater cash flow to the family member.

A family business is in a unique position to use and tailor these mechanisms to provide cash flow to owners and their family members. Other investments do not provide the same range of opportunities for providing cash flow to the owners and their family members and generally do not allow the investors the kind of meaningful input into cash flow decisions that is available to a family business owner.

3.1.1.b Wealth Accumulation

Wealth accumulation, or appreciation on invested capital, is another reason to participate in ownership of a family business. Although diversification in a marketable securities portfolio may lower risk, it also tends to lower potential return. Concentrated ownership of public company securities increases potential for appreciation, but usually at a level of risk that is undesirable for the investor, especially given that the average investor has little or no influence on the price or performance of public company securities.

In contrast, a family member often can invest concentrated amounts of capital in a family business with greater confidence in the potential for appreciation. Family business stock prices are not usually as susceptible to irrational market forces as publicly traded securities. Further, as a shareholder, director, or executive, the family business owner can have substantial influence on stock appreciation. Many authorities argue that privately owned businesses perform better than publicly traded companies over the long term because private company owners are less likely to emphasize short-term profits at the expense of long-term success.[1]

If the family business owner is willing to wait for a liquidation event over the long term, such as a redemption upon retirement or an eventual sale of the business to family members, employees, or a third-party buyer, then he or she may conclude that investing in the family business will provide a superior return over other investment options.

3.1.1.c Employment or Career Opportunities

Vocation is a third reason to participate in ownership of a family business. Family members often have occupational or career opportunities in a family business that would not be available to them as quickly or on terms that are as favorable in an unrelated business. For example, a family business that builds and manages hotels may provide family members with a wide range of occupational opportunities, including finance, marketing, design, legal, engineering, hospitality, restaurant/club management, and executive responsibilities. A family business also may be more willing to give its family member employees the time or flexibility they need to care for and raise their children, while continuing on their preferred employment or career track. For some family

---

1. *See, e.g.,* the discussion of the "short-termism" debate in David J. Berger et al., *Tenure Voting and the U.S. Public Company,* 72 Bus. Law. 295, 298–303 (2017).

members, basic job security and the goodwill and understanding of their employer may be all they are seeking from their employment, and they may be more likely to receive that in a business owned by their family.

3.1.1.d Family Legacy

Legacy is a fourth reason to participate in ownership of a family business. A family member who is proud of the family's business success and reputation in the community may wish to claim some share of that legacy, as a family business leader or even as a passive minority owner, or through involvement in the family's charitable activities.

3.1.2 Addressing Subjective Value

If family business owners can identify the reason or reasons why individual family members may want to participate in family business ownership and how they might prioritize those reasons, then the lawyer can help the owners create entity structures, governance systems, ownership rights, employment policies, charitable giving projects, and estate planning mechanisms intended to target and optimize the value of the business for individual family members. This process should make it easier for the owners to make decisions about succession and should make the resulting succession plan more satisfying to the owners and their successors.

The chapters that follow will refer back to this concept of individualizing business value for the owners and their family members, but the following are some simplified examples:

- If one of the owners' children is most concerned about cash flow but does not intend to seek employment with the family business, it may make sense to provide for that child to receive a lesser share of operating company ownership and a greater share of ownership in LLCs that own real estate or equipment that is leased to the operating company (and thus can provide a consistent cash flow to non-employee owners). To support that arrangement, the owners can put in place long-term lease agreements between the operating company and the LLCs that own the assets.
- If one of the owners' children is primarily concerned about employment in a friendly, flexible workplace but is not seeking an executive career, then it may be important to execute an employment agreement with that child and provide that child with a right of redemption under a funded buy-sell agreement in the event that his or her employment is terminated.
- If two or more of the owners' children expect to pursue an executive career with the business, it may be appropriate to ensure that they have representation[2] on the governing board and that the governing board has independent directors to make disinterested decisions about family member advancement and compensation.

---

2. Note that the concept of "representation" on a governing board can be confusing because, in most circumstances, every board member has the same fiduciary duties to the owners as a class and are not supposed to favor any particular owner, regardless of how the board member is appointed or elected. (See section 6.2.2.c.iv, which elaborates on this point.)

- If one of the owners' children does not want his or her capital to be invested in the family business but wants to enjoy association with the family legacy, the owners' estate plan can provide for him or her to receive a small amount of nonvoting shares and perhaps a prominent role in the family's charitable giving efforts.

Without identifying the subjective value of the family business for each potential successor, the result can be a one-size-fits-all plan, such as when the owners simply pass their ownership interests to their children in equal shares, or a winner-takes-all plan, in which control of the family business is granted to one successor who is then trusted to be fair to the other family members.

The one-size-fits-all plan can result in disputes among the successor owners because of their disparate needs or objectives and can lead to deadlocks in management or oppression of minority owners. Ultimately, such scenarios tend to result in litigation or hostile separations.

The winner-takes-all plan can lead to a disproportionate amount of the benefit of ownership accruing to the controlling successor, or, conversely, can lead to an unfair amount of the controlling successor's hard work accruing to family members who do not contribute in a meaningful way or whose input is actually counterproductive.

In contrast, a plan whose development and substance are guided by a knowledge of the subjective value, broadly defined, of the family business for each owner and successor can lead to a superior succession plan in which each owner and successor is more satisfied with his or her role in ownership and employment and in which disagreements among successor owners are rarer and are more easily resolved.

3.2 Market Value of the Business

The lawyer and the owners will be able to design a better business succession plan if they have a reliable understanding of the market value of the business.[3] Often, it is helpful to obtain a formal opinion of value from a qualified business valuation professional early in the process of developing a business succession plan. Although some business owners (and some advisors) believe that this is an unnecessary expense, if handled properly, it can be cost effective, can help avoid misjudgments in planning, and can yield a number of important benefits for the owners. Further, it may be necessary for gift tax reporting if the owners make transfers of ownership interests that may include a gift element.

3.2.1 Reasons for a Formal Opinion of Value

A formal opinion of the value of the family business can be beneficial in several important respects throughout the business succession planning process. These same benefits cannot be obtained from a mere estimate of value by the owners or from discussions with potential buyers.

---

3. For a thorough treatment of business valuation for lawyers, see JEFFREY M. RISIUS, BUSINESS VALUATION: A PRIMER FOR THE LEGAL PROFESSION (ABA 2007).

- **Realistic expectations.** A professional valuation can help the owners and their successors adopt realistic expectations about the economic benefit they could realize from joining or exiting ownership. For example, current owners can better understand how much they might receive in retirement from selling their ownership to the successors, or how much they might receive if they exit ownership for other reasons. Similarly, potential successors can better anticipate how much it might cost them to purchase a share of ownership or how it might affect the amount of other assets they might receive under the owners' estate plan if they opt out of participating in ownership.

- **Superior advice from advisors.** A professional valuation can help the lawyer and the owners' other advisors provide better advice. For example, reliable information about business value can help the owners make better decisions about levels of life insurance coverage and other mechanisms of funding redemptions or retirement, or addressing estate tax liability. Similarly, reliable information about business value can help the lawyer and the owners' accountants provide more dependable advice regarding estate planning and lifetime wealth transfers.

- **Equitable purchase price in family transactions.** A professional valuation can help ensure that family members perceive the price of ownership to be fair in transactions among them that occur as part of the succession plan or arising in the future under a buy-sell agreement. A key benefit of obtaining the assistance of a valuation professional is that he or she can assist in drafting the provisions of the buy-sell agreement that govern how purchase price is determined for ownership transactions among owners and/or successor owners. (For a more detailed discussion of purchase price provisions in a buy-sell agreement, see section 6.2.4.i.i.) Reducing uncertainty about the method of calculating purchase price is especially important if there is tension among potential successors. Often, when a family member exits ownership because of discord among the owners, valuation is the issue that leads to adversarial proceedings.

- **Accurate transfer tax planning and reporting.** If the owners are considering an immediate transfer of ownership interests as part of the business succession planning project, then a formal opinion of value of the transferred interests, prepared by a qualified valuation professional, may need to be filed with federal gift tax returns to report the transfer. The owners and their advisors will rely on that report when structuring the transaction to obtain the desired gift tax treatment. Even if the transfer is not intended to have a gift element, it may be prudent for the transferors to file federal gift tax returns to report the transfer and take the position that it did not involve a gift. If the facts of the transaction are fully disclosed on federal gift tax returns and the valuation report is filed with the returns, it should start the statute of limitations running on the ability of the Internal Revenue Service to challenge the value and attempt to impose an unwanted gift tax consequence on the transaction.[4]

- **Useful business insights.** In some cases, obtaining a formal opinion of value can provide the owners and managers with insights that may help them improve the business. This is especially likely if the opinion of value is much different from owners' expectations. In such cases, the business valuation professional may be able to help the owners and managers understand why the opinion of value is so much higher or lower than what they had assumed, and that information may help them make better decisions about operations or long-term planning. Even the numerical analyses that the valuation

---

4. IRC § 6501(c)(9) and Treas. Regs. § 301.6501(c)-1(f)(2).

professional will perform when preparing the report can reveal trends or phenomena that the owners or managers had not previously noticed.

3.2.2 Accountant's Opinion of Value

The cost of a professional opinion of value should not prevent the owners from obtaining one. It is possible that the business's accounting firm may be able to provide cost-effective valuation services. Presumably, the accounting firm will already have much of the needed information and familiarity with the business, which should create efficiencies. This can be a good option if the accounting firm employs qualified personnel. Note, however, that if the opinion of value ever became the subject of litigation, either among the owners or as part of an Internal Revenue Service challenge, the valuation personnel might be called upon to defend their work in depositions and court testimony. Even if that is a remote possibility, the owners should confirm that the accounting firm can provide litigation services before they engage the firm to prepare the valuation report.

Chapter Four:

Business Continuation Plan

This chapter discusses a business continuation plan that family business owners can develop, with the lawyer's guidance, to help avoid a disruption in business operations or damage to business value in case of the unexpected loss of a controlling owner or key owner-operator. This task arises at this point in the business succession planning process because it is a risk-management practice that the owners can adopt and then easily update as circumstances change.

In many cases, this is a stopgap measure until business succession can be properly accomplished, but it has value, it can be done simply, and it can be a learning experience for the owners, advisors, and key personnel in the business. Developing a business *continuation* plan can be done without the depth of analysis that the business *succession* process will require, but developing a business *continuation* plan will help begin a discussion about concepts and principles that will be useful later in the business *succession* planning process.

Simply put, the purpose of a business continuation plan is to provide for caretaker management of the business until the family successors are able to assume the responsibilities of leadership and ownership under a business succession plan.

4.1 The Concept

Many family businesses or business divisions are led by one of the principal owners whose daily contribution to the business is critical. (For purposes of this chapter, this person is referred to as the "Principal.") In some family businesses the Principal is the chief executive officer and chair of the board of directors, or even the sole director or managing member. A business continuation plan is a collection of measures that can be implemented immediately upon the loss of a Principal to minimize business disruption until leadership and ownership can transition to appropriate successors under a fully realized business succession plan.

4.1.1 The Risk of Losing the Principal

Upon the unexpected loss of the Principal due to death or disability, business operations may suffer a disruption. If the business does not yet have a comprehensive succession plan in place, the Principal's beneficiaries and the other owners may lose the value of their interest in the business while they try to establish new leadership, new governance structures, and new ownership agreements. Disruption to operations, and the potential loss of ownership value, can lead to discord among family members. These effects can exacerbate each other, with family frustrations mounting as business problems increase, and vice versa. Even the most well-intentioned family members may strongly disagree on how to proceed in such a crisis.

4.1.2 Managing the Risk

A business continuation plan can be a first step toward creation of a comprehensive business succession plan and can help preserve business value if the Principal dies or becomes disabled. Upon the loss of the Principal, a business continuation plan can be implemented immediately to enable the business to continue profitable operations with temporary management procedures until the owners settle on a more permanent succession arrangement. It can also address disruption to business relationships with other stakeholders, such as lenders and key personnel.

In form, a business continuation plan will consist of a memorandum describing business continuation measures and how they are to be implemented, and may include schedules and supplements that are updated from time to time. The business continuation plan likely will require corresponding modifications to the business's governing documents and the Principal's estate plan. The planning process might also identify contracts that should be changed or renegotiated to allow successful implementation of the business continuation plan.

The process of creating a business continuation plan also will identify many of the issues the owners and their successors will need to discuss to create a comprehensive business succession plan. A succession plan will substantially reduce the potential disruption of the unexpected loss of the Principal because it will remove uncertainty about succession of leadership, governance, and ownership. Even then, however, a business continuation plan will remain a useful means of addressing the most immediate problems that could arise upon the unexpected loss of the Principal.

4.2 Substance of the Continuation Plan

The following sections of this chapter discuss topics that the owners should consider addressing in a business continuation plan. It can be helpful if the lawyer provides the owners with a questionnaire or worksheet in memo form that explains a continuation plan, topic by topic, and raises questions that the owners can answer to help solicit information needed to convert the memo into the continuation plan itself. (See appendix C for a form of a business continuation plan worksheet.) This form of the business continuation plan is not enforceable or self-executing. To be most effective, it needs to be supplemented with corresponding changes to the business's governing documents, contracts, and the Principal's estate plan, as well as other specific tasks.

4.2.1 Business Structure and Ownership

To put the continuation plan in context, it should begin with an explanation of business structure and ownership. If the business has a multi-tiered organizational structure involving a parent company and one or more subsidiaries and affiliates, it may be helpful to supplement this section with a graphic illustration, such as an organizational chart, attached to the plan as a schedule. If some parts of the business, such as real estate, management companies, or vertical divisions, are held in separate entities, this section should describe their business relationship, such as leases, loans, and other contracts. These contractual relationships can also be shown on a graphic schedule. This section should also describe how each entity is owned. Ownership can also be shown on a graphic schedule, or a schedule can be attached consisting of a table of ownership for each entity.

As discussed in section 2.3.2, the lawyer will be obtaining this information early in the process of developing the succession plan, so preparing this as part of the continuation plan does not involve an additional task. However, the business structure and ownership may change as part of the succession planning process, and the completed continuation plan should be updated as that happens.

4.2.2 The Principal's Ownership Voting Rights

This section of the continuation plan states who would have authority to exercise the Principal's ownership voting rights if the Principal (a) were incapacitated or (b) died. This section must be supported by appropriate, enforceable documentation, such as powers of attorney and trust agreements, so it may be properly and immediately implemented in the event of the applicable contingency.

In most business entities, owners do not operate the entity by reason of their ownership or their voting rights. Ownership voting rights of a business entity primarily consist of the authority to elect directors (or appoint managers, if the company is a manager-managed LLC), amend governing documents, and approve a sale, merger, or other disposition or restructuring of the business. Further, ownership voting rights can be separated from beneficial, financial, or legal ownership in a variety of ways. (These concepts and distinctions are discussed in greater detail in chapter 6.)

For purposes of the continuation plan, it is important to be precise about voting rights and to distinguish them from the Principal's authority in other capacities, such as authority as a director or executive. This section of the continuation plan may need to be implemented, for example, to replace the Principal on the board, to replace the Principal as manager of an LLC, to amend governing documents to adopt new procedures that are needed on an interim basis, or to complete a transaction that requires owner consent. With those distinctions in mind, the continuation plan should address the following:

4.2.2.a The Principal's Incapacity

This section of the continuation plan should state who has authority to exercise the Principal's ownership voting rights if he or she is incapacitated, and it should explain how incapacity is to be determined. It also should identify the specific documents that grant the authority described, and the lawyer should prepare and execute those documents with the Principal. The documents that the lawyer drafts for this purpose should define incapacity and provide specific procedures for determining incapacity.

It might be that authority to exercise the Principal's ownership voting rights has already been granted under durable powers of attorney for financial matters that the

Principal has executed as part of his or her estate plan, but, upon further consideration, the Principal might conclude that such documents do not appoint the most appropriate individuals to serve as agent for these purposes, or that such documents require a process for determining incapacity that is too cumbersome or time consuming.

The Principal should consider adopting one of the following alternatives as a mechanism for granting the power to exercise his or her ownership vote:

- If the Principal is satisfied that the person named as agent under his or her general durable powers of attorney should have power to vote the Principal's ownership interest in the business, then the Principal can execute a modified version of the powers of attorney to include provisions that are specific to ownership voting rights and perhaps involve special procedures or a streamlined process for exercising such authority. For example, if the spouse is the agent, then perhaps the spouse should be allowed to exercise ownership voting authority without a determination of incapacity (but this may not be suitable if the spouse is not a parent of children who are in the business).

- The Principal could execute a special durable power of attorney that applies only to authority to exercise the Principal's ownership voting rights and names an agent different from the agent named under his or her general durable powers of attorney. In such a case, the Principal likely would have to amend the general durable powers to carve out the voting authority granted under the special durable power of attorney.

- The Principal could execute a proxy and keep it current, provided that it is consistent with the entity's governing documents.

- The Principal could hold his or her ownership interest in a revocable living trust, giving authority to a special trustee, a directing party, or a trust protector to exercise ownership voting rights. (However, for reasons discussed in section 8.1, holding ownership of family business units in a revocable living trust can sometimes cause unintended ambiguity with respect to buy-sell agreements.) (For more on the role of trust fiduciaries in voting family business units, see section 8.4.)

- In some cases, the Principal could hold his or her ownership interest, particularly if it is corporation stock, subject to a voting trust agreement for which the Principal is trustee, but which names successor trustees who have authority to act upon the Principal's incapacity. (For more on voting trusts, see section 6.2.1.e.)

The definition of "incapacity" can be tailored to focus on the cognitive abilities and mental or physical presence needed to exercise ownership voting rights. Many durable powers of attorney require a determination of incapacity by two physicians, but this may not be possible in an emergency. The Principal should consider providing a simpler procedure as an acceptable alternative, such as an affidavit signed by the authorized fiduciary, attesting a good-faith belief that the Principal is incapacitated. Also, the Principal should consider granting the authorized fiduciary a limited release under the Health Insurance Portability and Accessibility Act (HIPAA) to help ensure that the fiduciary can obtain prompt access to basic medical information if the Principal is hospitalized due to an accident or a sudden health impairment.

4.2.2.b The Principal's Death

This section of the continuation plan should state who has authority to exercise the Principal's ownership voting rights immediately after the Principal's death, and it should identify the specific documents that grant the authority described. Then, the lawyer should prepare and execute those documents with the Principal. The documents that the lawyer drafts for this purpose should allow implementation without probate or other cumbersome procedure or delays.

For example, if the centerpiece of the Principal's estate plan is a revocable living trust (which, in most cases, it should be), the Principal's ownership interest can be titled in a way that allows the appropriate fiduciary under the revocable trust to exercise the ownership voting rights without delay after the Principal's death. For example, the ownership interest can be titled to the revocable trust during the Principal's lifetime (but see concerns about that discussed in section 8.1, or the revocable living trust can be named as the TOD (i.e., "transfer-on-death") beneficiary of the ownership interest, which would allow the ownership interest to pass at the Principal's death by operation of law and free of probate.[1] The revocable trust agreement can provide special instructions regarding which fiduciaries are allowed to exercise ownership voting rights, such as a special trustee, a directing party, or a trust protector.) (For more on the role of trust fiduciaries in voting family business units, see section 8.4.)

In the alternative, the Principal could hold his or her ownership interest, particularly if it is corporation stock, subject to a voting trust agreement for which the Principal is trustee, but which names successor trustees who assume authority upon the Principal's death. (For more on voting trusts, see section 6.2.1.e.)

4.2.2.c Voting Instructions or Guidelines

The continuation plan should describe the voting mechanisms in place for the Principal's incapacity or death, and in some cases it may provide direction or guidelines as to how the agent or fiduciary should exercise the voting rights on a particular subject. For example, the continuation plan might advise the agent or fiduciary whom he or she should elect to replace the Principal as director on the governing board or as manager of an LLC. If the Principal is the company's sole director or manager, the continuation plan might provide guidance for populating a multi-member governing board of directors or managers.

Also, if the Principal's incapacity or death occurs before business succession planning has been concluded or before the successor owners have agreed on an optimal governance structure or a buy-sell agreement, then the continuation plan document should instruct the agent or fiduciary who is voting the Principal's ownership interest to vote to maintain consistent efforts to proceed with and accomplish the succession planning process.

To make these guidelines binding and enforceable, if it is desirable and prudent to do so, they must be incorporated into the trust documents or separate agreements, because the continuation plan document itself is only descriptive, not enforceable. For example, as a stopgap measure, the Principal could amend his or her estate plan to instruct the trustee

---

1. For the appropriate procedure, see the relevant state's version of the Uniform Transfer on Death Security Registration Act.

not to distribute ownership interests to trust beneficiaries until certain elements of the succession planning process, such as business restructuring, revisions to governing documents, and execution of buy-sell agreements, are completed.

4.2.3 Governing Boards

This section of the continuation plan states who should replace the Principal on the governing board of directors or managers for each business entity in the event of the Principal's incapacity or death. This section must be supported by appropriate, enforceable documentation so it may be properly and immediately implemented in the event of the applicable contingency.

If the Principal has the controlling ownership vote, then the arrangements made to exercise that vote in the event of the Principal's incapacity or death, pursuant to the previous section of the continuation plan, should be sufficient to address how he or she will be replaced on the companies' governing boards. However, if the Principal's ownership vote is not sufficient alone to elect a replacement, it may be desirable to collaborate with other voting owners to address this issue.

4.2.3.a Board Member Incapacity

If the consent or action of someone other than the Principal is required to install board members, then the continuation plan may need to include provisions addressing how incapacity is to be determined, how board members can be removed for incapacity, and how new board members can be appointed.

Board service is different from ownership voting rights because a board member usually cannot delegate his or her authority as a board member to any other person. Each board member must be able to act for himself or herself, or cease to serve. Therefore, the business continuation plan should define what may constitute a lack of capacity needed to serve as a board member and should provide a means for determining whether the Principal is suffering from such lack of capacity after an accident or a medical emergency. The continuation plan should provide a means for removing the Principal from the board (or suspending his or her board service if the lack of capacity is temporary) and replacing the Principal on the board under such circumstances.

When developing the continuation plan, if a company's governing documents do not already include the provisions described in the continuation plan regarding the incapacity of a board member, the lawyer should help the owners to amend the appropriate documents to include such provisions. Usually this will require an amendment to the bylaws for a corporation and an amendment to the LLC agreement for an LLC. Also, the Principal should grant a limited HIPAA release to a trusted person connected with the company, such as another board member, an officer, or another owner, who can help obtain medical information about the Principal's condition when a question of capacity arises.

4.2.3.b Board Member Death

Upon the Principal's death, his or her ownership shares will pass to new owners, consistent with the Principal's estate plan. The continuation plan should describe how the board of each company will be constituted after the Principal's death. If the *succession* planning process has not yet determined how the board will be constituted under successor ownership, then the *continuation* plan should provide for interim board authority to be held by an individual or individuals who will be able to govern the company until the successor owners have agreed upon a more permanent board structure.

To provide for an interim board and proper appointments as described in the continuation plan, the lawyer may need to help the owners to amend the companies' governing documents and the Principal's revocable trust or other mechanism that will control the ownership vote after the Principal's death, as discussed in section 4.2.2.b. If the company has an advisory board, it may be desirable to execute measures that would cause the advisory board to become the governing board immediately upon the Principal's death. In all instances, the owners should make sure that the board will have a mechanism to break deadlocks if the Principal's death may leave the board evenly divided.

4.2.3.c Affiliated LLCs with a Single Manager

If some of the business's components are LLCs for which the Principal serves as sole manager, it is possible to name either an individual, a board of individuals, or one or more business entities as the Principal's successor, upon disability or death. (Although the director of a corporate board must be an individual, the manager of an LLC can be another business entity.) Thus, for example, the family's primary operating company or a management company owned by the family could be named as successor manager.

If the family's primary business entity is named as the successor manager for affiliated LLCs, at least on an interim basis, then the primary entity's board can control the governance of the affiliated LLCs until a more permanent solution is reached. In the alternative, it may be appropriate to treat the role of sole manager of affiliated LLCs as an ex officio position that is always held by the chief executive officer of the family's primary business entity. Either approach may require a written action of the current manager, an amendment to LLC agreements, and consent of the LLC members.

4.2.3.d Member-Managed LLCs

If the Principal is a member of a member-managed LLC, the arrangements that the lawyer helps the owners to adopt regarding ownership voting rights upon the Principal's disability are also likely to apply to the Principal's management rights as a member. Upon the Principal's death, however, the applicable LLC statute or LLC agreement may not allow a substitute member without the consent of some or all of the other members. In such cases, the Principal's successor at death might not be able to participate in management of the member-managed LLC as a matter of right unless the lawyer helps the owners (i.e., the members) amend the LLC agreement to identify the Principal's successor owner, such as the Principal's revocable trust, as a permitted transferee. The Principal's estate plan can be amended to make reference to the disposition of the Principal's membership interest and the successor's participation in management as a permitted transferee.

4.2.4 Executive Authority

This section of the continuation plan states who should replace the Principal as the chief executive officer or president upon the Principal's disability or death. It also suggests how this may require changes to other executive appointments and responsibilities, and it identifies key personnel who should be incentivized to remain with the business during any disruption from the loss of the CEO/president.

4.2.4.a Interim or Successor CEO/President

When a company loses its chief executive, almost any delay in appointing a successor can harm the company. Empirical research demonstrates a clear correlation between the length of time it takes to appoint a successor and the amount of the resulting decline in the company's profitability and value.[2] It typically takes a company a couple of years to recover,[3] but sometimes the damage can be irreparable, such as when the chief executive is the company's founder or has unique expertise, or when the loss occurs during a key transaction or leads to acceleration of debt.

Therefore, if the Principal serves as chief executive, the business continuation plan should name a successor or interim successor to immediately assume the chief executive role and title if the Principal is suddenly unable to serve because of incapacity or death. The continuation plan should state the mechanism for the successor appointment, and the lawyer should draft the appropriate documentation for the owners or governing board to implement the chosen mechanism.

If loss of the Principal will not prevent or impede the governing board's ability to appoint the successor, then it may be sufficient to provide a mechanism in the bylaws or LLC agreement that enables the governing board to assemble electronically, without the usual formal notice of a board meeting, for the purpose of appointing the successor or interim chief executive (and perhaps address other pressing issues arising out of the crisis). Some state corporate law statutes expressly allow a corporation to adopt emergency bylaws, including shortened notice periods and lower quorum requirements.[4]

If the owners are concerned that the governing board will not be able to act promptly to appoint the successor or interim chief executive, it may be appropriate to use a more self-implementing appointment mechanism, such as a standing board resolution or an amendment to the bylaws, that triggers succession of a specific executive or board member as interim chief executive to serve until confirmed or removed by the board.

The business *succession* plan should allow promising family members or non-family executives to be trained over the long term to succeed to the chief executive role when the senior leaders exit the business. In contrast, the business *continuation* plan identifies a leader who is ready to serve as chief executive immediately in a crisis, even if that differs from the long-term succession plan. One of the benefits of having one or two retired executives on the business's governing or advisory board is that they may be able to step

---

2. Bruce K. Behn, David D. Dawley, Richard Riley & Ya-wen Yang, *Deaths of CEOs: Are Delays in Naming Successors and Insider/Outsider Succession Associated with Subsequent Firm Performance?*, 18 J. Managerial Issues 32 (Spring 2006).

3. *Id.*

4. *See, e.g.*, the ABA's Model Business Corporation Act (MBCA) § 2.07; *see also* Delaware General Business Corporation Law (DGCL) § 110.

in as interim chief executive in an emergency, without the expectation that they will be appointed as the long-term successor.

4.2.4.b Other Key Executives

Upon the loss of the Principal, other key executives may view their positions as insecure and may begin to seek other opportunities. The business continuation plan should identify those executives that are the most important to retain and provide guidance as to stay incentives (or deal bonuses for a successful sale of the business if the premature loss of the Principal will necessitate selling the business).

The owners also should consider whether noncompetition agreements signed by executives while the Principal is managing the business may make it easier to retain them after the Principal's incapacity or death. It may be easier for the owners to approach key executives about a noncompetition commitment if it is part of an agreement that also includes provisions for stay incentives in the event of the sudden incapacity or death of the Principal and other well-defined circumstances. (Before the owners offer these incentives, they should consider cash needs as discussed in section 4.2.7.) In many states, the law does not favor enforcement of broad noncompetition agreements signed by employees, so they should be limited as needed to make them enforceable and may need to be accompanied by some form of consideration.

4.2.5 Contracts

This section of the business continuation plan identifies economic relationships that may suffer adverse consequences upon the incapacity or death of the Principal, and it describes how such circumstances can be mitigated. (See a further discussion of these issues in the succession planning context in chapter 7.)

4.2.5.a Death or Change of Control

Some contracts, such as personal guaranties of business debt or franchising or distributorship agreements, may be in default or may terminate upon the death of the Principal or upon the transfer of the Principal's ownership interest as a result of death. The business continuation plan should identify these contractual relationships and suggest how the owners can mitigate their effects if the Principal dies unexpectedly.

In some cases, such as personal guaranties of business debt, the lawyer may be able to help the owners negotiate a procedure for avoiding default, such as by providing a partial pay-down or a suitable substitute guarantor within a specified time after the Principal's death. In other cases, such as with a franchising or distributorship agreement, the only possible approach may be simply to make sure that the owners understand the process required for approval of a successor owner-operator and are prepared to expedite application for approval when the Principal dies.

4.2.5.b Unwritten Agreements

In contrast, the owners may have economic relationships with family members or other affiliated parties that are not protected by a written agreement and that might not continue if the Principal is no longer personally involved. The business continuation plan should identify these situations and describe the owners' understanding of the parties' respective rights. Even better, if possible, the lawyer should help the owners put in place appropriate agreements to protect the proper arrangements. These relationships may include family member employment, other family member services, leases of family-owned property, and family member noncompetition expectations.

4.2.6 Notice

This section of the business continuation plan consists of a schedule of parties to be given notice that the Principal has suffered incapacity or death. The loss of the Principal may cause concern among parties who have an economic relationship with the business, such as employees, investors, creditors, vendors, and customers. Such constituents are less likely to act on their concerns to the detriment of the business if the business promptly notifies them of the loss and assures them that there is an effective plan in place for immediate leadership transition.

Sometimes (as discussed in section 4.2.5a), a contractual default or termination event may arise directly out of the Principal's death. In such cases, it may be especially important for the business to inform the other party of the Principal's death and begin discussions to continue the contractual relationship before the other party hears about the event from other sources and begins to execute defensive measures. The schedule used for this section of the business continuation plan may include the party name, relationship, individual contact person, telephone number, and the person whom the owners select to handle the initial phone call or meeting.

4.2.7 Cash Needs

This section of the business continuation plan consists of a discussion of the funds that would be needed by the business and the Principal's family to address the most immediate financial consequences of the Principal's incapacity or death. This section attempts to quantify those needs and identifies available sources of those funds.

4.2.7.a Cash Needs for the Business

While preparing the business continuation plan, the owners will realize many of the cash needs that would arise for the business upon the unexpected loss of the Principal. This section of the business continuation plan should describe those needs and attempt to quantify them.

For example, the business may need to pay down business debt to avoid a loan acceleration caused by a due-on-death clause in the Principal's guaranty, or the business may need to issue stay bonuses to keep key personnel in place until operations stabilize after the leadership transition. The business may need to come current with vendors who are reluctant to fill orders on credit without some reassurance of business stability.

In some cases, a business may address some of these cash needs with key person life insurance. Often, term insurance is a cost-effective approach to cover this contingency. It also may be possible for the business to reserve a line of credit to use for this contingency, but the owners should make sure that the business will still be allowed to draw on the line after the Principal's death.

This section of the business continuation plan also should state whether the business will rely upon a loan or a capital contribution from owners or their affiliates. For example, if a trust will receive life insurance proceeds upon the Principal's death and if the business expects to be able to access such proceeds for operations, then this section of the business continuation plan should discuss that arrangement. In such cases, the parties involved, including the trustee, should agree as to whether the arrangement should be in a form that is enforceable by the business or left to the discretion of trust fiduciaries.

4.2.6.b Cash Needs for the Family

Outside the business, the Principal's incapacity or death may give rise to cash needs for the Principal's family caused by a loss of the Principal's compensation or caused by the costs of health care or the assessment of estate taxes. In the context of either the business continuation plan or the Principal's estate plan, the Principal should advise his or her family and their fiduciaries whether they can expect to receive cash flow from the business after the Principal's incapacity or death, or, conversely, whether they should expect to provide additional cash to the business, as needed for operations after the Principal's incapacity or death.

Assuming that the family will need access to additional cash, in a lump sum or as cash flow, in the aftermath of the Principal's incapacity or death, the continuation plan should attempt to quantify that need, identify the amount that will come from the business, and describe the mechanisms to be used to facilitate the payment of the needed funds to the family. These mechanisms might include one or more of the following:

- The Principal's spouse could assume a portion of the Principal's compensation for services to be provided by the spouse, such as executive services, board service, or consulting services.
- The business could adopt a more generous dividend/distribution policy, assuming that would not violate the business's other obligations, including covenants with its lenders.
- The business could redeem a portion of the Principal's interests in exchange for cash or cash flow. (Note, however, that partial redemptions of corporate stock in some cases can have adverse tax consequences by causing the redemption proceeds to be taxed as a dividend rather than capital gains (which can be a significant difference depending on the relative tax rates and the Principal's basis in the stock to be redeemed.) In such cases, it might be possible to structure the transaction as a cross purchase of stock—i.e., purchase by other owners—to avoid the adverse tax consequences. Further, if the proceeds are used to pay estate taxes, it may be possible to execute a partial redemption under Section 303 of the Internal Revenue Code without the adverse income tax consequences.)
- The business could buy a property that the Principal has been leasing to the business, such as real estate or equipment.
- The business could loan money to the Principal's family, using the "applicable federal rate" under Section 1274(b) of the Internal Revenue Code as a low, safe-harbor interest rate for the loan.

With respect to estate taxes, the Principal should engage in appropriate planning to reduce the potential estate tax liability, as well as to fund the amount of the liability that cannot be eliminated. At this stage of the *succession* planning process, however, it may be prudent to emphasize such funding sources as life insurance rather than lifetime wealth transfers to avoid estate taxes. Until the lawyer is confident that the Principal has sufficiently addressed retirement needs for him- or herself and spouse (see chapter 9), the lawyer should be conservative about lifetime wealth transfers for estate tax planning. Term life insurance might be a cost-effective interim approach for addressing potential estate tax liability. A cautious approach to estate tax management at this point might focus on techniques that provide the Principal with cash flow during lifetime but have little or no value in the Principal's estate, including a spousal access trust or a self-canceling installment note. (These techniques are discussed in greater detail in chapter 10.)

Throughout the *succession* planning process, and particularly at points like this, a quality insurance professional can provide great value. If the owners intend to rely on disability insurance or life insurance for cash needs identified in the business *continuation* plan, they can be well served by an insurance professional who will guide them to coverage that is best suited for their needs and available resources. The insurance advisor can make better recommendations if he or she has a fairly complete understanding of the context in which the insurance will play a part. Some insurance advisors have experience or resources through their firm that can assist the owners in a variety of ways without additional charge. For example, they might be able to help with financial modeling, sample drafting, or planning around tax complications. If the owners ever have concern that a proposed insurance solution might not be appropriate but are unaware of suitable alternatives, it is possible to obtain an independent, fee-based analysis of a particular proposal.

4.2.8 Leadership Contingency Plan

This section of the business continuation plan consists of a summary of the plan that can be shared with business managers and staff members, without divulging sensitive material regarding financial matters, contracts, and specific succession plans. It can be included in the employee handbook and updated from time to time. It instructs employees what to do if they hear news of the incapacity or death of the Principal.

For example, it might identify specific managers or board members that employees should call for further information and direction. It might instruct employees not to discuss the matter with outside parties, except to provide the name and contact information for the managers or board members who are designated to communicate with outside parties about the occurrence, and then to promptly notify the appropriate manager or board member about the outside inquiry. It also might describe the process for convening an emergency meeting of the board or owners and instruct senior staff members on how to facilitate that. Finally, it also might direct senior staff members to contact the lawyer so that he or she can make sure that the complete, updated continuation plan is provided to board members and other key advisors and so that the lawyer can offer additional assistance to implement the continuation plan and help keep the business stabilized.

4.2.9 Beneficial Ownership

This section of the business continuation plan describes who will receive and hold beneficial ownership of the Principal's business interests after the Principal's death. It may be prudent to hold the beneficial interests in trust until the ultimate disposition of the business is determined.

As more fully discussed in chapter 6, an owner's voting rights can be separated from the beneficial or equitable ownership of business interests. Until the business *succession* plan is completed, it may make sense to provide for the Principal's ownership interests to be held in a single trust for the primary beneficiaries of the estate plan. This will give the other owners, the board, and the owners' advisors an opportunity to complete the succession plan with the trust fiduciaries before ownership interests are distributed to individual beneficiaries.

For example, if the business does not have an updated buy-sell agreement or updated governance structures, then holding the ownership interests in trust until a buy-sell agreement is executed among the beneficial owners and governance mechanisms are properly installed may help avoid owner disputes that otherwise might occur. Similarly, if a premature death of the Principal may necessitate a sale of the business, it may be easier to pursue a transaction while the business interests are held in trust, rather than after they are distributed to multiple individual family members.

One simple stopgap measure to implement at this stage in the *succession*-planning process may be to amend the Principal's estate plan simply to state that the trustees will not distribute ownership interests to beneficiaries until certain succession-planning tasks are achieved and key family members or trust fiduciaries decide not to sell the business.

4.2.10 Sale of the Business

This section of the business continuation plan states whether the business should be sold upon the unexpected loss of the Principal. If the Principal's children are too young to enter the business and if the Principal's spouse is not involved in the business, the owners may decide that the business should be sold if there is uncertainty about succession within the family.

If this is the case, then the business continuation plan should describe a process for selling the business. It might be helpful if the Principal keeps a list of potential buyers or potential investment bankers to handle the process. It may also be helpful if the owners could engage an investment banker or other consultant to advise the Principal and the board as to whether business operations, accounting, record keeping, or other practices should be changed to position the business better for sale to a third party.

Many business owners are reluctant to explore information or advice about positioning their business for sale because they do not want to alarm their employees or customers. However, if the business owner can explain that these exercises are being conducted in the context of contingency planning, they should not generate the same concerns.

In the alternative, the owners and the Principal might conclude that the Principal's interests should be sold to an insider, such as other owners, a management group, or an employee stock ownership plan. If these are possibilities, the owners should consider appointing a committee of the board or other appropriate individuals to explore the options and help position the business for the chosen transaction. In each case, obtaining funding for the buyers will be a key practical feature to explore.

4.3 Updates

It is prudent for the owners to review and update the business *continuation* plan on an annual basis, until leadership and ownership has transitioned under the business *succession* plan. After that, the successor owners should adopt a new business continuation plan that will protect the business until they have passed it on to their own successors.

Chapter Five:

Business Restructuring

This chapter discusses how to review and possibly organize the family business structure to create greater flexibility and economic efficiency for the business succession process. This stage of the business succession planning process provides the lawyer with an opportunity to yield an immediate, positive, and quantifiable financial impact on the owners, as well as provide other short-term and long-term benefits, while better positioning the business for ownership/leadership succession. It is essential for the lawyer to work with the business's accountants and tax advisors on this element of the succession plan, because they will best be able to assess the tax ramifications that particular business restructuring proposals may have on the business and its owners.

Often, when a family business is first established, its choice of entity and business structure is determined for reasons other than multi-generational ownership. Similarly, over time, as a family business grows, its business structure may develop haphazardly, as acquisitions or affiliated entities are added based upon immediate business needs or objectives rather than long-term succession planning. Therefore, taking a fresh look at entity choices and business structure, in the context of succession planning, may reveal many ways to substantially improve how the business is organized.

One important objective of restructuring the business is to create tax-efficient and diverse means of providing cash flow to facilitate owner exits. Another important objective may be to separate business operations and assets so that they can be disproportionately allocated among family members based on each individual's role and subjective interest in the business, including those family members who are not active in the business.

Business restructuring can have other advantages as well, such as protecting business assets and owner wealth against claims arising out of business operations, minimizing or eliminating owner guaranties of business debt, improving governance and management mechanisms, enhancing transfer tax planning techniques, and realizing immediate income tax benefits for the owners.

5.1 Overview

The lawyer can best accomplish business restructuring by collaborating with the owners' and business's accountants, personnel who understand the business's financial and operational dynamics, and the senior owners who are active in the business. Although this task precedes the discussion of business governance and succession of ownership in this book, it cannot be properly accomplished without an understanding of the owners' intentions and objectives regarding the whole succession plan.

This is one reason why the lawyer should draft the succession-planning outline, a template of which appears in appendix A, at the start of the project, and keep it updated after every substantial meeting with the owners. By keeping current on the owners' progress in all stages of the business succession planning process, the lawyer can provide better advice regarding business restructuring. Some elements of business restructuring might be so obviously correct that the lawyer and the other advisors may advise the owners to implement them immediately. Other elements, however, may be so dependent on how the rest of the business succession plan evolves that they should not be implemented until the lawyer and the other advisors can confirm that they are a correct fit, later in the succession planning process.

If the business consists of one entity, the lawyer should consider whether the business's form of entity should be changed and whether elements of the business should be segregated into new entities, either as subsidiaries of the business or as separate entities with affiliated ownership. If the business already consists of multiple entities, the lawyer should consider whether the form and function of each entity should be changed, and whether the entities' relationships with one another should be changed or augmented. All of these potential changes should be considered in the context of what is best for the business and the owners, at present and when ownership and leadership transition to the successors, as the owners develop their plan for succession.[1]

5.2 Getting Started

When working with the owners on the subject of business restructuring, it is helpful to start with the big picture. It is possible that the current business structure is appropriate. Ideally, the owners can provide a graphic illustration of all the entities in the business, their functions, the type of assets they hold, and how they interact with one another, as well as how they are owned. In the alternative, they could provide similar information in the form of a table or spreadsheet. Discussing that information with the accountants and one or two key managers or senior generation owners can provide a lot of insight, very quickly, on the topic of business restructuring.

This initial review might generate ideas for immediate restructuring, indicate that further review is needed, or at least identify ways in which future additions to the business might be treated differently from how acquisitions were treated in the past. For example, it may seem immediately obvious that the owners should form an LLC to hold business real estate that currently is owned by family members as tenants-in-common. If the property owners and the owners' accountants and tax advisors concur, the lawyer can memorialize the decision, and the reasoning, in the succession-planning outline and add the necessary tasks to the checklist.

In contrast, other changes might require further study. For example, if the business is taxed as a C corporation, and if the succession plan may require a tax-efficient source of

---

1. The discussion of "choice of entity" in this chapter is somewhat broad and fundamental. State law regarding business entities and state and federal tax law affecting business entities and their owners change frequently. It is prudent for the lawyer to stay current on this subject. For a truly deep dive into "choice of entity," see ROBERT R. KEATINGE & ANNE E. CONAWAY, KEATINGE AND CONAWAY ON CHOICE OF BUSINESS ENTITY: SELECTING FORM AND STRUCTURE FOR A CLOSELY-HELD BUSINESS (Thomson West 2019 ed.).

cash flow to a trust, the lawyer and the owners might ask the accountants to follow up with advice about the tax effect of (1) electing subchapter S treatment for the corporation (see section 5.7.1 for more on the subject of S elections) or (2) transferring equipment or real estate from the corporation to a separately owned LLC to produce cash flow through lease payments from the corporation. In such cases of uncertainty, the lawyer should update the succession planning outline to summarize the items that are approved for further study, along with the reasons why the changes might be desirable and the questions that must be answered before the advisors and the owners can make a final decision.

Sometimes, the initial review will reveal that a broad reorganization of the business and its components may yield current tax savings and operational efficiencies, as well as better serving the owners' succession planning objectives. In such cases it may be helpful to graphically represent how the business structure would appear after the reorganization, as well as writing a separate outline and checklist for this part of the business succession project. The restructuring graphic and the outline will help keep the owners and all their advisors updated as the details of the restructuring plan are refined and the restructuring is implemented.

Even changes that the lawyer and the other advisors strongly recommend may take time to implement. For example, new LLCs or other new entities may require agreement about buy-sell terms or may require agreement about leases or other contracts. Some changes might require lender approval or even refinancing. In each instance, the practical implications may affect the timing, and the changes may be implemented when circumstances allow.

One dramatic example of how circumstance can impede implementation of changes to business structure occurred in 2017, when owners of closely held corporations who wanted to elect subchapter S status had to wait until the Tax Cuts and Jobs Act was passed in December before their accountants could advise whether the S election would provide a net tax savings. In some cases, owners reversed course and decided not to make the S election for 2018 due to the effect of the new law on corporate income tax rates.

Finally, if, after the lawyer and the others involved in the initial review of business structure conclude that changes to the form of entities or business structure are not needed, then the lawyer should memorialize that conclusion and notify the owners that current action is not recommended on that item. This does not mean that the review was a wasted effort. As the succession planning process progresses, the lawyer should keep in mind the issues discussed in this chapter and be prepared to suggest revisiting these issues if new information or new circumstances might warrant.

The overarching questions for restructuring are whether business units, functions, and assets should be combined under one entity or should be owned in separate entities and then what form these entities should take. Following is a list of specific business organization and form-of-entity issues to consider when reviewing business structure. Each issue is discussed in greater detail later in this chapter.

• **Governance and management.** What business structure would provide the most appropriate governance and management structures? Should the business be held under a parent company that provides a central and prevailing governance mechanism? Should the business have a separate management company that provides executive management services to a portfolio of separate family entities? In the alternative, should various divisions of the business be separately governed and managed, either now or after succession?

- **Cash flow.** What business structure would provide appropriate mechanisms to meet the owners' cash flow needs or expectations, currently and after succession? Will cash flow be limited to compensation for services provided by owners who are also active in the business, or do the owners' expect to make cash flow available to inactive owners as well? Will the successor owners need cash flow to purchase the senior owners' stock or units when they exit ownership?
- **Asset protection.** What business structure could best protect business assets against liabilities arising out of operations? Further, what business structure could help reduce the need for owners, particularly inactive or minority owners, to provide personal guaranties for business debt, or at least mitigate the risk associated with such personal guaranties and other business liabilities?
- **Choice of entity/state of incorporation.** For each element of the business that is held as a separate business entity, which form of entity is most appropriate for its role in the business, and which state of incorporation or organization provides the most appropriate statutory rules to be applied to the entity's owners and fiduciaries.
- **Income tax treatment.** What is the most tax-efficient business structure and form of each entity to accomplish the owners' business purposes and succession plans?

These points should not be considered in isolation. Rather, if all of these points are included in the review of business structure, it should be possible to develop a structure that is appropriate in most or all of these respects.

5.3 Governance and Management

When reviewing the business structure, the lawyer should consider how the business could best be structured to facilitate governance and management mechanisms that are consistent with the business's operations, current leadership and ownership, and intentions for succession. (The subjects of governance, management, and successor ownership are further developed in the next chapter.)

If the owners anticipate that all components of the business should be governed by one governing board, then it may be best to consolidate the business under one parent company, with the governing board of the parent company having board oversight and authority over all business units.

Unified governance through a parent company may be desirable even if various business units will be separately managed. Consider the following example: A business has one ownership group and two distinct but synergistic business divisions. After succession, each division will be led by a different family member. In such a case, the business could be structured as a parent company that holds the separate divisions as two wholly owned subsidiaries. The appropriate family member could be appointed as chief executive of the subsidiary that he or she will manage, but the parent company's governing board could continue to have board oversight and authority over each subsidiary. The parent company also could employ executives and other staff who provide services to both business divisions. Under this structure, and in anticipation of the cash flow discussion in section 5.4 of this chapter, the parent company board would remain in control of cash assets of both subsidiaries.

If there are reasons not to consolidate business divisions or business assets under a single parent company, it may be possible nevertheless to create unified governance and management by creating a separate management company that is empowered to govern and operate the separate business entities by contract, such as a management agreement or executive services contract. Consider the following example: A family's business includes entities that hold individual properties or separate and diverse ventures. Specific successor owners do not wish to participate in ownership of all the properties or ventures in the same proportions as others, due to differences in cash flow, risk profile, or owner involvement. However, the separate entities could not each afford the quality of governance and executive staff that they could afford collectively. Under such circumstances, the owners could establish a management company with a governing board and executive staff that serves all the family entities. The management company also could provide family office services if that becomes part of the succession plan.

In contrast, it may be desirable to consider splitting up the governance and management of parts of the business that are currently owned and operated as a single entity. If separate business lines or units are not essential to one another and if each will be managed by a different family member after succession, it may be helpful to begin separating those lines or units in advance of succession. Consider the following example: A family owns a corporation that has two distinct lines of business, but they are not separated by formal divisions. After succession, each line will be managed by a separate family member who wants to have full control and ownership of the line of business that he or she will manage. With proper planning, it may be possible to untangle those lines of business and eventually split them into separate legal entities with separate ownership. In the right circumstances or given sufficient time to adapt business operations, it may be possible to accomplish the split without triggering income taxes.

Often, family business owners want to keep the whole family engaged in collective pursuit of all family business ventures. This can be accomplished through a parent company that functions as a kind of umbrella company that owns all of the family business ventures as wholly owned subsidiaries that are governed by the board of the parent company. Collective engagement in the family business, however, does not require lockstep or pro rata ownership of each of the family's lines of descent in each business venture. A family-owned management company can provide unified governance to a collection of family business ventures that are held in separate entities and owned by family members in different proportions.

Finally, sometimes it is best to allow the family business to be split into separate businesses to be owned and managed by different lines of descent. Such circumstances would not prevent the family from engaging in other collective projects, such as co-ownership of other business ventures or collaboration on charitable giving projects. If splitting the business eases tension among the family members, other collective family pursuits may be easier to sustain and may be more effective in fostering family cohesion through the next generation.

5.4 Cash Flow

When reviewing the business structure, it is important to determine where cash flow is needed and how the business can be structured to give the owners flexibility to direct cash flow to where it is needed.

5.4.1 Cash for the Business

Sometimes excess income produced by one element of the business is needed by another element of the business. In such cases, a consolidated entity providing tax-free flow of income and cash throughout the business may be the best structure. For example, if the business consists of several separate companies, it may be cumbersome to move cash from one company that has excess cash to one of the other companies that may need cash for expansion. In such cases, the transfer of cash might have to be treated as a loan from one company to the other, necessitating additional bookkeeping and producing taxable interest income. In contrast, if the separate companies are all wholly owned subsidiaries of a parent company, it may be easy to move cash around among the companies so that the business can use it where it is needed most. In such a case, the cash is transferred as a tax-free distribution from one subsidiary to the parent and then a cash contribution from the parent to the other subsidiary.

5.4.2 Cash Flow for Owners

In a family business, however, it is important to consider the cash flow needs or expectations of the owners. Cash flow is important to consider in succession planning because it may be the primary means of support for some family members and their dependents. Even family members who are not reliant on the business for support are likely to expect some level of present return on their investment in the family business; otherwise, they may wish to liquidate their ownership interest and invest in an alternative that provides a balance of current income and long-term appreciation.

Although consolidation of the business as a single company or as a portfolio of subsidiaries under a single parent company might be advantageous for cash flow within the business, it might be problematic for providing cash flow to the owners. In a family business, if some owners are compensated as employees of the business while the rest of the owners receive no current cash flow from the business, discord among the owners might arise about disparity in the economic benefits of ownership.

The governing documents of such companies could allow, or even require (within limits), the payment of dividends to the owners, but payment of dividends might cause the family to incur additional income taxes, which may be a waste of capital. In some cases, electing flow-through tax treatment for the company might mitigate the tax cost of distributing income to owners. (See section 5.7 for a more detailed discussion of tax considerations.) In a family business, however, dividends or income distributions usually must be made to the owners pro rata and thus might result in an excess of cash flow being paid to owners who are receiving both compensation and dividends or income distributions.

To make the allocation of income a little more flexible, it may be desirable to keep business real estate and equipment in entities that are separate from the operating company. This can provide cash flow from the business in the form of lease payments from the operating company to the separate asset companies. If family members who are employed in the business own a greater proportion of the operating company, and the family members who are not employed in the business own a greater proportion of the asset companies, the cash flow produced by lease payments can be distributed in a greater proportion to family members who are not receiving cash flow as compensation.

There may be other ways, specific to the owners' unique circumstances, to structure the business that will make it easier for the owners to direct cash flow to where it is most needed. There also may be ways to direct cash flow to an individual family member through services he or she provides to the business even if he or she is not an employee, such as board fees, guaranty fees, payment for services provided as a contractor, royalties for licensing of intellectual property, consulting fees or, for former employees, deferred compensation, severance benefits, or noncompetition payments. (These arrangements with individual owners are discussed in greater detail in section 7.1 and chapter 9.)

5.4.3 Cash for Owner Exits

When reviewing the business structure, it is important to consider how the business could best be structured to provide cash flow to the current owners after they retire and to successor owners, particularly those who are not employed by the business. In addition, if the succession plan or a buy-sell agreement among successor owners will require the successor owners to purchase the ownership interests of exiting owners, it is important to consider how the business could be structured to provide cash flow for these ownership transfers.

The cash flow from family-owned assets that are leased to the operating business may be useful for these purposes as well. For example, such assets could provide a senior owner with a source of income in retirement, even after exiting ownership of the operating company. Alternatively, such assets could provide the successor owners a source of cash flow to be used to purchase the senior owners' interests in the operating company. Similarly, such assets could provide cash flow to fund future buy-sell obligations.

Consider this example: A family business manufactures restaurant fixtures. The manufacturing operation is organized as a corporation, and each family member who owns stock in the corporation is also employed and compensated by the corporation. (The owners have decided that stock in the operating company should be owned only by family members who are active in the business.) The owners of the operating company also own the business's factories, equipment, and trucking fleet in separate flow-through entities, which generate cash flow by leasing the assets to the operating company. The owners can use the lease payments received by the asset companies in a variety of ways that may serve the business and the succession plan.

• **Reinvest in the business.** The owners can use cash flow from the asset companies to purchase new business assets, expand operations, or acquire new lines of business. The owners can contribute excess cash flow to the operating company as contributions of capital; or, the asset companies can loan excess cash flow to the operating company and create yet another source of cash flow (in the form of loan repayment) from the operating company to the asset companies or the owners.

• **Service a buy-sell obligation.** If an owner terminates his or her employment in the operating company, the remaining owners can use their share of cash flow from the asset companies to pay the exiting owner for his or her stock on an installment basis. Eventually, when the remaining owners have paid for the departed owner's stock in the operating company, they can then purchase the departed owner's interest in the asset companies as well.

- **Create a fund for future owner exits.** If an owner exit is not imminent, then the owners can use cash flow from the asset companies to create a separate fund of marketable securities as a source of cash to be used to purchase the operating company stock when any owner retires or otherwise leaves the employment of the operating company later during the life of the business. (Note that many buy-sell agreements are funded with life insurance, but many owner exits occur during the owner's lifetime, when the life insurance may not be as effective in funding the buy-sell obligation.)

5.5 Asset Protection

When reviewing the business structure, it is important to consider whether greater segmentation of business units and business assets into separate limited liability entities can help protect business assets against liability for claims arising out of one asset or one element of the business. Also, it is important to consider how individual owners and their personal assets can be protected against liability for claims of the business.

5.5.1 Limited Liability and Veil Piercing

If the business consists of one business entity, then claims against the business, whether claims of creditors under contract or of plaintiffs for an alleged tort, may be able to reach all of the assets of the business.

If such a claim is large enough and the claimant prevails, it could devastate the whole business. Even if the claimant does not succeed, a large claim brought against the whole business could tie up business assets during adversarial proceedings and could scare off lenders, vendors, staff, and other stakeholders. It could prevent the business from getting credit. It could suppress compensation and dividends. It could impair the owners' ability to sell the business or to raise cash by selling a business division or one of its assets.

Even worse, if the business owners do not keep proper separation between themselves and the business, and if a court agrees to pierce the corporate veil, the owners could be held personally liable for claims against the business, even if the business is held in a limited liability entity.

Therefore, when reviewing the owners' business structure, it is helpful to identify elements of the business, including different business functions and various business assets, that could be held in separate limited liability entities. For these purposes, parent companies, operating companies, and management companies should all be organized as limited liability entities. Real estate, even if it is owned by a parent company or the operating company, should be organized as a separate limited liability entity and held as a wholly owned subsidiary of the parent or operating company.

If different elements of the business are contained in their own limited liability entity, then a claim against one such company should not be able to reach the assets of the others, even if they have common ownership. In particular, a claim against a limited liability entity should not be able to reach its owner, whether the owner is a parent company or individual family members, unless a court allows the claimant to pierce the corporate veil.

Veil-piercing analyses vary from state to state, but in most jurisdictions, the following precautions can help owners avoid veil-piercing liability:

• **Identity.** When doing business of a particular entity, the business's employees and agents should clearly identify which business entity is party to the transaction, including its form of limited liability entity.

• **Capitalization.** Each business entity should be adequately capitalized (and insured) to carry out its business purpose and meet its expected obligations.

• **No commingling.** Cash of one entity should not be commingled or mixed with the cash of its owner or affiliated entities. Each entity should have its own cash accounts, and if cash passes from one entity to another, there should be a record of the event and the legal or business basis for the transfer, such as a distribution of a subsidiary to its parent or a capital contribution from a parent to a subsidiary or a loan between affiliated entities.

• **Corporate formalities.** Each entity should be governed with appropriate formalities for a free-standing business entity, including owner meetings, board meetings, and updated record books. Although LLCs don't typically require the same level of owner engagement and board formalities as corporations, it is simple enough for LLC management to keep a record book and update it at least once a year, and whenever the owners or managers take substantial action involving the entity.

• **Not a sham/fraudulent conveyance.** The owners should not expect a separate entity shield to be respected if they set it up to protect assets from an existing liability.

Note that a liability shield mostly runs in one direction. If someone has a claim against a limited liability entity (but not against its owner), then the liability shield should protect the owner's other assets from recovery for that claim; but if someone has a claim against the owner (but not the entity), then the liability shield will not necessarily protect the entity's assets from recovery for the claim against its owner. This is because a claim directly against the owner can be satisfied out of the owner's assets—even those unrelated to the claim—including the owner's interest in a limited liability entity. Nevertheless, even when the claim is against the owner, a limited liability entity can provide some asset protection. In some cases, a person who has a claim against the owner is not entitled to reach into a limited liability entity and recover its income or assets, but, rather, the claimant is allowed to reach such assets only when the limited liability entity distributes the income or assets to the owner in the ordinary course.

Consider this example: A family owns an S corporation that operates three restaurants. The S corporation owns the buildings where the restaurants operate, but it holds each building in a limited liability company (i.e., each as a wholly owned subsidiary of the S corporation). Someone has a claim against the S corporation, but does not have a separate claim against the family or the LLCs. If the S corporation's limited liability shield is respected, then the claimant should not be able to reach the family's other assets (such as other investments, real estate, cash) for satisfaction of the claim, but the claimant should be able to reach any assets held in the S corporation, including the wholly owned LLCs. In some cases, the claimant might be able to force a dissolution of the LLCs and a liquidation of its assets; in other cases, the claimant might only be granted a charging order against the LLCs, which would entitle the claimant to receive income and assets of the LLCs only when the LLCs distribute such income or assets to the S corporation.

Under a charging order, the LLCs could continue to own and operate the properties, and the claimant might receive only net rents that LLC management chooses to distribute to the S corporation.

Whether placing assets in a limited liability entity will protect the assets, to any extent, from claims against its owner will likely depend on the state law that applies and the facts and circumstances. Also, note that placing real estate into an LLC might generate a real estate transfer fee, which could be sizable if the property has a high value or if many properties are being placed into single-purpose LLCs at the same time.

5.5.2 Personal Guaranties

Owners' personal guaranties of business debt can help the business raise needed capital, but they also create a number of risks and can impede or disrupt the implementation of a business succession plan. Therefore, when the owners consider restructuring, they should try to determine whether their business could be restructured to reduce or eliminate the need for personal guaranties.

An owner guaranty of business debt creates a general and obvious risk for the guarantor, which is the possibility that the lender will recover the owner's personal assets for a loan default by the business. An owner guaranty, however, also creates potential problems for the business, its other owners, and its successor owners, including the possibility that the death of a guarantor will be treated as a loan default and give the lender the right to accelerate the loan and demand immediate payment in full. Another such problem is that if a guarantor wants to exit ownership but the lender will not release his or her guaranty, the guarantor's exit will be delayed or will be more costly to the owners and successor owners.

For these reasons, the owners should consider whether a new business structure would help reduce or eliminate the need for owner guaranties. For example, if business functions and assets currently are spread among separately owned entities, it may be difficult for any one of those entities to obtain a loan without owner guaranties because the lender concludes that the borrowing entity, standing alone, has an insufficient profile to warrant the loan or has insufficient unencumbered assets to satisfy the loan obligation if the borrower defaults. In such a case, the lender may naturally demand that the owners guarantee the loan so that the lender will have greater means of recovery if the borrower defaults. An alternative business structure, however, that consolidates the separate business entities under the ownership of a single parent company might allow the lender to conclude that the cash flow and unencumbered assets of the parent company (and its other subsidiaries) are sufficient resources for loan satisfaction, during the loan term and in the event of default, without owner guaranties, especially if the parent company is the borrower, co-borrower, or guarantor.

In contrast, sometimes the lender requires owner guaranties not because the borrower has insufficient cash flow or insufficient unencumbered assets, but because an owner guaranty intensifies the owner's commitment to make sure that the borrowing entity satisfies its loan terms. That might be a reasonable expectation for an owner-operator, but it might be meaningless and cumbersome to apply to owners who are not active in the business and cannot directly affect its performance under the loan (or otherwise). In such cases, the owners should consider a business structure that separates ownership of the borrowing entity from ownership of other parts of the business, so that the borrowing entity is owned only by the family members who are active in the business and are thus more willing to personally guarantee the borrower's obligations and more able to influence performance under the loan.

When reviewing business structure, considering the effect of owner guaranties does not necessarily produce conclusions about business structure that are contrary to those produced by considering asset protection (such as under the preceding section). This is because a loan, with owner guaranties, is a negotiated obligation that is set forth in a contract that clearly identifies the terms of the obligation and the parties who are liable. In contrast, the asset protection function of limited liability entities is primarily intended to protect the business owners and their companies from unexpected claims against one part of the business arising out of transactions, whether as contract claims or tort claims, that do not directly involve the owners and the other parts of the business.

5.6 Choice of Entity

In addition to reviewing the structure of the owners' business in its entirety, it is important to consider whether each component is organized as the most appropriate form of entity. In almost all cases, for reasons discussed in the preceding two sections, each component entity should be organized in the form of a limited liability entity, such as a corporation, limited liability company, limited partnership (with a corporation, LLC, or trust serving as general partner), or even a limited liability partnership or limited liability limited partnership.

Although the default rules of governance and the owners' economic rights differ among these forms of entity and from state to state, most of the default rules can be altered by the entity's governing documents. (Chapter 6 will look at governance and ownership rights in greater detail.) The most important difference among limited liability entities, therefore, is usually their tax attributes, which are discussed in detail in the next section.

Apart from taxes, the following considerations might influence choice of entity:

• **State of organization.** A business entity can be formed in any state, regardless of where it actually does business, and generally the law of the state in which the entity is formed will govern the entity's internal affairs, such as the form of governance, duties of managers, and rights of owners. Some rules exist only in the statutes of particular states. For example, the Delaware General Corporation Law has express rules allowing different directors to be granted different levels of voting rights, but the statutes of many states that have a version of the Model Business Corporations Act are silent on the matter.[2]

• **Formality or flexibility.** As between corporations and LLCs, the use of a corporation may be more predictable for its managers and owners. The default rules governing corporations generally are the most detailed and create the most formal operational procedures, and courts have been construing corporate law for centuries. In contrast, the default rules governing LLCs are relatively cursory and permissive, and LLCs have existed in most states for less than four decades. Therefore, owners may be able to tailor an LLC to their liking more completely than a corporation, but the permissive LLC statutes,

---

2. *See* DGCL § 141(d); *but see, e.g.,* MBCA § 8.24.

combined with the short history of court engagement with LLCs, may create greater uncertainty as to how the default rules or the governing documents will be given effect.

• **Diverse investment interests.** LLCs and limited partnerships are much more flexible than corporations in terms of creating different equitable rights and interests for owners, including the possibility of allowing some owners to participate in equitable ownership of some of the entity's assets or activities and not others. For example, family partnership entities can be set up with "side pockets" that hold investments whose return accrues to some of the owners but not others, or whose return accrues to the owners on an allocation that is different from the owners' pro rata ownership in the entity as a whole. Such features, for example, can be used for entities that hold family investment assets that are not directly related to the family business, or for life insurance held to purchase family business interests upon an owner's death, particularly when the entity holds life insurance on multiple owners. A series LLC is another type of entity that can allow an owner to participate in equitable ownership of the entity's several assets and investments in different proportions.

• **Societal benefit.** Recently, states have begun to create variations on traditional business entities, such as public benefit corporations,[3] public benefit LLCs,[4] or low-profit limited liability companies (also known as L3Cs),[5] that allow management to pursue objectives that benefit interests beyond those of the owners, even if pursuing those objectives may suppress the entity's profitability. For example, a family business might choose to be organized as a benefit corporation or LLC so that it can require management to emphasize the use of U.S. or local suppliers, keep jobs in a particular community, or reduce harmful effects on the environment.

Exploring these choice-of-entity features with the owners and their advisors can help the lawyer tailor the business's structure in ways that might be more appropriate than their current structure and in ways that the owners might not otherwise have known about. Whether the choice of entities leads to more appropriate governance, a more individualized design for equity participation, or adoption of a socially beneficial mission, addressing choice of entity in these terms can energize the owners with respect to the business succession project and can give them ideas for future family ventures.

5.7 Income Tax Efficiencies

An important goal of family business restructuring is to create income tax–efficient ways to use business cash for the benefit of the owners and other family members and to defer or eliminate capital gains taxes on transfers of assets or business interests within the family. Further, the possibility that the lawyer can help the owners realize immediate income tax savings through business restructuring can be a great opportunity to provide a present net financial value early in the succession planning process. Sometimes, the immediate income tax savings can exceed the cost of the business succession planning project in full!

---

3. *See, e.g.,* DGCL §§ 361–368.
4. *See, e.g.,* DGCL § 18-1201-08.
5. *See, e.g.,* 805 IL. COMP. STAT. 180/1-26.

The owners' and business's tax advisors and accountants, and the business's senior financial staff members should always be included in these discussions. These are the individuals who can most easily identify ideas for tax-efficient restructuring that have potential application to the owners' circumstances and promptly dismiss those that do not. This team can help the lawyer and the owners find tax efficiencies consistent with the other needs and objectives for restructuring, and can prevent the lawyer and the owners from making tax mistakes in the process.

Tax efficiency is important also because it is a way to keep more wealth and value in the business and the family in the aggregate. It is like reducing unnecessary operating costs or other wasteful financial practices. Often, cash flow is at a premium when family business succession is implemented, as exiting owners may continue to rely on the business for cash. In many instances, a buyout, deferred compensation, consulting fees, lease payments, or some other economic arrangement can supplement their resources in retirement. In the meantime, the successor owners will need cash in the business to continue to operate and grow, and will also need the business to compensate them sufficiently to meet the needs of their own families. By eliminating unnecessary tax liability, the owners can improve the results of the succession plan.

The following subsections are examples of some specific items that the business's and owners' advisors should review with respect to income tax efficiencies. The discussion is necessarily broad, selective, and generalized. Unless the family business lawyer practices as a tax lawyer, it is essential for him or her to collaborate with the business's accounting and tax advisors to properly navigate all of the state and income tax implications of choice of entity and business structure. The results in any given case will depend on the relevant tax law, both state and federal, and on the particular facts of the business and its owners, including the trusts that hold ownership interests. A truly qualified tax advisor will be able to help the lawyer find tax opportunities, solve tax complications, and, most important, avoid tax mistakes. A thorough treatment of all of the potential tax consequences of choice of entity and business structure is beyond the scope of this book.

5.7.1 Corporations: C or S?

For each corporation component of the family business, the advisors should determine whether the corporation would achieve long-term tax savings if it elected to be taxed as a subchapter S corporation rather than a C corporation (or, if it is already taxed as an S corporation, whether it should terminate its S election). Further, the advisors should determine the amount (if any) of the short-term tax cost of electing to be taxed as an S corporation. The correct answers depend on facts and circumstances. (Note that an LLC also can elect to be taxed as a C corporation or S corporation, but it usually elects to be taxed as a partnership for reasons discussed in the next section.)

In general, a C corporation incurs a tax on its income. In addition, when a C corporation pays dividends to its shareholders, the shareholders incur a tax on the dividend. For this reason, it is often said that a C corporation incurs two levels of tax. In contrast, an S corporation (and other flow-through entities) does not incur a tax on its income. Rather, the shareholders of an S corporation are taxed on that income, in proportion to their respective shares of ownership, whether or not the income is distributed to the shareholders. For that reason, when an S corporation distributes income or retained earnings, the shareholders do not incur a second tax on the distribution. (In respect to this distinction, payments from an S corporation to its shareholders often are referred to as "distributions" rather than "dividends.")

In general, a C corporation may be more tax efficient if the owners do not intend to take cash out of the corporation as dividends, such as when the shareholders are all employed with the corporation and thus are receiving income from the corporation in the form of compensation. Historically, the state and federal tax liability of C corporations have been assessed under rates and other rules that are more favorable than those that apply to the state and federal taxation of S corporation income (i.e., on a flow-through basis). Therefore, if the corporation is not likely to pay dividends to its shareholders (and thus the shareholders do not incur a dividend tax), then it may be more tax efficient for the corporation and its owners in the aggregate for the corporation to keep its status as a C corporation. In contrast, if the corporation will likely make regular distributions to shareholders (who may or may not be employed by the corporation) to provide cash flow for some of the cash needs discussed in sections 5.4.2 and 5.4.3, then it may be most tax efficient, over the long term, for the corporation to elect S status.

Note, however, that electing S corporation status might have an immediate or short-term tax cost to a business that has been operating as a C corporation. The lawyer should consult the business's accountants to identify and quantify these tax costs, so that the owners can take them into account when deciding whether to make an S election.

Note also that S corporations are subject to other rules that can limit their application. For example: an S corporation may have only 100 shareholders; most business entities and some types of trusts may not hold S corporation stock; gifts of S corporation stock to charitable entities may have much less favorable results than gifts of C corporation stock; and an S corporation is not allowed to have different classes of stock with different economic rights, such as preferred shares versus common shares.[6]

Based on these considerations, the owners might accomplish the greatest tax efficiencies from a C corporation or an S corporation in their business structure, depending on the purpose of the entity and the intended disposition of its cash flow. A C corporation could be appropriate for a business entity whose owners are all employed in the business and thus receive their cash flow from the business in the form of compensation, rather than dividends. In contrast, an S corporation might be an appropriate choice for an entity in the family business that has owners who are not employed in the business and who expect to receive cash flow from the business through "dividends" or distributions.

5.7.2 Flow-Through Entities: S Corporation or LLC?

During the tax analysis of the owners' business structure, the lawyer and the other advisors should also consider whether a particular business component should be organized as a limited liability company, and, if so, how that LLC should be taxed.

---

6. Note, however, that even with a C corporation it is difficult to use different economic classes of stock in the context of family business succession because of the provisions of section 2701 of the Internal Revenue Code, which imposes special, and arcane, rules for calculating transfer tax effects of gifts of family business interests when some of the stock or ownership units have special economic rights. Incidentally, to clarify, even though an S corporation cannot have classes of stock with different *economic* rights, it can have classes of stock with different *voting* rights, which will be discussed in chapter 6 and subsequent sections of the book.

From a tax perspective, a limited liability company may be the most flexible entity. For federal tax purposes, an LLC can elect to be taxed as a C corporation, or it can elect to be treated as an S corporation or a partnership, or it can be disregarded completely if it is owned by one person (or a married couple). If it elects to be taxed as a partnership, it will have the same advantages as an S corporation without the limitations on ownership, except that some of the cash distributions to owners who are employed by the business may be subject to self-employment tax.

An LLC taxed as a partnership has a couple of other tax advantages over corporations. First, an LLC that is taxed as a partnership often can distribute appreciated assets in kind to an owner without triggering a capital gains tax. In contrast, if a C corporation or an S corporation distributes an appreciated asset to an owner, the distribution will usually trigger a tax. In addition, when the owner of an LLC that is taxed as a partnership transfers his or her interest (or dies), the LLC can elect to adjust the LLC's tax basis on a pro rata share of the LLC's assets (i.e., pro rata based on the transferor's percentage ownership interest) to equal their fair market value at date of transfer (or death), which can be an advantage to the new owners for purposes of depreciating those assets or to reduce the capital gains tax liability when those assets are sold. Neither a C corporation nor an S corporation can make similar basis adjustments. These tax advantages can provide greater flexibility in succession planning because they eliminate or defer some of the tax costs involved in changing ownership of assets used in the family business.

Although an LLC taxed as a partnership may seem to be a better choice than an S corporation from a federal income tax perspective, the risk of self-employment tax on cash distributions to owner-operators may be a reason why, in some instances, the owners might choose to use an S corporation or an LLC taxed as an S corporation. Further, if a business entity was originally organized as a corporation, perhaps at a time before LLCs were statutorily enabled or widely accepted, the income tax liability incurred on converting an S corporation to an LLC might be too costly because it might be treated as a sale of the corporation's assets upon the conversion.

A limited partnership, limited liability partnership, or limited liability limited partnership can provide many of the same tax benefits as an LLC that is taxed as a partnership.

5.7.3 IC-DISC

If the owners' business exports its products outside the United States, either directly or through distributors or wholesalers, the owners should consider whether they could achieve tax savings through an Interest Charge Domestic International Sales Corporation (IC-DISC). In appropriate cases, the family business could pay a tax-deductible commission on export income to the IC-DISC, which the family would also own. The IC-DISC would not be subject to income taxes, and the dividends that the IC-DISC would pay to the family would be taxed at a 20 percent rate. As a result, family business income equal to the amount of the commission could be paid to the owners, with a tax savings for the family.

5.7.4 ESOPs

When reviewing the family business structure, the owners should consider whether they might establish an employee stock ownership plan (ESOP) at some time in the future as a device to assist in family exits, as well as a way to provide a benefit to employees. If they do, it might affect their decisions about whether to use a C corporation or an S corporation as part of their business structure, because the tax result is favorable for either C or S corporations, but in different ways.

An ESOP is a tax-exempt trust that holds shares of a corporation's stock in trust for the benefit of its employees. In a family business, an ESOP often is structured to hold a minority position, but it can acquire all of the stock if the family wants to exit ownership entirely.

Usually, when an ESOP is established, it borrows cash to purchase stock in the business from one or more of the owners. If the business is a C corporation, and if the ESOP owns at least 30 percent of the stock, then the selling shareholder can defer capital gains taxes on the transaction by using the sales proceeds to purchase other investments. The ESOP does not pay income taxes on dividends, so it can use the dividends and employer contributions to repay the loan it used to purchase the stock and to pay individual employee benefits when required.

If the business is an S corporation, then the selling shareholder does not have the right to defer capital gains taxes, but the ESOP's tax-exempt feature is still a great advantage. An S corporation is a flow-through entity, as discussed above, so if it has a tax-exempt ESOP as a shareholder, then neither the corporation nor the ESOP pays income taxes on a portion of the corporation's income proportionate to the percentage interest the ESOP holds. Consider the cash-flow advantages, for example, if an ESOP could pay back its acquisition loan using tax-free distributions from an S corporation.

5.7.5 Charitable Entities

In a family business, sometimes a family member who is not involved in the company can nevertheless participate in the family legacy of leadership in a community through participation in the family's charitable giving vehicle, such as a private foundation, supporting organization, or donor-advised fund. Further, family members sometimes want to make gifts of family business interests to the family charitable giving vehicle, either directly or through a split-interest trust, such as a charitable remainder trust or a charitable lead trust. It is also possible that a senior owner may want to make a charitable gift of closely held stock in exchange for lifetime income, such as through a charitable remainder trust or a charitable gift annuity.

The rules that govern the tax treatment of gifts to charitable giving vehicles, especially gifts of closely held business interests, depend on the type of charitable giving vehicle and the form of entity of the business whose ownership interests are the subject of the gift. If charitable giving will be an important feature of the senior owners' exit from ownership or other succession planning, the owners should consider how business restructuring could enhance those plans.

5.8 Tax-Free Reorganization

The lawyer can help the owners design an optimal business structure by considering how their needs and objectives may be best served, at present and after business succession, with respect to business governance and management, cash flow, asset protection, form of entity for various component parts, and, most dramatically, income tax treatment of the business and its affiliated entities and owners. The analysis helps create a better business succession plan but also a better business structure before and after succession.

It some instances, the business or the owners might not be able to restructure the business to adopt a particular new structure without incurring a tax in the process, but Section 368 of the Internal Revenue Code provides some specific means of accomplishing a tax-free reorganization under the right facts.

If the owners cannot accomplish a tax-free reorganization or a tax-free conversion of a particular entity, it might be possible to accomplish these steps with a lesser tax cost on a gradual basis or upon the occurrence of specific events, such as the death of an owner or the sale of an asset. Also, going forward, the most desirable choice of entity and the most appropriate function in the business structure should be applied to any new acquisitions and new ventures that can be added to the business structure without a tax cost.

Chapter Six:

Business Governance and Ownership

This chapter discusses how to review and possibly restructure the business's governance, management, and ownership systems to help the owners more appropriately allocate authority and benefit throughout the family business and affiliated parties. It is likely that the governance, management, and ownership systems that apply to the senior owners will not work as well, or might be harmful, when applied to the successor owners. Therefore, by designing new systems of governance, management, and ownership that are tailored to successor ownership, the owners can create a succession plan that will better serve the business and the successor owners.

In a family business, the separate roles and traditional checks and balances of corporate ownership and operation are often blurred or ignored. Founders and other senior generation owners often operate the business without regard to the fact that their economic interests and their activities as managers arise out of distinctly different sets of legal rights and obligations. However, by recognizing, formalizing, and articulating these rights and obligations, the lawyer and the owners can intelligently assign duties and rights and create an effective system of checks and balances that should maintain business operations at a high standard while also reducing and promptly resolving conflict among successor owners.

Family business governance should be tailored to the family and the business, but it also should be adjusted and adapted to best fit each new generation of owners. Off-the-shelf documents or statutory defaults are unlikely to best serve most family businesses, especially as ownership transitions to the next generation. Further, the exercise of working with the owners to create proper governance and ownership structures can provide them with additional insight they can use to refine their own ideas about specific succession decisions for their family. If the intended successors are old enough to meaningfully contribute or at least understand the conversations about governance and ownership, they should be included in this part of the planning process as well.

6.1 Overview of Corporate Governance and Ownership Roles

Business ownership is not the indivisible conglomeration of control, management, and economic interests that it may seem when the business is owned and operated by one individual or a small group of owner-operators. As a legal matter, what is often thought of as "ownership" is actually four separate and distinct classes of authority, duties, and rights that correspond to the following categories: owner voting rights; governing board authority; executive management authority; and owner economic rights. Although these categories are most formally defined in the law of corporations, they are relevant by analogy when considering LLCs, limited partnerships, and other business entities for which they can also be formally adopted.

When senior owners think about business succession within the family, they sometimes misperceive the task by conflating the questions of who will own the business and who will manage it. This arises out of the notion that the owners "run" the business and decide everything by majority rule. Under that model, it is easy to see how the senior owners might be confounded by succession planning if they have children who, respectively, have different talents, different levels of engagement in the business, different attitudes toward work-life balance, different levels of risk tolerance, different economic needs, different personality types, and perhaps have relationships among one another that are not always pure amicability.

For example, if a senior owner has three children, the senior owner may believe that his or her only choice is to let each child acquire a specific percentage of ownership that will grant such child a proportional right to vote as an owner, participate in governance, and enjoy an owner's economic rights. Consider how unsatisfactory that choice would be if the senior owner believes that all decisions must be made by majority rule or unanimous vote, and if the children also will be expected to guarantee debts of the business, so that the economic risk of those business decisions will run to each child's entire individual wealth. In many cases, there would simply be no correct allocation of percentages that would provide an appropriate outcome. In many cases, a simple allocation of ownership by percentages might result in deadlock, real or perceived oppression of a minority owner, costly negotiations and compromises, or perhaps litigation.

In reality, however, senior owners do not need to allow the number of shares of stock (or other ownership units) that the senior owners transfer to a particular successor owner to determine proportionally all of the successor's rights to participate in decision making, governance, daily operations, and economic benefits. Rather, the senior owners can consider each of the attributes of ownership separately for each successor owner, and allocate each of those attributes in amounts best suited to that particular successor and the successor group collectively. The succession plan and its implementation will document those allocations to be clear, effective, and enforceable.

As the senior owners review these attributes of ownership and consider how to allocate them to their successors, they should consider the reasons for participating in ownership of a family business, discussed in section 3.1.1, and how each successor might prioritize these reasons: cash flow, wealth accumulation, employment/career opportunities, and family legacy. Some of the attributes of ownership and governance roles will be better suited than others to satisfy each successor's reasons for participating in the family business.

6.1.1 Four Levels of Governance and Ownership

Under corporation law, the attributes of an entity's governance and ownership roles can be divided into four distinct categories or levels of authority and economic benefit. This analysis can also be applied to LLCs and limited partnerships, but it is less formally imposed on those entities by relevant law. This chapter will describe the corporate model because it is a useful way to understand governance and ownership of businesses and because the corporate model can be applied to LLCs and other common business entities.

Reference to "corporate model default rules" means statutory default rules under the ABA's Model Business Corporations Act (MBCA).[1]

Under corporate model default rules, the separate categories or levels of governance and ownership, which will be discussed in greater detail throughout this chapter, can be summarized as follows:

6.1.1.a Share-Voting Rights

Shares of stock in a corporation carry one vote per share. Generally, shares can be voted on matters of governance process or existential matters, such as adopting or changing governing documents, electing directors to serve on the governing board, and selling or merging the corporation. These are important voting powers, but they do not entitle the shareholders, as owners, to "run" the business. In fact, as described below, share-voting rights are two steps removed from involvement in managing the corporation's day-to-day business affairs. Further, share-voting rights can be separated from economic ownership of the shares, so that someone other than the shareholder is empowered to exercise voting rights for specific shares, and some shares may carry no votes at all. The corporation's governing documents can expand or limit the subject on which owner voting rights are to be exercised.

6.1.1.b Governing Board Authority

Directors (i.e., members of the corporation's governing board) are generally elected to serve on the board by the persons exercising share-voting rights. Directors cannot exercise board authority by acting individually; rather, the board must act as a body, based on the results of collective deliberation and voting. Under the corporate model's default rules, a shareholder does not have an enforceable right to serve as a director, and directors can serve without owning shares.

Directors do not manage the corporation's day-to-day operations. The board appoints officers and senior executives to manage the corporation's operations, and the board oversees their activities and holds them accountable. Other typical board powers include authority to approve business plans and budgets, authorize transactions that are not in the ordinary course of business, issue dividends, issue new shares or admit new shareholders, and suggest changes to governing documents.

6.1.1.c Executive Management Authority

Officers and executives are appointed by and serve at the pleasure of the board of directors. Officers and executives manage the day-to-day business of the corporation, but their authority is limited, and they generally cannot engage in transactions that are outside the scope of the corporation's ordinary business except to the extent that the board empowers them to do so. Under the corporate model's default rules, a shareholder does not have an enforceable right to serve as an executive, and executives can serve without owning shares.

---

1. Many states have adopted a form of the ABA's MBCA. Delaware is not one of them, but many of the default rules under the DGCL are similar to those of the MBCA.

6.1.1.d Shareholder's Economic Interests

Generally, although a corporation is operated for the benefit of the shareholders, the shareholders, as owners of equity, have little or no direct influence on business decisions or operations, especially shareholders whose share-voting rights are separated from their shares' economic rights and are exercised by another person. In such instances, shareholders are mostly passive beneficiaries of the activities of fiduciaries, directors, and executives, who may have no ownership interest in the corporation. This is a far cry from the common perception, even among business owners, that the shareholders run the business.

6.1.2 Governance Hierarchy

Under the corporate model, the hierarchy of authority and accountability for corporate performance and operations can be illustrated as shown in figure 6.1.2. Share-voting powers, regardless of who has power to exercise them, are exercised to elect the directors and hold them accountable. Next, the board of directors, acting as a body, appoints the senior executives, oversees them, and holds them accountable. Finally, the senior executives manage the business and hold their staff and employees accountable. At the bottom of this hierarchy sit the owners of share equity, who have virtually no authority by reason of their ownership of equity in the corporation.

Figure 6.1.2: Governance Hierarchy

Share Voting

Elects the directors and holds them accountable
through removal power.

Board Authority

Appoints officers/executives, directs and oversees their
performance, and holds them accountable
through removal powers.

Executive Management Authority

Exercises powers of day-to-day management that determine
return available to beneficial owners.

Share Equity

Benefits from exercise of authority of all levels above
but has no authority.

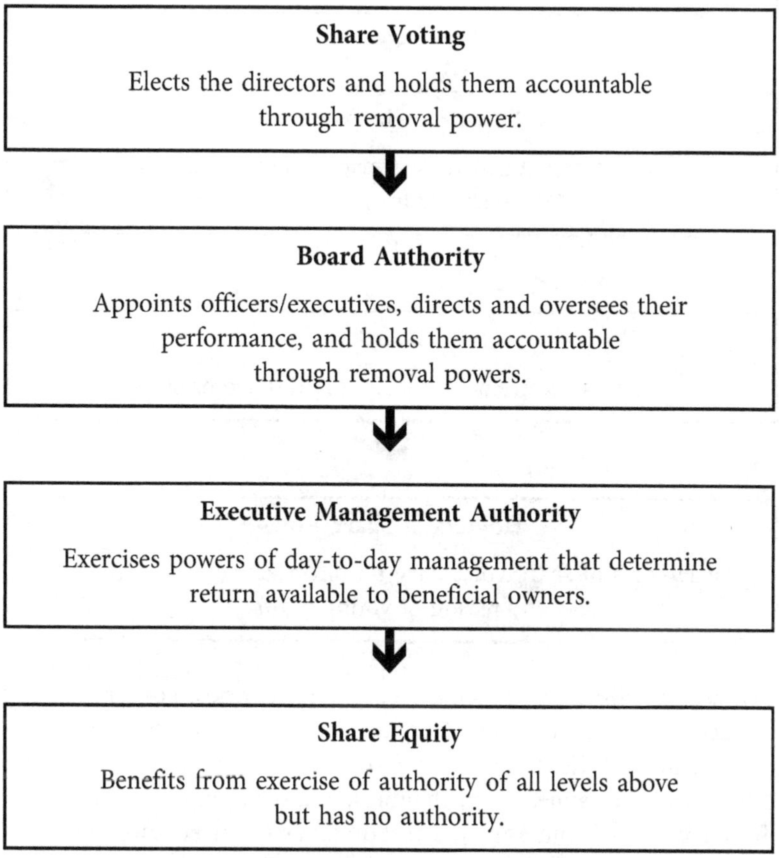

6.1.3 Economic Hierarchy

In the illustration of the corporate governance hierarchy, share voting is at the top and share equity is at the bottom, consistent with the flow of authority. In contrast, an illustration of economic interests might be inverted, consistent with the flow of economic benefit. A graphic illustration of economic interests could appear as shown in figure 6.1.3.

This inversion occurs because the owners of share equity are entitled to the profits and net appreciation of the corporation. Regardless of their lack of authority, the shareholders should receive the greatest economic return from a successful family business. Next down would be the executives, who receive compensation, benefits, and bonuses for their fulltime employment managing business operations. Farther down would be the directors, who are paid board fees for their role in governance, but board service is not a full-time occupation, so the corporation pays them much less than the executives. Finally, if share-voting powers are exercised by someone other than the owner of share equity, the persons voting the shares might receive no compensation from business operations at all.

Figure 6.1.3: Economic Hierarchy

Owners of Share Equity
Owners of share equity entitled to unlimited economic enjoyment of profits or net proceeds.

Executive Management
Executives entitled to reasonable compensation and benefits for services.

Board
Directors receive a fee for limited time commitment.

Holders of Share Votes
Holders of share votes have no direct economic interest by reason of voting rights.

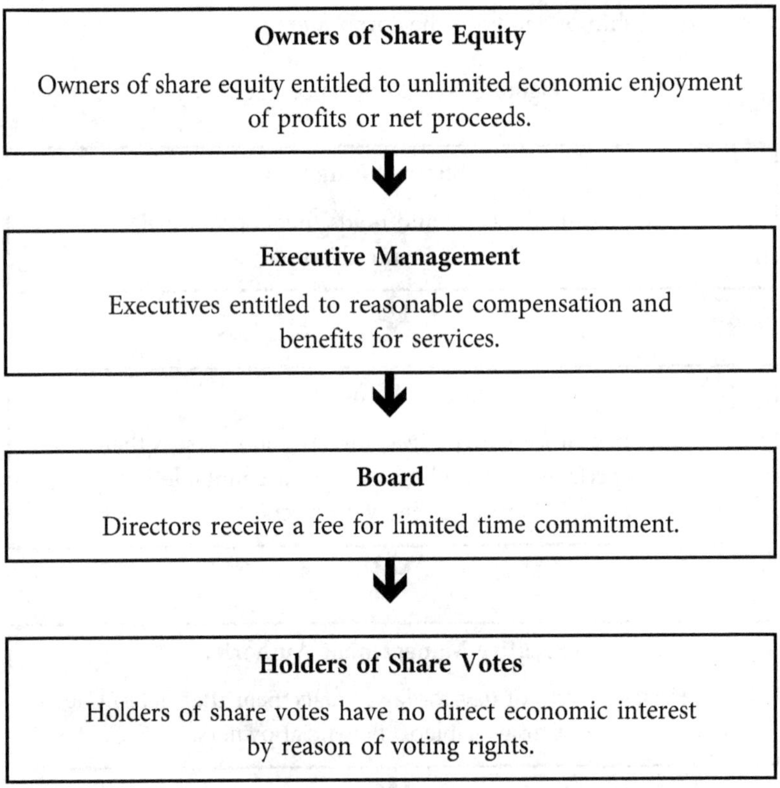

Summarized simplistically, under the corporate model, a corporation is managed through a tiered system of checks and balances for the economic benefit of the relatively powerless equity interests. In this sense, a corporation is similar to a trust, with trustees managing the trust's investments, expenditures, and distributions, all for the benefit of the trust beneficiaries. As with a trust, a corporation's managers owe fiduciary duties to the beneficial owners. Using the trust analogy may be an effective way to help owners understand the structure of and the rationale behind a corporation's division of governance authority and equitable interests.

6.1.4 LLCs and Other Entities: Governance and Economic Structure

An LLC is different from a corporation in that the statutory defaults tend to collapse the four separate levels of ownership and control and vest their attributes in the same person or persons without the formalities of separate levels. Under statutory defaults, LLCs are owned by members and can be managed by the members or by one or more managers who are appointed by the members. LLC statutes, however, allow LLC organizers or owners to create a governance structure that replicates the corporate structure, with member voting powers that can be exercised to elect a board of managers or directors, which in turn appoints officers/executives to run the day-to-day business of the LLC for the benefit of the beneficial owners.

If a business organized as an LLC is operated using the simple member-managed structure while its founder (or other senior generation family member) is running the business as sole owner, it can nevertheless adopt a corporate model of governance as part of the business succession plan before successor owners are admitted. This can allow the current owner-operator to benefit from the simplified, less formal structure of an LLC while he or she is in control, but then utilize the checks and balances of a corporate structure when the business is passed on to the successors and beneficiaries. Also, LLCs held as subsidiaries of family-owned parent companies can function under the simple member-managed governance structure, while the more complex corporate governance mechanisms are utilized for governance of the parent company.

Limited partnerships and most other business entities can also utilize a corporate-style governance and ownership structure. Even the owners' rights to manage property owned as tenants-in-common can be altered by agreement (and perhaps the assistance of a trust) to tailor decision-making processes and separate management from beneficial ownership.

6.2 Succession Planning at Each Level of Governance and Ownership

As with business restructuring (discussed in the preceding chapter), the lawyer should help the owners consider how they could make changes to governance mechanisms and ownership rights to yield immediate benefits at present, and to apply to successor owners in the future. If governance mechanisms and ownership rights will change after succession, then that change should be effected by the documents that implement the succession plan.

If the owners understand the attributes of each level of governance and ownership, as well as how those attributes can be enhanced or limited, they can more easily decide how governance mechanisms and ownership rights should be changed at present and after succession. This task can be most effective when it is combined with an explicit understanding of what each owner and the potential successors hope to receive from their participation in family business governance and ownership.

With that foundation, the objective of this stage of planning is to structure a way to confer the economic benefits of the business on the owners and their successors in proportions that meet the owners' intentions and expectations, and then to secure those economic benefits by allocating governance and management authority in a manner that establishes the most effective leadership and system of checks and balances under the particular circumstances at present and after succession, and during a transitional phase if succession will not occur all at once.

Although succession planning at this stage may be oriented toward identifying specific individuals to serve in specific roles or receive specific economic benefits, it should also create a process that will produce appropriate results as facts and circumstances change. In other words, the established governance mechanisms and ownership rights, including buy-sell agreements, should include processes that will produce appropriate results for decision making, replacement of fiduciaries, transfer of ownership, and dispute resolution after the senior owners no longer have power to change the operative documents. The processes that the senior owners establish, and the means to adapt those processes, should be designed to effectively serve future generations of owners as long as the business remains in the family.

Following are some important notes about how this section is organized:

First, this section is organized consistent with the hierarchy of authority described above. It addresses each level of control in order of figure 6.1.2. Therefore, the discussion starts with unit voting. In practice, however, it is often most effective for the owners to start designing governance structures by deciding how the governing board should be composed and elected. This is true because the board plays such a critical function in representing and protecting the interests of the owners. For the most part, owners in the corporate model do not owe fiduciary duties to one another, but the board owes fiduciary duties of due care, good faith, and loyalty to the company and its owners as a class. Therefore, board composition and the mechanisms for appointing and removing specific directors can be the most important part of the governance discussion and thus can be the key to the whole governance and ownership structure.

Second, this section is intended to be fairly exhaustive on the features of each topic. In most cases, however, the owners will not need to address every possible nuance raised in this section. Based on knowledge of the facts, the lawyer should be able to select which particular dimensions of each topic should be presented to the owners for consideration.

Finally, this section discusses governance and ownership of the business as a single company. If the family business consists of more than one company, these governance and ownership issues may be most important with respect to the primary company in the business, such as the parent or operating company. Usually, the owners should design a governance and ownership structure for succession of the primary business first, and then address governance and ownership for succession of affiliated entities and other family ventures.

6.2.1 Share Voting

Under corporate model default rules, voting rights are important but limited, and they can be separated from the economic benefits of share ownership. This section discusses how the owners can specify the matters that will be subject to share voting and how to design share voting as a power that can be held separate from the economic benefits of share ownership.

Specifically, when reviewing share-voting rights, the owners should consider the following items:

- What matters are put to a vote of shares?
- What are the mechanics of share voting?
- Do all shares carry the same voting rights?
- Do any events affect a share's voting rights?
- Will some shares be bound by a voting agreement?
- Will shares be voted by a fiduciary?
- Will voting shares be held in trust?
- Can a creditor vote shares?

The owners should answer each question for the present circumstances and then as applied to ownership after succession. If succession will be a gradual process, the owners also should consider what rules should apply or how the rules should be applied during the transition.

6.2.1.a Matters for Share Voting

Under corporate model default rules, shareholders, by virtue of the power to vote their shares, do not "run" the business and have no direct effect on day-to-day management or operations. Under corporate model default rules, the matters on which shares can be voted are important but limited. However, the matters that require a vote of shares can be increased by the corporation's governing documents, voting agreements, or board resolutions.

6.2.1.a.i Default Rules: Matters for Share Voting

Under corporate model default rules, shares can be voted to:

- elect and remove directors;
- amend the corporation's governing documents; and
- approve fundamental transactions affecting the existence and form of the corporation (such as to sell or merge the corporation).

6.2.1.a.ii Additional Matters for Share Voting

Corporate model default rules allow the corporation's governing documents or board resolutions to expand the matters that must be put to a vote of shares, thereby increasing the influence of share votes on the business decisions of the board of directors and the executives.

Note that corporate model default rules apply to large corporations whose stock is publicly traded, as well as to closely held family business corporations. Therefore, the statutes are conservative as to the matters that must be submitted to share voting for approval. It would be cumbersome if a public corporation had to reach out to all of its shareholders for approval of anything other than the most fundamental governance questions. Further, many of the shares of a public corporation are voted by persons who do not have sufficient knowledge to make business decisions for the corporation, and some of those persons may have objectives that are not consistent with the corporation's best interests. These same concerns about expanded unit voting may not apply to a family corporation.

A family business governance structure can be designed to ensure that the persons who are voting the corporation's shares consist of a small group of well-informed voters whose interests are aligned with the purposes and objectives of the corporation. Further, in a family business context, some business decisions might disproportionately affect the shareholders' economic well-being, and therefore it is appropriate to require share voting for such decisions.

For example, if shareholders have personally guaranteed corporation debt, it may be appropriate to require approval by share vote before the corporation increases the debt that is supported by the guaranties. Similarly, it may be appropriate to require approval by share vote before the corporation expands its business purpose and pursues a potentially riskier business line.

The lawyer can start the discussion with the owners about the scope and content of share voting by providing the owners with a list of matters that share voting is entitled to decide under default rules and suggestions for items that the owners might want to add. The following is a list of some additional matters that may be appropriate for share voting in a family corporation, along with comments about why each matter might be important to the shareholders.

• **Changing or expanding the business purpose.** A new business purpose might entail greater risk, less reward, or a longer period of illiquidity for the shareholders. Further, a new business purpose might be morally objectionable to some of the shareholders, or the shareholders may view the change in business purpose as inconsistent with family legacy.

• **Issuing more shares.** Under corporate model default rules, if the number of shares authorized under the articles of incorporation exceeds the number of shares outstanding, usually the board can issue those additional authorized shares on terms it considers appropriate. Issuing more shares, however, could have the effect of changing the relative economic or voting rights of the shareholders and outstanding shares.

• **Admitting a new shareholder.** Allowing shares to pass to a non-family shareholder could undermine some of the advantages of family ownership or inhibit pursuit of the family's objectives that may not be purely profit-oriented.

• **Redeeming a shareholder.** Redemption of shares could change the relative economic or voting rights of the shareholders or outstanding shares. For example, if one of three equal shareholders is redeemed, the remaining two shareholders could be at risk of deadlock on electing directors or taking other action.

• **Requiring additional capital contributions.** If the board can unilaterally make capital calls, shareholders might be forced to invest further capital or face dilution of their interests.

• **Borrowing over certain limits.** If the board's power to authorize debt does not require consent of shareholders, debt service could depress annual dividends/distributions or impair share value, especially if the lender imposes restrictive covenants. Also, if shareholders have guaranteed the corporation's debt, additional debt could increase their risk of personal liability.

- **Distributing profits as dividends/distributions.** For a family business in which share ownership is concentrated and which may constitute a large percentage of a shareholder's wealth, the decision to pay or withhold dividends/distributions can have a substantial effect on the cash flow and personal tax liability for individual shareholders.

- **Allowing certain related-party or insider transactions.** Transactions with family members and their affiliates that can be executed without broad scrutiny or approval may be viewed as abusive by shareholders. Sometimes, senior owners may feel that they or their successors will lose control of the business if the governing board includes seats for non-family, independent directors. One way to address this concern is by expanding the matters that require approval by a vote of shares, as described above, thereby imposing a corresponding limit on board authority. Another way to address that concern is to allow shares to be voted at any time to remove a director with or without cause.

Provisions in governing documents that limit the board's authority might not be enforceable if they constrain directors from complying with their fiduciary duties, especially without the consent of all the shares (or shareholders). Also, an expansion of share voting rights cannot allow shareholders, as shareholders, to participate in the day-to-day management of the business or sign contracts or otherwise engage in transactions on behalf of the corporation.

6.2.1.b Procedures for Share Voting

Procedures for voting shares under corporate model default rules are rudimentary and may not be well suited to voting shares of a closely held corporation with a small number of persons entitled to vote, especially if the decisions that require share voting have been expanded beyond default rules. Fortunately, share-voting procedures can be altered and tailored in many respects to better fit family businesses, as long as the procedures are transparent and fair for the parties involved.

6.2.1.b.i Default Rules: Procedures for Share Voting

Corporate model default rules anticipate that it will be rare for the corporation to resort to share voting in the ordinary course. In fact, default rules require only one meeting of shareholders each year, and that is for the purpose of electing directors to fill any open seats on the board (or replacing or re-electing directors whose terms have expired). A corporation can call special meetings of shareholders if a share vote is needed at a time other than the annual meeting.

Under corporate model default rules, each shareholder is entitled to one vote for each share that he or she holds, and most matters that are put to a vote of shares require the affirmative vote of at least a majority of shares voted at a shareholders' meeting at which a quorum (i.e., a majority of share votes) is present. Other matters have different voting thresholds under default rules. For example, directors are usually elected by plurality (i.e., the candidate who wins the most votes cast is elected, even if he or she did not receive a majority of the vote), and decisions to sell the corporation (in one form or another) generally require approval by a majority of shares (which is a higher standard than a majority of shares represented at a meeting at which a quorum is present). Also, shares can be voted without a meeting, but the statutory default may require written consent representing all the shares entitled to vote on the matter.

6.2.1.b.ii Amended Rules: Procedures for Share Voting

Many of the default rules for share voting can be changed by the governing documents, or, in some cases, persons who have power to vote shares can enter into binding agreements on how they will vote in particular circumstances. Voting rights of particular shares can be increased, reduced, or eliminated, and voting rights can be completely separated from the equitable ownership of shares. In some cases, arrangements can be made to allow share-voting rights to be exercised by persons who do not own any shares or who have no beneficial interest in shares.

The corporation's governing documents can control who can call special meetings of shareholders, how many share votes must be present at a meeting to constitute a quorum, and how many shares must vote in the affirmative to take each type of action that is put to a vote. These elements of share voting may affect, for example, whether shares can be voted to change the governing documents without action of the board, whether to remove a director before the end of his or her term, or whether to expand the board (i.e., add more board seats) when the board is considering a critical matter.

Consider that if a corporation relies on default rules to define a quorum at a shareholders' meeting, which could be as small as 50 percent of the voting shares plus one, and to determine whether a vote of shares at a meeting was sufficient to constitute shareholder consent (i.e., a majority of shares represented at the meeting), then a matter put to the vote of shares could be approved with the affirmative vote of only 25 percent of voting shares plus one. That procedure may be appropriate for a public corporation with many shareholders who own a small amount of shares and do not attend shareholders' meetings or otherwise participate in corporate governance, but it could be disruptive to a family business if share approval could be attained by an affirmative vote of less than 26 percent of the voting shares for something that does not actually enjoy a majority consensus. For a family business, it may be best to define the threshold of share votes that are required for shareholder approval based on the number of voting shares outstanding, rather than allow it to be affected by the unpredictable variant of attendance at a meeting.

With these concepts in mind, the owners should consider the following means to define standards for matters that require approval by share voting:

• **Majority voting standard.** The owners could adopt a standard rule that provides that, unless the governing documents or controlling statutes require otherwise, matters that are put to a vote of shares require approval of a majority of shares outstanding, voted at a meeting at which more than 50 percent of the voting shares are represented. This preserves the quorum requirement for a meeting but does not allow attendance to affect the level of approval for an action by share vote.

• **Class voting approval.** The owners could create different voting classes and then require a particular item to be approved by a majority of each class. (See section 6.2.1.c for a further discussion of voting classes.) For example, some matters could require approval by a majority of voting shares in each line of descent (such as siblings and their respective issue), or some matters could require approval by a majority of shares voted on behalf of shareholders who are active in the business or a majority of shares voted on behalf of shareholders who are not active in the business.

- **Supermajority approval.** The owners could provide that some of the matters that are put to a vote of shares require supermajority approval. Usually decisions that are "permanent" or change shareholders' rights should require approval by more than a simple majority of voting shares. For example, a decision to increase or withhold dividends in a given year might be appropriate for approval of a simple majority of voting shares, but a decision to issue additional voting shares to a new owner perhaps should require approval of a large percentage of the shares whose voting rights will be permanently diluted by the transaction.

- **Unanimous approval.** The owners could provide that some of the matters that are put to a vote of shares must be approved by all of the voting shares, but such a requirement can be problematic if it would, in effect, give a unilateral veto to a person who votes a small percentage of voting shares. In a family business, however, the circumstances of a particular decision might have a disproportionately negative effect on a minority shareholder in a way that does not constitute actionable conduct by the other shareholders and thus gives the minority shareholder no recourse. For example, if a minority shareholder is elderly, ill, impoverished, or not employed in the business, a particular decision might affect him or her adversely, even though it is otherwise in the best interests of the corporation and the shareholders collectively. In such situations, rather than require unanimous approval, it might be preferable to require approval of a large supermajority of shares, but then grant a "put" option (the right to demand redemption) for shares that are voted in opposition to the supermajority.

- **Approval without a meeting.** The owners could allow shareholder approval to be provided by written consent, without the need for a shareholders' meeting. The owners could require the written consent to be signed by persons representing at least the same number of voting shares as would be required for approval at a shareholders' meeting. However, if share approval can be provided without a meeting, it might prevent the shares that oppose the action from attempting to persuade the other shareholders not to approve the action. Therefore, the owners might want to require advance notice to all shareholders and an opportunity to comment before share approval is obtained by written consent.

- **Electing directors.** There are many variations for how shares can be voted to elect directors, depending on how the board is constituted. (See section 6.2.2.c for a discussion about board composition and share-voting mechanisms.)

6.2.1.c Voting Classes

Corporate model default rules allow a corporation to establish different classes of stock with different voting rights, as long as that fact is disclosed in the corporation's articles of incorporation. Although S corporations cannot have more than one class of stock with respect to economic attributes, they are allowed to have different classes of stock as to voting rights.[2] A class of stock can have one vote per share, more than one vote per share, or even no voting rights at all, for certain matters or for all matters that are put to a vote

---

2. Treas. Regs. § 1.1361-1(l)(1).

of shares. The only requirement is that all outstanding shares, in the aggregate, must possess 100 percent of share-voting rights.

Classified stock can be used in a family business to allocate board seats and otherwise divide share voting equitably among different populations of shareholders, such as classes based on lines of descent. For example, shares could be classified for ownership by a brother and sister as "B" shares and "S" shares, respectively. The board seats could then be designated to be filled by vote of the B shares, the S shares, or both. This would ensure that, as the shares pass down to the brother's or sister's issue, such issue would continue to be able, as a group, to fill the board seats that were designated for election by their line of descent. In addition, the governing documents can provide that particular decisions require the majority approval of the shares of each class, rather than a majority of the total outstanding shares. This would prevent one line of descent from dominating the other with respect to a particular action. For example, if each class consisted of 50 shares, a decision might require approval of at least 26 shares of each class.

Also, it is possible to use a class of nonvoting shares to limit voting rights to a small percentage of the corporation's stock, so that it is easier to control the allocation and succession of voting control. For example, if a corporation issues 99 nonvoting shares for each outstanding voting share, then the voting stock will constitute only 1 percent of the equitable ownership of the corporation (assuming the classes carry the same economic rights). This can allow the owners to transfer much of the economic benefit of share ownership broadly throughout the family while retaining voting control for themselves (until they are ready to release voting control) or while allocating voting control to a smaller subset of family members. In the example used above, the owners could transfer 99 percent of equitable ownership to children and grandchildren but allocate all voting control to the remaining 1 percent ownership interest held in a trust to be voted by particular family members or other fiduciaries.

6.2.1.d Lapsing or Vesting Voting Rights

A corporation's governing documents, stock subscription agreements, or voting agreements can provide for voting rights to lapse or vest upon the occurrence of a particular event.[3] For example, voting rights might lapse if an owner ceases to be an employee of the corporation, or voting rights might be granted or enhanced if the corporation fails to satisfy an obligation with respect to particular shares, such as payment of a dividend or satisfaction of a redemption right.

6.2.1.e Fiduciary Voting

Under voting trusts, common-law trusts, or proxies, fiduciaries can be appointed to exercise the voting rights of particular shares. Shares of minors and incompetent individuals are often held in trust so that their voting rights can be exercised by a trustee or other fiduciary, but empowering fiduciaries to exercise share-voting rights can be used in a variety of circumstances, and it can be temporary or it can be relatively permanent.

---

3. Caution: If stock is transferred within the family, lapsing or vesting voting rights might trigger the special valuation rules under sections 2701 or 2704 of the Internal Revenue Code and create unintended consequences for transfer tax liability.

Under these arrangements, the fiduciary generally is required to vote the shares in a manner that is in the best interests of the beneficial owner.

Fiduciary voting can be a way to ensure that only qualified family members or other individuals can exercise share-voting rights. For example, shares could be held subject to a voting trust whose trustees must be family members who are employed in the family business.

Fiduciary voting also can be used to allocate voting rights among multiple individuals in a way that is different from share ownership. For example, the owners could provide that all of the shares owned by members of a particular line of descent within the family will be voted by one representative of that line of descent, acting as a proxy or elected to serve as trustee of a voting trust.

Many states have codified the concept of "directed trusts," under which a party other than the trustee has authority over the investment of trust assets and voting of securities held by the trust. This is becoming more and more common as a way to obtain the administrative services of a professional fiduciary or corporate trustee while allocating to other parties control over the disposition and voting of the family business share held by the trust.

The concept of fiduciary voting includes the application of fiduciary duties to the persons who have power to vote the shares. Under most fiduciary voting arrangements, the person who is empowered to vote the shares owes the fiduciary duties of due care, good faith, and loyalty to the beneficial owners of the shares. In most cases, the person who can vote the shares does not owe those same duties to the corporation or the other shareholders.

In the documents that empower fiduciary voting, it may be prudent to explicitly refer to fiduciary duties as a reminder to the fiduciary and the beneficial owners, or it may be possible to alter or limit the fiduciary duties. For example, if the trustee of a voting trust also owns shares in his or her own name, the voting trust document could explicitly allow this apparent conflict of interest but nevertheless require the trustee to vote the trust shares exclusively in the best interests of the voting trust's beneficial owners, not in service of the trustee's personal interests as a shareholder.

Note that if a corporation's shares are divided into voting and nonvoting shares, the persons who own and vote the voting shares generally have no fiduciary duties to the nonvoting shareholders. In this way, such an arrangement differs from fiduciary voting mechanisms. This fact might affect the owners' decisions about how to separate share-voting rights from equitable share ownership.

For example, if the owners want equity of the corporation to be owned equally by seven owners, but they want only three of the owners to have voting power, the owners' choice could be framed as follows:

Option A: The corporation may issue three voting shares and four nonvoting shares (i.e., one share for each shareholder). The shareholders who own the voting shares will have all the voting rights, but they will not owe fiduciary duties to one another or to the nonvoting shareholders. (Note that if a voting majority acts in a manner that is abusive of the rights of other shareholders, it might create a basis for liability under a cause of action for minority oppression, but such are special circumstances, usually applying to behavior that is egregious and intentionally inequitable.)

Option B: The corporation may issue seven shares (i.e., one for each shareholder), all of which carry one vote, but title the shares to a voting trust under which three of the owners will serve as trustees and vote all seven shares. Under this option, the shareholders serving as trustees will owe fiduciary duties of due care, good faith, and loyalty to all seven shareholders when voting the shares.

In a family business context, the fiduciary model may be a superior way to allocate voting authority while protecting the economic interests of the beneficial owners. Under that model, however, it might be possible for a beneficial owner to cause disruption by alleging breach of fiduciary duty whenever he or she disagrees with the voting trustees' actions. Owners can consider ways to mitigate that risk by exculpating fiduciaries from liability for actions taken in good faith and by providing for alternative dispute resolution mechanisms to resolve the claims of beneficial owners without formal adversarial proceedings.

6.2.1.f Debt Holder Voting

In some instances, holders of debt can be given voting rights through the terms of debt instruments, pledge agreements, or proxies. Debt instruments issued by the corporation can provide for conversion of debt to voting shares at the election of the debt holder or upon the occurrence of an event. These types of arrangements can be used in a family business to provide a voice to family members, including senior owners, who are redeemed in exchange for payments over time.

6.2.1.g Voting Agreements

In many cases, owners can execute voting agreements among themselves that govern how they will vote on specific matters. Voting agreements can be part of other agreements affecting owners as well, such as shareholders' agreements with buy-sell provisions, trust agreements, stock subscription agreements, loan documents, or stock pledge agreements. If shares are not classified, a voting agreement can be an alternative means of ensuring that members of a particular branch of the family vote their shares in the aggregate, rather than as smaller, fragmentary share percentages.

6.2.1.h Implementation

After the owners address the issues raised in this section 6.2.1 and thus make decisions about share-voting rights, the lawyer must implement their decisions in appropriate documents, to be effective immediately or only upon transfer of ownership to the successor owners. The documents should include provisions for how they can be amended, and such provisions should be consistent with the voting rules that they are drafted to impose.

In most instances, the documents can be given effect immediately, in a way that does not necessarily change the rights of current owners but will have the desired effect after succession because of how the voting shares are allocated among the successors and because of who may be appointed to serve in fiduciary voting roles.

6.2.2 Board Authority

A board of directors oversees management of the corporation and makes high-level decisions about business strategy, finances, and growth. Directors cannot exercise board authority individually, but must act collectively as a board. This section discusses how the owners can specify matters that will require board approval and decide how the board will be constituted.

A governing board, if appropriately constituted and properly used, can be a great resource for a family business and can be a key element to its long-term success. The governing board can help the business identify and seize opportunities, avoid or mitigate risk, and resolve existential threats as soon as they arise. Talented and sincere directors also can help resolve discord among the owners before it degenerates into adversarial proceedings.

Unfortunately, many family businesses fail to see the potential benefits of a well-constituted board, and as a result, they have no independent directors and hold no formal board meetings. The lawyer can provide long-term value to the owners and their successors by educating them on the proper role of a governing board and helping them develop a quality, functioning board.

Specifically, when reviewing the role of the board, the owners should consider the following items:

- What matters require board approval?
- How is the board constituted?
- How are directors elected?
- What are the directors' fiduciary duties and potential liability?
- What documents control authority (and how can they be amended)?

The owners should answer each question as it applies to present circumstances and then as it should apply after the transition to successor owners. If succession will be a gradual process, the owners also should consider what rules should apply or how the rules should be applied during the transition.

6.2.2.a Board Function and Powers

The owners should review a board's function and powers under default rules and then decide whether to expand or curtail the board's function and powers.

Under the corporate model default rules, a company's board determines business strategy, oversees management of the business, and authorizes transactions that are outside the ordinary course of business (such as expansions or joint ventures). The board appoints or removes officers and top executives, determines their compensation, and defines the scope of their responsibility and authority. The board can cause the corporation to issue new shares or redeem shares at prices that the board deems appropriate, and the board can cause the corporation to pay or withhold dividends/distributions. The board can only act as a group. Individual directors usually do not, in that capacity, sign contracts or otherwise engage in transactions on behalf of the corporation.

The corporation's governing documents can limit or expand the board's function and powers. To assist the owners' decision making on this topic, the lawyer can provide the owners with a list of board functions and powers and then add or delete items according to the owners' decisions.

Typically, a governing board meets four to six times a year. The primary purpose of each meeting is to take action by vote of the directors. In support of that purpose, a board meeting may include presentations of information and deliberations relevant to a matter before the directors vote.

Although the board is not involved in the day-to-day operations of the corporation, it is not simply a passive institution. The board, acting on its own initiative, can generate and assign tasks or projects to be pursued by a board committee or the executive team which the board deems necessary for future action.

For example, the board might require the executive team to present an amended budget or business plan due to the sudden loss of a major customer. The board might form a committee to work with the executive team to assess cybersecurity deficiencies and develop a plan to reduce the risk of a data breach. The board might retain special counsel to investigate allegations of sexual harassment or hiring discrimination by executives or personnel under their supervision.

Here are some of the more important board functions and powers that the owners should consider:

• **Business strategy.** The board's influence over business strategy is a pervasive function that does not consist of voting on a single matter. In most cases, the board should require the executive team, working alone or with a committee of the board, to create a strategic plan for board approval. Thereafter, the board's decisions will be guided by the strategic plan. Either the board, the committee, or the executive team can initiate amendments to the strategic plan, and it can be reviewed on an annual basis. Business performance can be measured against the strategic plan, and executives can assume that they have authority to take action that is consistent with the strategic plan.

• **Budgets and financial reporting.** In most cases, the executive team should submit annual and longer-term budgets to the board for approval. Executives can assume that they have authority to expend the corporation's resources consistent with the budget. For example, the executives may assume that they can add personnel as long as they do not exceed the budget for payroll. Then, at each board meeting, the executives will present actual results as compared with the budget. Based on actual results, the executives or the board may seek to amend the budget or create variances to respond to dynamic situations.

• **Risk management.** In most cases, the board should be apprised of risks that threaten the health, profitability, or sustainability of the business in all areas of operations, and should require the executive team to develop means of addressing those risks.

• **Crisis management.** In the case of a crisis, the board may have emergency bylaws and other procedures that allow directors to take an active role in operations or to take action on behalf of the corporation as needed to manage the crisis and minimize the damage to the business. For example, if the CEO dies unexpectedly, the board may empower one of the directors to serve as interim CEO until the board can find a successor.

• **Authorize transactions.** Usually, a corporation's officers or executives must obtain the board's express authorization to bind the corporation in a transaction that is outside its ordinary course of business. Usually the board must authorize particularly large expenditures, unusually large debt obligations, or the sale of particularly valuable assets. The corporation's governing documents can be specific about when such transactions require board authorization. In some cases, the owners may want to require shareholder approval, not just board authorization, before the corporation incurs additional debt or engages in any other significant transaction. For example, if shareholders guarantee the corporation's debt, they may not want that debt to be increased without their consent.

   • **Selling or merging the business.** A business can be effectively sold by means of a stock sale, asset sale, or merger. In some cases, the board may have the power to initiate or veto a particular sale of the business or certain elements of the transaction. The owners should decide what role, if any, the board should play with respect to a sale of the business, regardless of the form of the transaction.

   • **Oversight of executives.** Generally, the board has power to appoint officers and top executives, review their performance, and determine their compensation. In a family business, the owners can diminish tension surrounding the issue of family member employment if decisions about the advancement, employment, and compensation of family members are made by a committee of independent directors or with the help of an independent consultant.

   • **Issue and redeem shares.** If shares that are authorized in a corporation's articles of incorporation have not all been issued, then the board can issue the unissued shares to any person that the board deems to be appropriate. For example, if a corporation's articles of incorporation authorize 10,000 shares but only 2,000 have been issued and remain outstanding, then the board can issue up to 8,000 more shares without seeking consent of the shareholders. In a family business, however, the owners prefer to keep tighter control over who becomes an owner. In such cases, the board's authority to issue additional shares can be further proscribed by a provision in governing documents that grants the shareholders a right of first refusal to acquire such shares, or allows shareholders to avoid dilution by the issuance of new shares, or simply prevents the board from issuing new shares without shareholder consent.

   • **Pay dividends.** Under the corporation model default rules, the board has discretion to withhold dividends (or distributions, if it is an S corporation) or to pay dividends/distributions in an aggregate amount that the board determines. In a family business, however, the owners tend to want to have direct input regarding dividends or distributions. In particular, if the corporation is an S corporation with flow-through income tax liability, the shareholders may be dependent on distributions from the corporation to pay their share of tax liability. Family business governing documents can require dividends or distributions of a particular minimum amount, and then give the board discretion to authorize additional dividends or distributions with or without approval of the shareholders.

6.2.2.b Board Composition

Board composition relates to how many directors sit on the governing board; whether directors must have any special qualifications; how each director is elected, removed, or replaced; and when each director's term begins and expires. The owners should tailor their board using these elements of board composition. In family business succession planning, board composition may be the single most important decision the owners will make.

   Corporation model default rules generally do not impose requirements about who may serve as a director or how many directors there must be on the board or a committee. Such requirements, however, can be imposed by a corporation's governing documents. The governing documents may fix the number of directors and how that number may be changed. The governing documents may require a certain number or proportion of "outside" directors (i.e., directors who are not employees or shareholders) or "independent" directors (i.e., outside directors who have no economic relationship with the corporation) to be on the board or serve on any particular committee. For example, the governing documents could require the board to have a majority of independent directors, or a charter approved by the board could prohibit any inside director from serving on the personnel committee, which would make employment and compensation recommendations to the full board.

Under the corporation model default rules, a board must have at least one director but may have many more. Shareholders and employees may be directors, but persons who are neither also may be directors. Directors are elected by plurality vote of all the share votes at the annual shareholders' meeting. However, these default rules regarding board powers, board composition, and director elections can be changed in the governing documents and other agreements. When making decisions about board composition, the owners should keep in mind the board's function and powers, as addressed under section 6.2.2.a.

6.2.2.b.i Family Directors

In a family business, it is desirable to ensure that key elements of the family are represented on the board. Such key family elements may include each generation, each line of descent, family members who are active in the business, and those who are not. Family members who might soon sit on the board, perhaps after the occurrence of a particular event, might be permitted to train for board service as junior board members or as board observers.

Family member directors can bring the perspective of family legacy to board deliberations. Further, they can bring the perspective of investors who may be seeking a more robust dividend policy or who may wish to use earnings to aggressively grow the business and thereby cause their shares to appreciate in value. A family member who has personally guaranteed company debt may wish to serve on the board to protect his or her interests as a guarantor as well as shareholder. Similarly, a family member who is owed a substantial amount by the corporation or other shareholders after being bought out in exchange for an installment note may wish to sit on the board until his or her note is paid off. In many cases, when a key senior owner retires and sells his or her shares to the successors, the withdrawing owner may remain on the board as an active chair or a nonvoting emeritus director to assist with the transition.

6.2.2.b.ii Independent Directors

Non-family directors, particularly qualified independent directors, can provide substantial benefit to a family business. The owners should consider designating a minimum number of seats on the board to be filled by independent directors.

Note that there is a difference between "outside" directors and "independent" directors. An "outside" director connotes an individual who is not an employee or shareholder in the corporation, but is a service provider or has some other ongoing transactional relationship with the corporation. For example, an accountant who provides services to the corporation may be an "outside" director, but not an "independent" director. Generally, an "independent" director is a director whose only nexus with the corporation is his or her board service.

Many of the comments in this section can apply to outside directors as well as truly independent directors, but sometimes an outside director's other relationship with the corporation can diminish or impair his or her objectivity when it is needed most. In particular, it is understandable if the owners ask their lawyer, as their trusted advisor, to sit on the board. The lawyer may be positioned to provide unique value to the owners as a director because of his or her broad knowledge of the family, the business, and the succession plan. In some instances, however, particularly if family members on the board are at odds and the lawyer has not been able to mediate a consensus, it might do more harm than good if the lawyer were forced to vote against the wishes of one side or the other. Thus, if the lawyer serves on his or her client's board, it should be understood that the lawyer does not serve the same function as a truly "independent" director and reserves the right to recuse himself or herself from a particular matter when family members on the board are in conflict. (Also, see section 2.1.4 regarding ethical considerations when the lawyer serves on a client's board.)

Independent directors can provide the following benefits to a family business:

• **Expertise.** An independent director can be selected to provide expertise that is not otherwise available within the business or among the owners. Such expertise may involve knowledge of the substantive market in which the corporation does business, such as real estate, hospitality, automotive, pharmaceuticals, or aerospace. In the alternative or in addition, such expertise may involve a knowledge of corporate services that the corporation does not have in-house, such as law, accounting, information technology, human resources, or marketing. Using board seats to obtain access to needed expertise can be especially effective if the shareholders choose directors whose skills are complementary rather than duplicative.

• **Outside experience.** An independent director can bring the corporation fresh ideas and perspectives about business operations based on experiences that he or she has had with other businesses.

• **Contacts.** An independent director may be a new source of contacts for the business in its industry or market, or among other potential transaction partners, such as lenders or acquisition targets.

• **Credibility.** The presence of well-qualified independent directors on the board may add to the credibility of the business in its market and industry. This may be helpful after ownership of the corporation is transferred to the successors, who might not yet have achieved the reputation of the exiting owners. It may be particularly important if ownership passes to the successor by reason of an unexpected death or disability of a key owner.

• **Impartiality.** Perhaps the most compelling reason to have independent directors on the board of a family corporation is their ability to be objective and disinterested when the board needs to make a decision that might affect family members disproportionately, or when family member directors do not have a consensus. For example, if some owners are active in the business and some are not, the inactive owners may be more accepting of decisions about compensation of the active owners if those decisions are made by the independent directors. Further, if a dispute among owners threatens to become disruptive, the independent directors can intervene immediately as informal mediators or, with the consent of the parties, as de facto arbitrators. Further, it is much more difficult for a disgruntled minority owner to mount a legal challenge to a board decision if it is made by (or includes the unanimous consent of) directors who have no conflict of interest in the matter.

6.2.2.c Election of Directors

Under the corporation model default rules, each year, at the annual meeting of shareholders, each director is elected or re-elected to a one-year term by plurality vote of the shareholders (i.e., the candidate receiving the most votes, even if not a majority, is elected). These defaults can be changed by the articles of incorporation and bylaws of the corporation in a variety of ways.

The appropriate changes to consider will depend, in part, on board size and the percentage of shares being voted together. For example, if the board is large and if no one person has power to vote more than 10 percent of the shares when electing directors, then the best approach to electing directors might be very different from the best approach for a corporation that is owned by three or four equal shareholders. The owners should try to adopt rules that will allow them to convene and maintain a quality board, but they also should try to avoid rules that could be abused or could unintentionally cause unfair or unproductive results.

The following are some provisions to be considered.

6.2.2.c.i Longer Terms

In a family business, in which many of the directors are selected from a small group of family members and in which ownership of voting shares changes usually only on the time scale of generations, a one-year term for directors may be much too short. In such cases, directors' terms can be lengthened to a greater number of years, or some directors could be allowed to serve until the occurrence of a particular event. For example, the bylaws could allow each outside or independent director to serve for a three-year term (with a possibility of multiple terms) and allow each inside director to serve until he or she is removed or is no longer an employee or shareholder.

6.2.2.c.ii Staggered Terms

In a family business, it could be disruptive if the terms of all the directors, or, for example, all the independent directors, ended at the same time. Therefore, if the bylaws allow each director's term to run longer than one year, then the bylaws also can provide for board terms to be staggered so that the terms of only some of the board members end in any given year. Under such an arrangement, if those directors are not re-elected, the board may nonetheless remain more stable as it absorbs new directors. Note that if some of the bylaws adopt some of the other approaches described below, then staggered terms may be less important, or even counterproductive.

6.2.2.c.iii Ex Officio

The bylaws can provide for board seats that are automatically granted to individuals who have particular positions with respect to the corporation. For example, there may be an ex officio seat on the board for the individual who serves as CEO or president of the corporation. Similarly, if the corporation is a parent company, the board may include an ex officio seat for the individuals who serve as presidents of key subsidiaries.

6.2.2.c.iv Constituent Directors or Classified Seats

A "constituent director" is one who is elected or appointed by a specific person or group, and a "classified seat" is a board seat that may be filled only by a director who is elected by a specific class of shares. The bylaws or a voting agreement can provide for constituent directors or classified seats to ensure that the board includes representation of the interests of particular shareholders or other stakeholder who do not hold a majority of voting shares.

For example, if a senior generation owner sells voting control to successors in the family in exchange for payment over time, then the successors might agree that the seller may continue to sit on the board, or appoint a representative to do so, until the purchase price is paid in full. (Note: The owners should confer with tax advisors if this right is granted in the context of a redemption of the seller's shares (i.e., rather than a cross purchase). If it causes the transaction to be treated as less than a full redemption of the seller's shares, it could have unintended tax consequences.)

The use of classified seats may be especially appropriate when the clients wish to maintain a balance of influence among distinct branches of family ownership. For example, in a corporation owned by four siblings, if a board seat is classified for each sibling and his or her line of descent, then each line of descent may continue to have at least one seat on the board, regardless of the relative numbers of offspring, as long as the classified shares remain in the line of descent. Similarly, board seats could be classified for election by a class of shareholders who are also employed in the business and by a class of owners who are not employed in the business.

Note, however, that a constituent director, including directors elected to classified seats, does not owe a special or superior fiduciary duty to the persons or class of persons who elected him or her. Rather, all directors have the same fiduciary duties of due care and loyalty to the corporation and all the common shareholders collectively. The value of a constituent director or classified seat is that it allows persons in the minority to select a director they trust to provide prudent input on the board and, presumably, to raise the alarm if the board might pursue a course that is reckless or improper—the alarm to be raised in a manner that is consistent with the director's other duties, including a duty of confidentiality owed to the corporation.

6.2.2.c.v Majority Voting or Cumulative Voting

Other variations for electing directors include majority voting requirements or cumulative voting, or virtually any other voting mechanisms that the shareholders may agree upon.

A majority voting requirement would allow a director to be elected to the board only if he or she received a majority of votes by some measure, such as a majority of the shares voted, a majority of the shares outstanding, or a majority of the shares of each class. A majority voting requirement is intended to ensure that each board member has broad support.

Cumulative voting allows a shareholder to aggregate his or her votes in a particular election and cast them to fill fewer than all the seats that are open. For example, if a shareholder has ten voting shares and there are three open seats, then, under the default rules, the shareholder would have thirty votes in the aggregate, but would only be able to cast ten votes to fill each seat. Under cumulative voting rules, however, the shareholder would be allowed to aggregate his or her votes and thus cast all thirty votes to fill one seat, or otherwise freely allocate the votes among the open seats. The purpose of cumulative voting is to allow minority shareholders a means to fill at least one or two seats on the board, rather than be outvoted as to each seat.

6.2.2.c.vi Nonvoting Board Members and Board Observers

If it is not practical or desirable to allow board seats for particular minority owners, it may be possible to allow them to appoint nonvoting board members or board observers to attend board meetings on their behalf. A nonvoting board member may speak at board meetings but may not vote as a director; a board observer may attend board meetings but has no right to address the board and cannot vote as a director. Although nonvoting board members and board observers will not be able to directly affect board action, and thus they will not owe the same fiduciary duties to the corporation and the shareholders as governing directors do, they nevertheless should be bound by an express standard of conduct, including a duty of confidentiality and a prohibition on competing with the corporation. These rules should be adopted in writing by the board and signed by the individuals who will be bound by them. As with constituency directors, it is expected that nonvoting directors and board observers will share some board-level information with the shareholders who have appointed them, but those communications can be limited by reasonable confidentiality parameters that protect sensitive business information without defeating the purpose of allowing these individuals to attend the board meetings.

6.2.2.c.vii Junior Directors

To assist with board succession within the family, the board can select junior generation family members to attend board meetings as junior directors. Junior directors typically would not be allowed to vote as directors, but by attending board meetings and participating on committees, they can become better prepared to serve as governing directors if and when they are asked to do so. As with other nonvoting board members, rules for their service should be adopted by the board in writing and signed by each junior board member who serves.

6.2.2.c.viii Standards to Qualify

To help maintain the quality of directors serving on the board, the owners may agree upon a written standard for family member directors and for outside directors. The corporate model default rules provide only minimal standards for who can serve as a director. Therefore, the owners should consider adopting basic standards, including mental capacity, levels of education or training, quantity of business experience, and, for independent directors, a definition of independence. In particular, by defining a mental capacity requirement, the standards for service on the board would cause a director's term to cease automatically if he or she no longer met the mental capacity requirement. (This should not invalidate any action taken by the board before it was aware that the incapacitated director's term had ceased.)

6.2.2.c.ix Removal

The power to remove directors without cause is a way to preserve a standard of quality on the board and allow shareholders to hold directors accountable for failures or transgressions that might not warrant more punitive remedies. The number of votes required to remove a director should be no fewer than the number needed to elect the director. In addition or in the alternative, it might be appropriate to allow directors to be removed by a supermajority of the board itself. For example, it may be desirable for a supermajority of the board to be able to remove a director who has become disruptive or who has violated standards of conduct, such as confidentiality or noncompetition commitments.

6.2.2.d Board Procedures and Standards

The corporation model default rules govern procedures for board action and standards for directors' conduct, but many of these defaults can be augmented or changed by a corporation's articles of incorporation or bylaws.

6.2.2.d.i Board Action

Under the corporation model default rules, most board actions require the affirmative vote of at least a majority of directors in attendance at a meeting at which a majority of directors (i.e., a quorum) are present, but the corporation's governing documents can increase or reduce quorum and voting requirements for meetings. Each director is entitled to one vote on any matter that comes before the board, except in special circumstances (such as conflict of interest transactions), but the corporation's governing documents may be able to increase or decrease the voting powers of particular directors.

Under the corporation model default rules, if the board is acting without a meeting, then the action requires the directors' unanimous written consent, but the corporation's governing documents can provide for written action to be effective if it is signed by no less than two-thirds or even a simple majority of directors. The primary reason to require unanimous written consent of directors for board action taken without a meeting is because if an action does not have the support of the full board, then perhaps the board should not take the action without a meeting to hear arguments in opposition. If the owners choose to require less than unanimous consent for board action, they should consider some other safeguard, such as requiring the written consent to include at least a majority of independent directors.

6.2.2.d.ii Delegation and Committees

Directors cannot vote by proxy or otherwise delegate their voting rights. However, a corporation's board may delegate some of its powers to committees, whose authority and responsibilities are governed by charters approved by the board. Committees are composed of directors, but they may include advisors or employees who attend their meetings but do not vote. In some cases, a committee can be delegated the power to exercise the authority of the full board as to specific matters. Common committees include executive, governance, finance, and personnel/compensation. In a family business, it may be deemed most equitable to require decisions about family member employment and compensation to be determined by a board committee composed of independent directors. Also, consider that many projects, such as information and technology risk management, that would be unwieldy for the full board may be handled more effectively by a committee of the most qualified board members.

6.2.2.e Fiduciary Duties and Director Liability

At all times, directors owe fiduciary duties to the corporation and all the shareholders (i.e., in the aggregate) to be loyal and to act in good faith and with due care. These duties cannot be eliminated, but their scope can be narrowed, and directors can be protected from liability for claims arising out of some of these duties. The owners should try to find a balance by adopting mechanisms that elicit prudent and equitable board decisions, but do not subject the directors to intimidation or abuse.

For example, reliance on the threat of shareholder litigation as a means to discourage poor conduct by directors is cumbersome and potentially damaging to the whole enterprise. In contrast, precautions such as independent directors, board observers, conflict of interest procedures, and unanimous consent for written action can reduce the opportunities for directors to inadvertently or willfully misuse their powers. Further, in many cases, the power to remove a director without cause can be a sufficient means to address truly bad behavior without resorting to litigation.

6.2.2.e.i Director Liability, Exculpation, and Indemnification

Under the common law of many states, shareholders can bring direct actions (i.e., on behalf of themselves) or derivative actions (i.e., on behalf of the corporation) to hold directors personally liable for loss caused by breach of fiduciary duties. Such litigation can enable shareholders to hold directors accountable, but it also can be a disruptive and costly force that damages the corporation and adversely affects all of its stakeholders. The corporation model default rules allow corporations to utilize mechanisms, such as exculpation and indemnification of directors, to reduce the likelihood that shareholders will resort to litigation, except in the most egregious circumstances.

If directors must operate under the threat of personal liability, they may be unable to properly exercise their business judgment and may govern too conservatively, opposing even a reasonable level of business risk to avoid litigation. They may be unable to resolve shareholder conflict or even may be reluctant to take any position that is not unanimously supported by the shareholders. Under such circumstances, some talented individuals might refuse to serve as a director. For these reasons, the owners should try to create an environment in which directors will not be punished for decisions they make in a good-faith effort to pursue the best interests of the corporation and its shareholders collectively.

The corporation model default rules allow a corporation to protect its directors from the costs of litigation, and the potential liability arising out of such litigation, by exculpating them (i.e., exonerating them in advance) for claims arising out of actions they take in good faith and by indemnifying them for losses they may incur in any litigation except for successful claims involving their intentional wrongdoing. Indemnification of directors often will include an advance of litigation costs and may be funded with errors and omissions insurance for directors and officers (often referred to as "D&O insurance").

6.2.2.e.ii Conflict of Interest Transactions

Another means to help directors avoid personal liability for board action is to adopt special procedures for approval of transactions that involve a conflict of interest, such as transactions between the corporation and a director or controlling shareholder. If a director engages in conduct that involves a conflict of interest for him or her, either personally or by reason of a relationship with another party, such conduct may imply that the director did not act in good faith. As a result, exculpations and other protections for good-faith conduct might not apply. In a family business, however, there may be many instances in which the corporation should be allowed to engage in transactions with directors, shareholders, and related parties. Such transactions may include compensation decisions, stock redemptions, or transactions between the corporation and a business owned by one or more of the directors. Therefore, a corporation can adopt procedures to help ensure that such transactions are fair to the corporation and are fully enforceable. For example, the governing documents may provide that interested directors must recuse themselves from voting on a conflict transaction or that disinterested shareholders also must approve the transaction. Such procedures should clearly define a "conflict of interest," based on applicable law.

6.2.2.e.iii Advisory Boards and Board Members

To assist its governing board, a corporation may appoint advisory board members or create an advisory board. Advisory board members may assist the directors in making decisions or pursuing committee projects, but they do not vote and they do not have fiduciary duties.

Advisory board members can be helpful to the board if they bring special expertise or knowledge, whether technical knowledge or simply knowledge about the needs and objectives of shareholders. For example, if a corporation holds or manages a substantial position in alternative investments (perhaps as a collective investment venture for the shareholders and their families), the board might appoint one or more individuals with venture capital or private equity experience as advisory board members to help the board oversee those investments.

In other family businesses, especially those that are still primarily owned and operated by the founder, the shareholders might conclude that they do not want outside directors to have any enforceable authority that might intrude on the family's autonomy to govern its own enterprise. In such cases, an advisory board still can provide many of the advantages of outside directors on a governing board, such as expertise, experience, networking, and enhanced credibility. Further, an advisory board can transition to a governing board with outside directors as ownership circumstances change. For example, the advisory board may serve only in an advisory capacity until the founder retires, and then the individuals on the advisory board may be formally appointed to the governing board. Such an arrangement can be an effective mechanism for governance succession, especially if a change of ownership happens unexpectedly. In that instance, the governing board can be populated immediately by members of the advisory board who already are familiar with the corporation and its shareholders.

6.2.2.f LLCs and Other Business Entities

Although statutory defaults for LLCs do not require an LLC to have a board, an LLC's operating agreement can establish a board of managers or board of directors that can be structured and can operate the same as a board of directors of a corporation. Similar mechanisms can be used to govern limited partnerships and other business entities.

For LLCs and other companies that are wholly owned subsidiaries of a parent corporation, the owners of the corporation may choose not to have a governing board at the subsidiary level but rather allow the parent company board to appoint a manager (or other officer) to manage the subsidiary pursuant to instruction from the parent company board. If the subsidiary has business operations that are unrelated to the parent or sibling companies, however, the corporation's owners may conclude that the subsidiary should have its own governing board. (When a parent and its subsidiary are governed by the same board, the companies should be especially diligent in taking precautions against attempts to pierce the corporate veil, which could cause the parent company to become liable to satisfy obligations of the subsidiary.) (See the discussion at section 5.5.1.)

6.2.3 Executive Authority

Officers and executives of a corporation serve at the pleasure of the governing board and conduct the corporation's day-to-day business. Officers and executives have the authority granted to them by the board, both in general terms and in specific instances. This section discusses how the owners can allocate executive authority, recognizing that family members, from time to time, may occupy some of those executive positions.

Specifically, the owners should consider the following questions:

- What are the officer and primary executive positions, and what are their functions?
- What are the officers' and primary executives' terms of employment and service?

The owners should answer each question as it applies to present circumstance and then as it should apply after the transition to successor owners and managers. If succession will be a gradual process, the owners also should consider what rules should apply or how they should be applied during the transition.

6.2.3.a Key Positions

Under the corporation model default rules, officers and executives are appointed by the board and have authority to manage the day-to-day business of the corporation. The scope of authority of any officer or executive is determined by the bylaws, board resolutions, and common usage. The board can delegate powers to officers or executives to the extent that delegation may be prudent and the bylaws may permit. Officers and executives typically cannot engage in transactions that are outside the ordinary scope of the corporation's business without approval of the board.

For the most part, each officer and executive owes fiduciary duties of due care, good faith, and loyalty to the corporation and all the shareholders when performing his or her duties. However, officers and executives may be exculpated and indemnified, like directors, to protect them from personal liability for actions they take in good faith. (See section 6.2.2.e.i.)

Most corporations have a president, at least one vice president, a secretary, and a treasurer, but the bylaws and the board may establish other officer and executive positions that may be appropriate for that corporation's particular structure and business. Many corporations also use executive titles. For example, the president often also serves as chief executive officer, and the treasurer often also serves a chief financial officer (or, in a smaller business, controller). Titles are not governed by statutes and usually can be tailored by the board to serve the purposes of the corporation.

For each office and executive position, the board should adopt job descriptions, including powers, duties, and reporting assignments. These positions should be incorporated into a visual organizational chart. It is particularly important to be express about job descriptions for positions held by family members, because confusion about a family member's authority and duties in the business can create personnel problems, which can lead to discord among owners. Further, it is difficult for the board or others to evaluate the job performance of a family member if his or her responsibilities are not clear.

In most corporations, the role of board chair is simply a member of the board whom the board elects to conduct board meetings and otherwise take the lead on board procedural matters. In a family business, however, the title of "Chair" is sometimes given to the founder or other key senior owner when he or she begins to transition away from daily involvement in the business and no longer serves as the president or CEO. In such cases, the Chair is sometimes granted some residual executive powers that do not require a daily presence.

6.2.3.b Terms of Service

The board determines compensation of officers and top executives and can terminate them without cause. An employment agreement, approved by the board, can further define the terms of an officer's or executive's service, including the scope of his or her authority, duties and responsibilities, and the amount and form of his or her compensation.

Although a board should not (and perhaps cannot) relinquish its right to remove and replace any officer or executive, an employment agreement can control the consequences of termination. For example, an employment agreement can provide severance benefits to an officer or executive who is terminated without cause. Addressing the consequences of termination may be especially important with respect to employees who are family members. An employment agreement can also include noncompetition and non-solicitation agreements that will apply if the officer or executive is terminated. Note, however, that if the employee is also an owner, noncompetition and nonsolicitation provisions might be easier to enforce if they are part of the ownership buy-sell agreement rather than in an employment agreement. The law tends to be more protective of employees on such contract issues because of the imbalance of power between the employee and the employer. In contrast, that imbalance of power is not assumed to be present in the context of agreements between owners.

6.2.3.c LLCs and Other Business Entities

The members or managers of an LLC also may appoint officers and executives to manage the day-to-day business of the company. In the case of a manager-managed LLC, the president or chief executive might serve as the manager, or a governing board may serve as a board of managers, with power to oversee the service of the officers and executives. Limited partnerships and most other business entities also can appoint officers or executives to manage their day-to-day business activities.

6.2.4. Equity Ownership

Ultimately, a corporation is operated for the economic benefit of the shareholders. The shareholders generally are entitled to receive dividends or distributions of profits, and the shareholders are entitled to receive a return of their investment and any appreciation when the corporation is sold or liquidated. In a family business, however, some shareholders may want to exit ownership and recover the value of their interest when the corporation has not been sold or liquidated. Appropriate provisions in governing documents and a well-tailored buy-sell agreement among the shareholders is the best way to prepare for and manage owner exits in a way that does not disrupt business operations. This section discusses key concepts for buy-sell agreements as they apply to family businesses.

Specifically, when collaborating on a buy-sell agreement, the owners should consider the following questions, which are discussed in greater detail below:

- Who can be a shareholder?
- What cash flow will shareholders receive each year?
- When can or must a shareholder exit ownership?
- What will a shareholder receive upon exit?

The owners should answer each question as it applies to present circumstance and then as it should apply after the transition to successor owners.[4]

6.2.4.a Allocation of Profits

Under the corporation model default rules, a corporation has one class of common stock, and the economic rights of ownership are allocated pro rata among the shareholders based on the number of shares of stock they own. The default rules allow the owners of a corporation to agree to allocate the owners' economic interests differently, but such alternative allocations can cause unintended tax consequences. Therefore, clients should

---

4. The buy-sell components of owners' agreements can be difficult to draft because they must cover a broad range of possible circumstances, and they must be thorough and internally consistent to be truly effective, particularly when an owner exit occurs because of owner discord. One excellent resource on this subject is LOUIS A. MEZZULLO, AN ESTATE PLANNER'S GUIDE TO BUY-SELL AGREEMENTS FOR THE CLOSELY HELD BUSINESS (ABA 3d. ed. 2017).

consider all of the economic interests of family members in the business and allocate the economic benefits among the family members in ways that are tax efficient. The lawyer should work with the owners' accountants and tax advisors when reviewing this issue.

For example, if an S corporation creates different classes of economic ownership, such as classes of preferred stock, this will result in mandatory termination of the corporation's subchapter S election. In contrast, if a family member were to loan cash to the corporation or rent property or equipment to the corporation, that arrangement might accomplish a similar result for the family (e.g., fixed payments to a particular family member having priority over distributions of profits to the other shareholders) without the adverse tax consequence to the corporation's subchapter S election.

Similarly, if a family business entity has different classes of economic ownership, the special valuation rules of Section 2701 or 2704 of the Internal Revenue Code (IRC) or the estate inclusion provisions of Section 2036 of the IRC might be invoked by the Internal Revenue Service to impose unintended and adverse transfer tax consequences on the family when ownership interests are gifted or pass at the death of an owner. Again, alternative arrangements developed within the totality of the family business often can produce the desired economic effect without the adverse transfer tax consequences. Sometimes the desired economic effect can be achieved by separating elements of the business to be owned by family members in different proportions or by entering into contractual arrangements (such as loans or employment or consulting agreements) with some family members, rather than creating different classes of ownership of a single family business entity.

Another important point for clients to consider is that most family members who acquire an interest in a family business, at some point, may want to liquidate that interest in exchange for its value, even if he or she received the interest by gift or other gratuitous family transfer. An owner's desire to liquidate his or her interest while the business is a going concern may be inconsistent with or even disruptive to the needs of the business and the objectives of the other owners. Therefore, owners should not plan to transfer an ownership interest to a family member without a plan for how that family member could liquidate his or her interest in the future without forcing the business to be sold. The owners ultimately may decide that family members will not have the right to realize a value for ownership if they wish to liquidate their interests before the rest of the owners in the family are willing to sell the business. In such a case, the owners should consider using a trust to own the business interests (and manage family member expectations accordingly).

6.2.4.b Dividends/Distributions

The amount and frequency of dividends or distributions is usually determined by the board, but the owners can set standards or parameters for dividends/distributions in the company's governing documents. Usually the allocation of dividends/distributions from the company to its shareholders will be allocated pro rata based on the number of shares of stock (or other ownership units) they own, but there are other means of providing shareholders with cash from the business on a non-pro rata basis.

6.2.4.b.i Amount of Dividends/Distributions

The owners' policy on payment of dividends or distributions will depend in large part on tax features of the corporation (or other business entity).

- **C Corporation.** A C corporation's income is taxed at the level of the corporation, and the corporation pays the tax liability. When a C corporation pays a dividend to shareholders, the dividend does not reduce the corporation's income tax liability, but the shareholders incur a tax on the dividend as ordinary income. The aggregate tax cost of the tax on dividends will depend on the corporate and individual tax rates in a given year, as well as any special rules in the tax code that might apply to certain closely held C corporations, but payment of C corporation dividends will almost always increase the family's net tax liability. Therefore, it may not be advisable for clients to adopt a mandatory dividend provision in the governing documents of a C corporation. It may be best to allow the board or the shareholders to decide each year whether the corporation should pay a dividend, based on the state of the tax code and other relevant economic factors. One such factor might be whether there are more tax-efficient means to share the corporation's profits with the shareholders. This is one reason why the C corporation may be more appropriate for a business whose shareholders are all employed by the corporation and thus can receive cash flow from the business through compensation, rather than one that is owned by a number of shareholders who are not active in the business and may expect to receive cash flow from this business through dividends.

- **S Corporations and Other Flow-Through Entities.** A corporation that operates under a subchapter S election does not pay taxes on its income but rather passes the tax liability through to its shareholders, who incur a tax on the corporation's income, even when the corporation has not distributed any of that income to the shareholders. (Note that payment of corporate profits to shareholders of a C corporation is referred to as a "dividend," but payment of profits to shareholders of an S corporation (or owners of any other flow-through business entity) is referred to as a "distribution.") The same is true of LLCs (except those that elect to be taxed as a C corporation) and other flow-through business entities. If the S corporation has taxable income in a given year but does not distribute cash to the shareholders, then the shareholders will have to pay the income tax on their share of the flow-through income using other income or investments. This can be frustrating (or distressing) to the owners, especially because payment of a distribution from a flow-through business entity is not a taxable event (i.e., it generally does not cause any additional tax liability for the entity or the owners). Therefore, it may be desirable for the owners to adopt a mandatory distribution provision in the governing documents of an S corporation or other flow-through business entity, requiring the company to make annual or quarterly distributions in amounts sufficient to cover the owners' flow-through federal and state income tax liabilities. The governing documents can give the board or the owners, perhaps by supermajority vote, discretion to withhold distributions in a given period or to make distributions over and above amounts needed to cover the owners' flow-through tax liability.

6.2.4.b.ii Allocation of Dividends/Distributions

For reasons discussed above, it is difficult for a family business entity to provide for allocation of dividends or distributions among the owners other than pro rata based on the number of shares of stock (or other units of ownership interest) they own without causing an unwanted income tax or transfer tax consequence. Therefore, clients most likely should accept that dividends or distributions will be paid to the owners pro rata and then provide for a disproportionate allocation of business income using other means.

6.2.4.c Sales Proceeds or Liquidating Distributions

The most substantial economic right of stock ownership, along with the potential for dividends or distributions of profits each year, is the right to realize the value of the stock when the stock is sold, or the corporation sells its assets and the proceeds are distributed to the shareholders. In most cases, the value of the corporation (e.g., the sale proceeds) will be allocated pro rata among the owners, as with dividends and distributions.

6.2.4.c.i Decision to Sell the Company

The governing documents or agreement among the shareholders should control who can require the business to be sold, as a stock sale a merger, or an asset sale, followed by a liquidation. Although proceeds from the sale of the business likely would be divided pro rata among the shareholders, the value of continuing to own the corporation may differ substantially among the shareholders because of their different roles in the business. Owners who are employed in the business and whose children are or perhaps someday will be employed in the business may value continued family ownership of the business much more than an owner who is not active in the business. Therefore, it may be most equitable for the owners to give the greatest discretion as to when to sell the business to the owners who benefit the most from continued ownership. If they do that, however, they should then give the other owners a means to exit ownership on an individual basis. (See section 9.2 for a discussion of owner exit mechanisms.)

6.2.4.c.ii Allocation of Sales Proceeds or Liquidating Distributions

Due to income tax and transfer tax considerations, the owners most likely will have to accept the principle that if the business is sold, or the assets are sold and the proceeds are distributed to the owners, the proceeds will be allocated pro rata, based on the number of shares of stock (or other units of ownership interest) they own at the time of sale, without regard to classes of ownership.

This should affect the owners' decisions about how ownership should be allocated among successors. For example, members of the family who are active in the business may resent the idea that some of the appreciation of the business's value resulting from their skill and efforts will be realized by inactive owners if the business is sold. Conversely, inactive owners may be frustrated that their ownership interest may decline in value due to poor performance by the owners who are operating the business, and that the burden of such loss should not be borne disproportionately by the active owners when the business is sold. A class of preferred stock for the inactive owners perhaps could address the respective concerns of the active and inactive owners, but it is not likely that this would be possible without adverse transfer tax consequences.

One alternative to preferred stock for inactive owners would be to provide for the company or the active owners to buy out the inactive owners in exchange for an installment obligation that is paid off over a very long term. This would provide an inactive owner with a fixed return for his or her share of the business. The selling owner would be paid interest for the time value of money and perhaps some risk of default, but the value of the selling owners' interest would not be increased or decreased by the performance of the active owners. If the business were sold, the owner who previously sold his or her interest would be paid off in full at that time. Perhaps, for purposes of nominally continuing to participate in the legacy of family ownership of the business, the selling owner could keep a small number of nonvoting shares. (Note that a partial redemption of a shareholder's corporation stock can cause adverse income tax consequences at the time of redemption, but such rules do not apply to a cross purchase (i.e., the purchase of shares by one or more of the other shareholders).)

In a family business, the business may not be sold for many years—perhaps a generation or two. Therefore, the fact that each owner is entitled to a pro rata share of proceeds upon a sale of the business is more likely to be significant for purposes of determining a purchase price when a single owner wants to exit ownership and the company or remaining owners wish to purchase his or her interest. This is discussed in greater detail in section 9.2 with respect to individual shareholder exit mechanisms.

6.2.4.d Raising Capital; Anti-Dilution

The owners should provide rules for how successor owners can raise capital for the business, particularly as it may affect voting and equity interests. The owners also should address the possibility of owner loans to the business.

6.2.4.d.i Capital Calls

The corporation model default rules provide that a corporation cannot require the shareholders to make additional contributions of capital unless the governing documents permit. A corporation's governing documents can allow the company to require capital contributions as the board may decide or with the shareholders' approval, perhaps by supermajority or unanimous consent. Incidentally, a decision to require capital contributions might be a rare instance in which the corporation should be required also to obtain some measure of consent of the "nonvoting" owners. In the ordinary course, it may be equitable to allow the voting owners to have unilateral rights to appoint board members and even decide when to sell the business, but a family company should rarely be able to require its owners to invest their own assets in the business without their consent.

Note also that if the corporation could require capital calls, then shareholders might become liable for creditors' claims against the corporation to the extent the corporation would otherwise be insolvent. Therefore, all provisions regarding capital contributions should be limited to protect the corporation's liability shield for the shareholders.

6.2.4.d.ii New Shares

If the owners decide to use a high bar for shareholders' approval of capital contributions, then they might wish to give the corporation an alternative means of raising capital by allowing the board to sell additional shares of stock to new or existing shareholders. In such instances, the other shareholders (particularly the voting shareholders, in the case of voting stock) should have the right to acquire additional shares, on the same terms, in amounts that will prevent their voting or economic rights from being diluted. The process of selling new shares to family members and determining the purchase price should rely on consent of independent directors or at least some of the shareholders who will not be involved in the transaction, because it is in the nature of a conflict-of-interest transaction, particularly if one of the buyers is a shareholder who serves as an executive or sits on the company's board.

6.2.4.d.iii Shareholder Loans

Finally, the owners may wish to establish rules regarding loans from shareholders to the business. As discussed in section 7.1.d, such loans should be formally documented, and perhaps secured, to ensure that they will be respected vis-à-vis the rights of the corporation's other creditors. Again, the owners might want the rules to require approval of independent directors or other shareholders if the lender is an executive or director of the borrower.

6.2.4.e Share Transferability

Under the corporation model default rules, a shareholder can freely transfer his or her stock in a corporation to other persons, and the transferee will succeed to all the rights of a shareholder. (Transferability of ownership interests in LLCs and other business entities usually is more limited.) However, the owners likely will want to adopt appropriate transfer restrictions for family business interests.

6.2.4.e.i Transfer Restrictions: Reasons

In a family business, there are a number of reasons to restrict an owner's right to transfer his or her shares outside the family (or even within the family in some cases).

- **Harmonious ownership group.** Most family business owners want to prevent outsiders from owning an interest in the family business, as they believe that outsiders are less likely to hold the objectives and values that the family needs the owners to share for optimal benefit to the family unit. That often is a valid perception. In many cases, owners will work with a greater sense of commitment and even altruism if the other owners are family members. However, membership in the family does not guarantee harmony or commitment to the business.

- **Adverse owners.** Transfer restrictions can help prevent creditors, competitors, ex-spouses, or other adverse persons from obtaining ownership of family business interests and using that ownership to harm or harass the other owners. Minority shareholders do not have a fiduciary duty to the corporation or the other shareholders, and therefore they have much more latitude to exercise ownership rights in a way that is not in the best interests of the corporation or its other shareholders. Even owners with a small percentage of shares can create costly distractions because they may have the right to demand records or accountings, or to veto decisions that require unanimous consent of shareholders. They may also have standing to bring lawsuits against the directors and officers through direct or even derivative lawsuits. Adverse owners might refuse the other shareholders' efforts to acquire their shares, except at a premium price. Further, if another shareholder is redeemed, then the adverse shareholder's interest might increase, or if new shares are issued, the adverse shareholder might have an anti-dilution right to acquire some of the new shares.

• **Economic simplicity.** Sometimes, it is economically simpler if all the owners are employed in the business. For example, if all the owners are receiving compensation from the business, then the company might have no reason to pay dividends or discretionary distributions. This can be an especially compelling reason to restrict ownership if the owners are also required to personally guarantee business debt, or if the company has contracts with franchisors or manufacturers requiring ownership by owner-operators.

6.2.4.e.ii Types of Transfer Restrictions

The owners may agree to transfer restrictions in a form that is binding on future owners and potential transferees. Transfer restrictions are less likely to be a source of future controversy if they are focused on keeping out unwanted owners rather than preventing owners from liquidating their interests.

6.2.4.e.ii.a Outright Prohibition

The owners can agree that an owner cannot transfer his or her interest to any other person without the consent of the company, board, or other owners. An absolute prohibition against transfers, however, may not be legally enforceable if it leaves an owner with no right to liquidate his or her interest, especially in an entity that is organized without a termination date. The law is generally sympathetic to a company's desire to limit its ownership group and even to ensure that it can use its owners' capital for a reasonable period of time, but at some point an owner should be granted a return of capital, or the right to otherwise liquidate his or her interest.

Therefore, a prohibition against transfers is more likely to be enforceable if it is for a fixed period of time, or if the owner has other means to liquidate his or her interest, such as a put option (to require the company or the other owners to purchase the interest) or exceptions for broad categories of permitted transfers.

If the owners wish to prohibit transfers, it may be possible to achieve their objective by agreeing that if an owner transfers his or her interest in violation of the prohibition, the only "penalty" is that the transferee will not have the full rights of an owner but will be entitled only to the economic rights of an assignee of the ownership interest. This can be a somewhat effective defense against the disruption that an adverse owner could cause.

6.2.4.e.ii.b Right of First Refusal

A right of first refusal is a more common, and more likely enforceable, restriction on transfers. Under this agreement, if an owner voluntarily or involuntarily transfers his or her ownership interest, the company or other owners can purchase the interest at a price and on terms that are set forth in the agreement. This is a way to limit the ownership group while also granting each owner the right to liquidate his or her interest upon the occurrence of certain triggering events.

Triggering events might include any or all of the following:

• An owner sells his or her interest to a person who is not in the class of permitted transferees.

- An owner's creditors take action that affects his or her ownership interest.
- An owner's employment with the business is terminated for cause or because of disability, or the owner begins participating in a competing business.
- Upon the divorce of an owner, his or her ex-spouse's share of property division includes some of the ownership interest.
- The owner dies and his or her share passes to someone who is not a permitted transferee.

If clients use a right of first refusal mechanism to restrict the ownership group, they should also consider adopting precautions against certain unwanted consequences that can arise from exercising the right or declining to exercise the right (as described in the next point).

• **Reallocation of ownership rights among remaining owners.** If an owner triggers a right of first refusal and the company or the other owners exercise the right, it may have the effect of disturbing the allocation of voting rights or economic rights among owners or groups of owners. For example, if one owner holds 45 percent of the voting stock, and if the company redeems an owner who holds 20 percent of the voting stock, the first owner will hold an outright majority of voting stock after the redemption, and the remaining owners may be forced into a "permanent" minority position without even a swing vote to influence owner action. One way to address this potential problem is to adopt some protections for minority owners, such as class voting. For example, if the company has issued different classes of ownership interest, then perhaps the right of first refusal with respect to interests in a particular class should be available first to the other owners in the same class.

• **Price, terms, and funding for purchase option.** The owner agreement that creates the rights of first refusal should establish a clear mechanism for determining a price for the option to purchase. The purchase price may differ for different triggering events, but in a family business, if it is less than fair market value, it may create unintended transfer tax consequences. Before adopting the provisions for determining purchase price, it can be helpful to confer with a business valuation professional for input. In addition, provisions setting forth the terms of payment, if payment will be seller financed, should be clear and complete, because additional terms usually cannot be imposed when the option to purchase is exercised. For example, the number of payments, the interest rate, the use of security or guaranties, subordination of the debt to other creditors, and remedies in the event of default should all be addressed in detail if they are to be part of the option transaction. Finally, the company or the owners who might exercise the option to purchase should make plans for how to fund payment under the option. For example, a purchase option triggered by the death of an owner could be funded by purchase of insurance on the owner's life, but life insurance may not be a substantial aid when the option is triggered by something other than death. Often a plan for funding an option to purchase could involve several approaches, including cash from a sinking fund (i.e., a fund of cash or marketable securities set aside and increased over time for this purpose), proceeds from the sale of a nonessential asset, a loan or line of credit from a commercial lender, and the rest addressed through seller financing.

• **Rights of a third-party transferee.** If the company and other owners are not able to exercise the right of first refusal, it is possible that an undesirable third-party transferee may acquire an ownership interest, which could be disruptive to the business, especially if the transferee's objectives are inconsistent with or opposed to the objectives of the remaining owners. To mitigate the harm from such a result, the owner agreement should provide that such a transferee will not have the full rights of an owner, but will be entitled only to the economic rights of an assignee of the ownership interest. It also should provide that all transferees, assignees, and successor owners will be bound by the ownership agreement, as though they had been one of the original parties to the agreement.

6.2.4.e.ii.c Permitted Transferees

Usually transfer restrictions will list categories of persons who are "permitted transferees." These are persons to whom an owner can transfer an ownership interest without violating any transfer restrictions or triggering any rights of first refusal. In a family business, the following persons or classes of persons are often defined as permitted transferees:

- An owner's lineal descendants.
- Other owners. Note, however, that if an owner can transfer voting interests to another owner, the transaction could consolidate majority vote in one owner without providing any way for the other owners to prevent it. For this reason, it may be prudent not to allow transfers to other owners without consent of all the owners.
- The owner's living trust. Note, however, that holding an ownership interest in a living trust can create confusion about application of other elements of the owners' agreement. For example, if the owner's death or termination of employment should trigger a purchase option, ownership by a living trust could impair application of such provisions because a living trust does not die and is not (most likely) employed by the business. If ownership by a living trust is to be allowed, the owner agreement should clarify that the parties will look through the trust to the grantor as owner for all purposes until the trust becomes irrevocable.
- An irrevocable trust for the owner's lineal descendants or spouse, provided that a distribution from the trust to a beneficiary who is not a permitted transferee will trigger the right of first refusal. Sometimes the provision allowing the transfer to a trust may also impose restrictions on who may serve as a trust fiduciary. For example, the company and its owners would not want a trust fiduciary to be a person who is involved in a competing business.

If the company is an S corporation, no trust or person should be a permitted transferee who is not a permitted shareholder of an S corporation (i.e., if their ownership of S corporation stock would terminate the corporation's S election).

6.2.4.f Expulsion

Another way to restrict the ownership group is to give the company the right to expel an owner without cause. Many family businesses reserve the right to purchase an owner's ownership interest if he or she ceases to be employed in the business, but the company can reserve the right to redeem (or allow the other owners to buy) an owner's interest for other reasons as well. An expulsion right can be used as a supplement to rights of first refusal (or if it is otherwise applicable) in only limited circumstances and if economically fair to the owner who is expelled.

For example, the company might reserve the right to redeem (or allow the other owners to purchase) an owner's interest under the following circumstances:

• **Termination of employment.** If an owner who was employed in the business has been terminated or has left the company voluntarily, the company or other owners could be given the right to acquire the departing employee's ownership interest. This would be particularly appropriate if all the other owners are employees of the company, or if the departing owner's separation has occurred because of wrongdoing or an atmosphere of discord.

• **Assignee.** If an owner has transferred his or her ownership interest to a person who is not a permitted transferee and has not been admitted as an owner, and therefore has the status of only an assignee, the company could retain a right, exercisable at any time, to acquire the assignee's interest at a price equal to the fair market value of the interest. This would be helpful in case the company and other owners were unable to exercise their right of first refusal (or for some other reason chose not to exercise their right of first refusal) when the assignee acquired the interest.

• **Litigant.** If an owner brings a lawsuit against the company or its managers or against other owners, it could trigger a right in the company to redeem the owner's interest. This would prevent the owner from having standing to pursue a derivative claim or other claims that are relevant only to existing shareholders. The owners should be careful about adopting this type of expulsion provision because sometimes, unfortunately, litigation (or at least the threat of litigation) may be the only tool that a minority owner has to address very real wrongdoing by a majority owner or managers.

• **Owner in breach.** The company could retain the right to redeem (or allow the other owners to purchase) the interest of any owner who has breached the owners' agreement, the company's governing documents, or any contract between the owner and the company, including a confidentiality or noncompetition agreement. This would allow expulsion.

• **Nominal owner.** The company could retain the right to redeem (or allow the other owners to purchase) the interest of any owner whose interest is less than some minimal threshold, such as 5 percent or 10 percent. Spreading ownership among many family members representing multiple generations can be a meaningful way to grow and perpetuate the family legacy in a large enterprise. In a smaller family business, however, nominal owners, especially those who are not otherwise involved in the business, can be an administrative burden and can give rise to anomalies in governance, operations, tax planning, and strategic planning. Too often business decisions that may benefit the primary ownership group, especially those who are active in the business, will seem to be at odds with the interests of a nominal owner. This may be particularly likely if the business consists of other family-owned entities in which the nominal owner does not hold an interest.

6.2.4.g Owner Exit Rights

Family business owners should consider providing exit rights for owners who wish to liquidate their interest, either because they need the liquidity or because they are at odds with the other owners.

6.2.4.g.i   Owner Retirement

If a family business is to continue to operate for multiple generations, then it should have a plan for the retirement of senior generation owners. (See chapter 9 for a more detailed discussion of this subject.)

Ideally, a senior owner will have resources for retirement that will not include the value of the family business interests. In such cases, the senior owner likely will transfer his or her ownership interest to his or her lineal descendants through means that have a substantial gratuitous component and do not place an economic burden on the company or its owners.

Other senior owners, however, may not have the resources to retire without realizing the value of their interest in the family business or otherwise retaining an ongoing economic benefit from the business. In such cases, it is best for both the owner and the business to have a comprehensive plan for owner retirement. The plan might include a combination of rights that the owner is granted under the owner agreements and his or her employment agreement.

6.2.4.g.ii   Owner Put Options

An owner put option gives an owner the right to require the company (or the other owners) to buy his or her ownership interest at a price and on terms that are governed by the option agreement. The purchase price either is predetermined or is determined based on a method or formula that is set forth in the option agreement. A put option can be a means to ensure that a minority owner's input or wishes regarding the business will be respected or the minority owner will have the right to liquidate his or her interest and invest it elsewhere.

Sometimes reasonable minds among ownership can differ. A put option can prevent such differences from becoming sources of litigation. If an owner who holds a minority position has the right to liquidate his or her interest through a predetermined, equitable process, then he or she has less reason to fight the majority on how the business should be run or whether the family should continue to own the business or sell it.

A put option can be limited with respect to how much of a person's interest he or she can require the company (or other owners) to purchase in a given period or it can be limited by other metrics to ensure that exercising the option will not place an undue burden on the business. Note, however, that if the company is a corporation, a partial redemption could cause the redemption proceeds to be taxed as a disproportionate dividend/distribution, and in such cases it might be better to structure the transaction as a cross-purchase. Also, if the selling owner is part of a class or particular group of owners, it might be most appropriate to give other owners of the same class or group the first right to buy the interest and thus cause less change to how attributes of ownership are allocated among family members. Finally, if the company is taxed as an S corporation, which is not allowed to have more than one economic class of stock, the owners should be cautious about giving economic rights (such as a put option) in an owners' agreement to one owner that are different from those of other owners because they might be inadvertently create a de facto second economic class of stock.

6.2.4.h Selling Control

The sale of a business can be accomplished through a "stock" sale, an asset sale, or a merger. A company's governing documents and owners' agreements should be clear about who has authority to require the business to be sold in various contexts, and there should be a high level of consistency about who has that authority regardless of the form of transaction.

In the context of a stock sale, many owner agreements will provide that if owners of a majority of the voting interests wish to sell their interests to an unrelated third-party buyer, the sellers may require the other owners to sell their interests as well, and, similarly in such cases, the other owners may have the right to require the buyer to buy their ownership interests at the same price and on the same terms as he or she is offering for the majority ownership interests.

6.2.4.h.i Drag-Along Rights

Sometimes a person who wants to buy a company through a "stock" sale wants to buy all the ownership interests, not just a controlling interest, because the buyer does not want to co-own the business with minority family owners who refuse to sell. Therefore, many owners' agreements will include "drag-along rights," which provide that if a controlling majority (or higher percentage) of owners wish to sell their ownership interest to a third-party buyer for fair value in a good-faith transaction, the owners who wish to sell can require the other owners to also sell their ownership interests for the same price per share and on the same terms. Drag-along rights are intended to prevent minority owners from having the de facto authority to veto a stock sale that the majority wishes to pursue.

6.2.4.h.ii Tag-Along Rights; Dissenters' Rights

If owners who hold voting control decide to sell their shares to an unrelated third-party buyer, the remaining owners may not want to continue to own their ownership interests as minority owners with the new majority owner. (This is the flipside of the concern addressed by "drag-along rights.") Therefore, many owners' agreements will include "tag-along" or "piggyback" rights, which provide that if owners who hold voting control wish to sell their ownership interests to a third-party buyer, then all other owners have the right to sell their ownership interests to the buyer for the same price per share and on the same payment terms. In the case of a merger, in which the "buyer" is a business entity and the sellers will receive ownership interests in the buyer instead of cash, the owners' agreement can provide that minority owners who oppose the merger can require their ownership interests to be redeemed for cash, based on their pro rata share of the value of the company at the time of the merger, so that they do not have to become owners of the surviving entity. Such rights are similar to dissenters' rights, which are available to some minority owners under statutory defaults. The concept of dissenters' rights can be modified or adapted in an owners' agreement to avoid litigation that sometimes arises when a company (the "target") merges with a buyer without unanimous support of the target's owners.

6.2.4.i Purchase Price

In all instances when some owners or the company may exercise a right to buy an owner's interest, or an owner may exercise an option to put his or her ownership interest to the company or other owners for purchase, the owners' agreement should provide a mechanism for determining the purchase price of the interest at issue. Without such a mechanism, the value of the interest can become the subject of adversarial proceedings.

6.2.4.i.i Methods of Determining Share Value

The appropriate method for determining purchase price will depend on the characteristics of the company and the intentions of the owners. For example, net asset value might be an appropriate approach for a company that simply holds real estate or equipment that is leased to an affiliated family business, but it may not be appropriate for a service company with several key employees.

The following are several common methods of determining share value under family business owners' agreements:

• **Fixed value, updated periodically.** The owners' agreement can provide that the owners will agree upon a share value annually or biennially, and that share value will be used for determining purchase price for any put or call transaction under the owners' agreement that is triggered within the period in which the share price applies.

Often the owners' agreement will provide a methodology for the owners to use when they agree to a purchase price. For example, the owners' agreement might include a formula to be used, or might require the purchase price to be based on an opinion of value submitted by the company's accountants or a business valuation professional.

If the fixed share price cannot be adopted or updated by all of the owners, then the owners' agreement should make it clear that the owners who oppose the share price are nevertheless bound by it, and the methodology should involve objective standards or independent persons, such as the opinion of an independent valuation professional or review and approval by independent directors.

Using a fixed value that is updated periodically is advantageous, because it sets realistic expectations for owners who are thinking about an exit, it creates a clear target for funding mechanisms, and it can substantially reduce grounds for litigation about purchase price.

• **Objective formula share value.** The owners' agreement can provide for share value to be determined by an objective formula that leaves little room for subjectivity. For example, the share value could be a multiple of the average (or weighted average) of the past few years' earnings before interest, taxes, depreciation, and amortization.

Any such formula written into the owners' agreement should be based on advice and input from the company's key financial personnel, the company's accountant, and a business valuation professional within or outside the company's accounting firm. Each year, the company should provide the board and owners with a pro forma application of the formula so they can determine whether the formula continues to provide reasonable results or whether they should consider amending it before it must be used in an actual transaction.

Also, sharing a pro forma application can help keep owner expectations in line with reality, can help owners with their financial and estate planning, and can help the company and owners develop appropriate funding mechanisms.

• **Opinion of value.** The owners' agreement can provide a procedure for an objective, qualified business valuation professional to determine the share value at the time a put or call is triggered under the owners' agreement. This mechanism is most likely to generate a challenge because it may seem the most subjective, and because the results might not conform to the expectations of one or more of the parties to the transaction. Also, because its results may be surprising, this process may cause the purchase obligation to be underfunded or overfunded, which is inefficient and can create the appearance of inequity. For example, if the valuation leads to a purchase price at the death of an owner that is much less than the life insurance proceeds that the company will use to purchase the deceased owner's interest, then the deceased owners' spouse or children may feel that the company received an unfair windfall.

If the share value will be determined by an opinion of value rendered when the put or call is triggered, then it might be best to draft it in the owners' agreement as though it is an arbitration provision, with all of the elements needed to make the process enforceable as a binding arbitration. Such precautions should render the result enforceable in court, absent fraud or malfeasance by the independent person who renders the determination of value.

• **Bidding.** Sometimes, owners might adopt a bidding process to resolve disputes about share value in the event of a put or call or governance deadlock, but bidding for ownership (especially with features that encourage game theory tactics) may be inappropriate for family business owner agreements because ownership of the business may affect the family in many different ways. In particular, if family members have committed themselves to a career with the family business, ownership succession should be predictable and should not be dependent on contests arising at random times in the life of the business.

6.2.4.i.ii Purchase Price Adjustments

Although the purchase price used for puts or calls under the owners' agreement may be based on a determination of share price, the purchase price might not be the same in every circumstance. The owners' agreement might provide that in some instances, such as death of an owner, the purchase price is based on the share price without taking into account discounts for lack of control or lack of marketability, but in other instances, such as termination of employment for cause, specific discounts will be applied in determining the purchase price.

It is common to apply discounts to the purchase price for purchase options that are triggered by involuntary transfers, but if a discounted purchase price is to be used to acquire shares that have passed to an owner's spouse or ex-spouse, then it may be advisable to obtain the spouse's advance written consent to be bound by such provisions.

Owners might decide that the owners' agreement should provide for no discount to be applied to share value or purchase price if the put or call is triggered by the death or disability of an owner because (a) in such circumstances the owner's family may have financial needs that warrant a purchase price that is not discounted, and (b) purchase obligations in such circumstances can be funded with insurance, thus providing ready liquidity for the transaction. In contrast, owners might want valuation discounts to apply at the death of an owner so as not to increase the value of the deceased owner's interest for estate tax purposes.

Generally, the Internal Revenue Service is not bound by the valuation provisions of an owners' agreement for purposes of determining the value of an ownership interest for transfer taxes—although the IRS often will respect and take into account provisions of an owners' agreement that increases the value of the shares. To avoid a disconnect between the purchase price of a deceased owner's shares and the value used for estate taxes, family business ownership agreements will often include a savings provision stating that the purchase price under the agreement will be no less than the value of the interest as finally determined for estate tax purposes. This is intended to prevent a deceased owner's estate from paying an estate tax on share value that the estate does not realize when the shares are purchased under the owners' agreement.

6.2.4.j Terms of Payment and Funding

The owners' agreement should assume that any put or call under the agreement will be fully seller-financed, except to the extent that the owners agree to mandate a specific funding mechanism, such as life insurance, for specific circumstances. As part of the ongoing attention to business succession, however, the owners should try to make other plans for funding an owner's exit.

6.2.4.j.i Installment Obligation

The seller-financed part of the share purchase provisions should include the following:

- Amount of down payment. (If the parties agree to a funding mechanism that is not sufficient to pay the full purchase price, the funding mechanism might nevertheless define the minimum down payment.)
- Amount and number of installment payments.
- Interest rate (or how it is to be determined).
- If and how future installments will be secured or guaranteed.
- Seller's rights in the event of default.
- Seller's position vis-à-vis other creditors (e.g., will the obligation to the seller be superior or subordinate to the buyer's obligation to other creditors?).
- Seller's right to be removed from guaranties of business debt.
- Buyer's covenants (such as limitations on dividends and bonuses that the owners may receive while installments are owing; subordination of new debt; prepayment upon a change of control).
- Seller confidentiality, noncompetition, and nonsolicitation commitments.

Often it can be helpful to include, as exhibits to the owners' agreement, a form of share purchase agreement, form of installment note, and form of pledge agreement. If a particular term, condition, or consideration of a share purchase is not required in the owners' agreement, it is not likely that one of the parties can insist that it be included when the share purchase provisions are triggered and given effect.

6.2.4.j.ii Other Funding and Financing

When the owners' agreement is drafted and from time to time after it is signed, the owners should try to plan for the use of funding and financing mechanisms in addition to seller financing, particularly with respect to owners who hold more than 20 percent of the shares outstanding. Such funding mechanisms can include the following:

- Insurance on the life of an owner (including policies whose cash value can be used toward purchase of shares during the insured's lifetime).
- Insurance that pays on the disability of an employee-owner.
- Commercial financing, including a reserve line of credit.
- A sinking fund, consisting of cash and marketable securities owned by the company or co-owned by the owners.
- Non-essential assets that can be sold to generate cash for a share purchase.
- An inside market, such as an employee stock ownership plan. (See the discussion of ESOPs in section 9.2.g.)

If other owners (rather than the company) will be the buyers under a share purchase provision of an owners' agreement, the owners should identify a source of cash flow that they can use to pay down any debt obligations they incur as part of the transaction. If the company is a C corporation, it may be costly, from a tax perspective, to rely on dividends for that cash flow. This may be a reason to consider an S election or to arrange for cash flow from other sources, such as rent that the company may pay to lease a building or equipment owned by the buyers.

6.2.4.k Alternative Dispute Resolution

Owner agreements should provide means of resolving disputes about owners' rights that involve litigation. Litigation sometimes can be a necessary last resort (or at least a looming threat) to remedy abuses of power, enforce agreements, or realize economic rights in a family business context, but litigation can inflict unnecessary damage on both the business and the family. There are alternative means to resolve disputes that owners should adopt in the owners' agreements.

• **Objective standards or independent experts.** Share value and other key terms can be predetermined in the owners' agreement (such as specific purchase price discounts), can be based on an objective formula or standard (such as prime rate or applicable federal rate for interest), or can be delegated to an independent expert to decide (such as a qualified business valuation professional).

• **Independent directors.** If the company has independent directors, the owners' agreement can delegate decisions to a board committee composed of independent directors or can otherwise provide special quorum and voting rules for the board with respect to issues that involve a conflict of interest for family members who serve on the board. Such arrangements may require or may warrant corresponding provisions in the company's governing documents. Even if decisions are not formally delegated to independent directors, disputes under the owners' agreement can be informally mediated by independent directors, whose knowledge of the business and the family put them in a unique position to try to help the parties find common ground. This is one of the many reasons to have independent directors.

• **Mediation.** The owners' agreement can require that parties to a dispute under the owners' agreement must make a good-faith effort to mediate the dispute with a qualified, independent mediator. Although mediation does not always produce a resolution, it may be superior to arbitration in a family business context because it gives the parties an opportunity to compromise and collaborate, perhaps in a way that does less damage to family relationships.

• **Binding arbitration.** The owners' agreement can provide that the parties will submit disputes to binding arbitration rather than resort to litigation. Although binding arbitration sometimes can be almost as expensive and time consuming as a bench trial, it has several advantages over litigation, including the following:

➤ Most important, the parties can choose an arbitrator or panel of arbitrators who are independent and who are experts in the subject area of the dispute, as opposed to appearing before a judge who, in many courts, may not have any special understanding of business law, business valuation, taxes, accounting, or other relevant subject matter.

➤ Arbitration can be less expensive than litigation because the procedural rules can be better tailored to the proceedings and the dispute.

➤ Arbitration decisions cannot be appealed, absent fraud or malfeasance by the arbitrator; therefore, the parties avoid the expense and delay of one or more appeals. Further, the fact that the decision cannot be appealed sometimes causes the parties to focus on settlement much sooner in the process than they otherwise would.

➤ Arbitration can be more private than litigation in courts, whose records are open to the public. Parties to arbitration can more easily and effectively agree to protect confidential family information and business information that is disclosed in the course of the proceedings.

➤ Owners can include a tailored fee-shifting provision in the arbitration clause. They could provide that the losing party must pay the arbitration fees and expenses of the prevailing party, or they could provide that the arbitrator will equitably allocate the fees and expenses among the parties, based on the arbitrator's discretion or based on a standard set forth in the arbitration clause.

6.3 Putting It Together

Proper business succession planning must include a plan for structures, governing documents, and agreements that define the rights and obligations of participants in the family business with respect to four distinct roles: share voting, board authority, executive management, and owner equity. These issues should be addressed for each company that is a component or affiliate of the family business, but they should be addressed with a view to the family business as a whole. This stage of the planning may benefit from or may warrant restructuring the business, consistent with concepts discussed in chapter 5.

Although this part of the project focuses on planning for successor owners, the current owners should consider which of these plans could be implemented to help the business immediately (such as adding independent directors to the board) and whether they should adopt transitional measures that would make the succession plan easier to implement (such as establishing a voting trust, creating an advisory board, or purchasing life insurance on potential successor owners).

In some cases, the potential successor owners will not be old enough or have sufficient experience to meaningfully participate in the succession planning process, but if the successors are already working in the business or are otherwise experienced enough to understand the concepts that drive business succession planning, they should fully participate in the planning process. In fact, if the senior owners are nearing retirement, the successor owners may take more of a role in planning the future governance and ownership rights than the senior owners.

6.4 Family Council

Some families benefit from forming a family council, particularly families with multi-generational involvement in the family business, family investments, and family charitable-giving entities. A family council is not a legal entity or a business governance mechanism. Rather, a family council usually is a means of formalizing family gatherings to help maintain family unity around shared economic and charitable ventures and to perpetuate family values and family legacy.

A family council may be a representative body, with participants from various family branches, or it may be a collection of all adult family members, sometimes including in-laws, regardless of each family member's level of participation in any specific family business entity. A family council can be especially effective in using family resources to collaborate in ways that uniquely benefit family members, educating junior family members with respect to family business and financial matters, and addressing misunderstandings or dissenting opinions among family members before they become disruptive.

Often, family councils are organized around a family constitution, which expresses shared family values, beliefs, and objectives, and a family council charter, which provides rules and guidelines governing family council membership, functions, and procedures. In many cases, a family business consultant may be the best service provider to assist a family in creating a family council and conducting its events.

6.5 Family Office

A family office also is not a business governance mechanism. Rather, a family office is a term that loosely describes a variety of structures that can be used to coordinate the delivery of family financial services, ranging from financial advice, collective investing of family wealth, individual tax advice and compliance, trust administration services, and estate planning. Families with sufficient wealth can create a free-standing business entity to provide most of the family office services in-house, but other families may choose to maintain a family office that is more of a virtual presence whose services are outsourced to a corporate trustee, bank, or other financial services firm that operates a multifamily office model. Although a family office can operate parallel to the family business, perhaps the greatest advantage of a family office is that if the family business is sold, a family office provides the family with a way to collectively invest and manage the sales proceeds as a new family venture, which can help continue family cohesion around economic collaboration, opportunity, and entrepreneurism.

Chapter Seven:
Key Contracts

This chapter discusses how to prepare key contracts for family business succession, including those with related parties and third parties. In some cases, it may be desirable to establish written agreements that do not currently exist. In other cases, it may be desirable to amend contracts to be more consistent with the succession plan. In still other cases, if it is not possible to amend an existing contract, it may be desirable to take steps to mitigate how the contract might adversely affect the succession plan.

7.1 Related-Party Contracts

If a person affiliated with the owners provides goods or services to the family business, that relationship should be formalized in a written contract to the extent that the owners would want that relationship to continue after the business transitions to the successors. Consider the following examples:

7.1.a Real Estate and Equipment Leases

If one of the family's companies leases real estate or equipment from a related individual or another family-owned company, the owners should sign a written lease that will continue to apply after ownership succession. In most cases, it should be a long-term lease, with automatic renewals and periodic rate enhancers that are specified in the lease or are tied to an objective measure, such as an appropriate consumer price index.

Leases should allow one party or the other to terminate the lease obligation if a particular change of circumstances occurs. For example, it may be appropriate for a building tenant to have a right to terminate the lease if the building is sold to a buyer outside the family. Similarly, it might be appropriate to grant the lessee a right of first refusal if the leased asset (e.g., building or equipment) is sold to a buyer outside the family.

Note that if the asset and the lessee currently are owned by the same owners, then there may be tax efficiencies or cash-flow considerations that dictate the optimal lease terms as long as the ownership remains the same. (The owners should consult their accountants and tax advisor regarding these arrangements.) In such cases, the lease should be reviewed as part of the owners' estate planning process. If ownership of the leased asset and ownership of the lessee business will or may diverge under the succession plan, then the owners should arrange for their successors to be bound by a lease that is equitable to both lessor and lessee.

7.1.b Service Agreements

If one of the family companies provides services to other family companies that are owned by different owners, or by the same owners but in different proportions, then the companies should execute a service agreement to ensure that the service relationship is equitable and will continue under similar terms. For example, if the family owns a portfolio of real estate, with each property in a different LLC, and the properties are managed by a separate management company also owned by the family, then service agreements will help ensure that the management company has cash flow that it needs to compensate employees and for other expenses of operations.

7.1.c Employment Agreements

Family members who have chosen to work for the family business in a substantial capacity might assume that their employment status with the business and their compensation will not be adversely affected by ownership succession, but if they do not have an employment agreement, they may be at risk of being treated as an employee-at-will who may be terminated, demoted, or geographically displaced by a successor board or new management.

    Therefore, if there are family members who rely on their employment with the family business and compensation at a particular level (sometimes including a history of bonuses), it may be appropriate to protect such family members with employment agreements that state they cannot be terminated or demoted without cause and that establish a minimum level of compensation, including perhaps cost-of-living increases and terms of bonus practices. The employment agreement also can provide for severance compensation and benefits upon a change of control (such as a sale of the business to an unrelated third party) or other change of circumstance that may warrant separation without cause.

    If the employee is not an owner, it may be best for the business to include confidentiality, noncompetition, and nonsolicitation language in the employment agreement, but if the employee is an owner or may become an owner, then the confidentiality, noncompetition, and nonsolicitation agreement might be better addressed in the owners' agreement. In many states, broad noncompetition provisions in an employment agreement are harder to enforce than similar provisions in an owners' agreement. Further, if an employee is an owner, it may be appropriate to provide that if his or her employment with the business terminates, then the business or other owners may purchase his or her ownership interest. (See the discussion of owners' agreements at section 6.2.4.)

    Finally, although it usually is desirable to include alternative dispute resolution provisions in all family business agreements, an arbitration clause in an employment agreement might not be enforceable in some states.

7.1.d Debt Obligations

If the business owes any sum to an owner or other family member or affiliated business, then the existence and terms of the debt should be clearly and formally documented. This will help ensure that successor owners and management will honor the obligation; it will help ensure that the payments are treated properly for taxes; and it will help ensure that the obligation will be given proper priority vis-à-vis the business's other creditors. Such obligations may arise, for example, if an owner lent cash to the business, or if the business purchased assets from an owner on an installment basis, or if the business redeemed an owner's shares on an installment basis.

In some cases, it may be desirable to grant the lender security (perfected, such as by recording a mortgage or filing UCC statements) to give the lender priority as against a tort creditor or in the event of the borrower's bankruptcy. It is likely, however, that the lender will have to agree that the obligation will be subordinate to existing third-party debt. (Commercial lenders do not want their rights to be subordinate to, or even *pari passu* with, insider obligations.)

7.1.e Contingent Liability

If owners have personally guaranteed debt of the business, each may be at risk of a disproportionate loss under his or her guaranty, unless the owners execute a reimbursement agreement with the business and contribution agreements among one another. This is particularly important for an owner who is exiting ownership but has not been released as a guarantor.

Under most commercial loan facilities, guaranties are joint and several, and in the event of a default, the lender can proceed against any one of the guarantors for the full amount, even without trying to collect from the borrower or the other guarantors. In fact, often the lender is allowed to release the borrower or a guarantor without the consent of the other guarantors. Further, a default may be something that neither the borrower nor the guarantors can control, such as the death or bankruptcy of one of the guarantors.

For these reasons, an owner who guarantees debt of the business should execute a reimbursement agreement granting the guarantor the right to be reimbursed by the business for any losses incurred under the guaranty. The lender may need to consent to a reimbursement agreement and will probably not allow it to be enforceable until the lender is satisfied in full.

Similarly, the guarantors should execute a contribution agreement among one another. A guarantor's common-law right to seek contribution from other guarantors for losses he or she incurs under a guaranty usually are not particularly effective. Often, they do not reflect the guarantors' expectations. Under a contribution agreement, however, the guarantors can be clear about what percentage of the loss each guarantor will contribute and how the loss will be measured. As with the reimbursement agreement, the guarantors may need the lender to consent to the contribution agreement, and it may not be enforceable until the lender is satisfied in full.

7.1.f Tort Liability Indemnification

Owners who serve as directors and officers or managers of the business should be protected against liability for their service for acts taken in good faith. (See section 6.2.2.e.i.) Usually such provisions appear in a company's articles, bylaws, or operating agreement. These should be drafted to include protection for directors and officers who are no longer serving in that capacity. If such fiduciaries are covered by directors' and officers' insurance, either directly or as a way to fund the indemnification, the coverage should include former fiduciaries as well.

7.2 Third-Party Contracts

Business ownership and leadership succession can disrupt relationships with unrelated stakeholders, such as key employees, and can have unintended consequences under the terms of third-party contracts, particularly those that are guaranteed by an exiting owner or that contain a change-of-control provision.

7.2.a Employment Contracts and Benefits for Key Employees

Successor owners and leaders likely will be more successful if they can keep key employees after the ownership transition. For this reason, it may be prudent to negotiate employment contracts and stay incentives with the most valuable non-family employees.

Non-family employees may be anxious about how succession will affect their careers and their financial security. The owners can reassure a key employee about his or her post-succession prospects with the business by defining the employee's role, minimum compensation, eligibility for bonuses, and employment benefits, as well as providing severance benefits for termination without cause or if the business is sold outside the family.

Key employees could be offered bonuses for longevity at the job or deferred compensation that vests over time, and the amount of such bonuses or deferred compensation can be based on growth or profitability of the business or other metrics. Incentive mechanisms like nonqualified profit-sharing plans, stock appreciation rights, or phantom stock can create stay incentives and reward employees for contributing to the financial success of the business. Such mechanisms can allow key employees to feel as though they are investors in the business without actually owning an equity interest.

In return for these stay and performance incentives, it usually is reasonable for the business to ask the employee to agree to confidentiality, noncompetition, and non-solicitation covenants. (Note that in some states, such agreements may not be enforceable unless the business has provided the employee with consideration in exchange for these covenants. Continued employment may or may not be deemed to be adequate consideration under applicable state law.)

7.2.b Personal Guaranties

If senior generation owners personally guarantee business loans from commercial lenders, they usually should renegotiate these guaranties in advance of succession so that their exit (or a corresponding change of control) is not defined as a default and so they do not continue to be at risk under the guaranty after they cease to have influence over the management and performance of the business.

A commercial lender may resist releasing the exiting owners from their guaranties, unless it considers the successor owners to be suitable substitute guarantors. If the business's lenders will not agree to release owners upon their exit, then the business should try to negotiate this accommodation if the business has an opportunity to refinance its debt in advance of succession. Often, the subject of personal guaranties will not arise until after the business has selected a lender or, worse, not until the loan closing. At that point, the business has little leverage to negotiate on the issue of personal guaranties, and the lender usually will charge the business for attorneys' fees the lender incurs to negotiate and revise its standard forms regarding personal guaranties.

Therefore, in anticipation of ownership succession, the business should always address the issue of personal guaranties when it is shopping a loan or a refinancing and when potential lenders are competing with one another on terms. The business should ask competing lenders to address personal guaranties in their offers, in addition to more common terms, such as interest rates, amortization, and collateral. In particular, the business could seek one or more of the following features with respect to personal guaranties:

- No personal guaranties.
- Nonrecourse carve-out guaranties that the lender could act upon only in the event of certain specific breaches, such as "bad boy" activities like fraud or other specified malfeasance by the borrower or the guarantors.
- Guaranties limited as to dollar amount or specific percentage of the obligation.
- Release of guarantor who exits ownership (perhaps contingent on a suitable substitute).
- No default upon the death of a guarantor (perhaps contingent on a suitable substitute).

If the senior owners are not released after they exit ownership, they should execute a reimbursement agreement with the business and the successor owners to compensate them for any loss they may incur by reason of the guaranty. (See the discussion of reimbursement and contribution agreements in section 7.1.e.) Further, if the loan terms allow the lender to accelerate payment upon the death of a guarantor, the business would be wise to maintain life insurance coverage on key senior-owner guarantors so that upon the guarantor's death, the business would have cash to pay down some of the debt and be in a better position to negotiate a waiver of the lender's due-on-death rights.

7.2.c Franchise and Dealership Contracts

Under many contracts for franchises or dealerships, the franchisor or manufacturer requires the franchise or dealership to be owner-operated by an approved person. In addition, franchise or dealership contracts often limit the percentage of equity in the franchise or dealership that may be owned by persons other than the owner-operator. In such a case, if the franchise or dealership undergoes a change of control, its contract could be terminated unless the franchisor or manufacturer approves the successor.

Unfortunately, most franchisors and manufacturers will not formally approve franchisee or dealership succession plans until they are given effect. However, many franchisors and manufacturers encourage their franchisees or dealerships to engage in succession planning, and they provide support and resources for such efforts.

Therefore, when planning for succession of a franchise or dealership, the business should be familiar with the requirements for a successor owner-operator and should collaborate with the franchisor or manufacturer to establish a succession plan that the franchisor or manufacturer is most likely to approve.

In addition, the uncertainty created by the right of the franchisor or manufacturer to reject a new owner-operator increases the importance of thorough planning in all other elements of the succession plan. For example, upon the death of the owner-operator, disruptions caused by a lender accelerating its loan, the defection of key employees, an incapable board, or uncertainty about who may exercise owner voting rights will make it difficult to maintain the confidence, goodwill, and cooperation of the franchisor or manufacturer needed to obtain their approval to keep the business in the family.

7.2.d Other Contracts Affected by a Change of Control

The business should review and attempt to mitigate or address change of control provisions that may be imbedded in any other important contract that might be inconsistent with the succession plan. For example, if the business recently acquired a new division, in a seller-financed transaction, payment to the seller might be accelerated by a change of control. The business could work with the other party to the contract to obtain an exception for the succession plan; conversely, the business should have a plan to mitigate the effects if the other party enforces the change of control provision.

Chapter Eight:

Estate Planning

This chapter discusses means of updating senior owners' estate planning, consistent with plans for management and ownership succession of a business. In particular, this chapter considers estate planning updates that specifically implement the succession plan and how trusts can be used to enhance the results of business succession planning. (For purposes of the next three chapters, the terms "ownership interest," "ownership units," or simply "units" will mean shares in a corporation or units of ownership interest in an LLC, LP, or other business entity.)

This chapter focuses primarily on estate planning for dispositions at death, rather than lifetime wealth transfers. (For estate planning that involves lifetime wealth transfers, see chapter 10.)

The business succession objectives of estate planning include the following:

- Avoiding probate of ownership interests;
- Allocating ownership units to specific beneficiaries, consistent with business succession objectives;
- Providing liquidity for payment of debts, taxes, and bequests to beneficiaries who will not receive ownership interests, including a spouse who will not be involved in business ownership;
- Using trusts to hold ownership units; and
- Identifying appropriate fiduciaries and means of appointing successor fiduciaries.

The discussion in this chapter assumes that the senior owners still hold substantial amounts of ownership interests that will be affected by their estate planning. If the senior owners subsequently transfer ownership interests to successors (see chapter 10), their estate planning documents should be reviewed and updated to take account of the effect of such lifetime transfers.

8.1 Probate Avoidance

Probate administration of family business ownership units can cause problems for business succession in several ways. It may delay the fiduciaries' ability to exercise unit voting rights. It provides a mandatory, one-size-fits-all approach to addressing creditors' claims. It creates an easy procedural mechanism for challenges to the estate plan. It often requires public disclosure of the value of ownership interests. For these reasons, an owner's estate plan should provide a means to avoid probate of ownership units.

A business owner, the business, and the beneficiaries usually are best served if the business owner creates a living trust to control the disposition and administration of assets that otherwise would be probate property. (For purposes of this discussion, a living trust is a trust that does not become irrevocable until the grantor's death.) Unlike a will, a living trust does not need to be filed with a probate court, and its terms do not have to be publicly disclosed unless it becomes the subject of litigation. If the substantive and administrative provisions of the owner's estate plan are contained in a living trust, and if his or her will simply provides for all of the owner's probate assets to pass to the living trust upon the owner's death, then the details of the owner's estate plan, such as the allocation of assets among family members and the terms of ongoing trust administration, can remain private.

To avoid probate administration or probate court disclosure of family business ownership interests, the owner should title all ownership units to the living trust or provide for the units to pass to the living trust by non-probate means, such as transfer on death (TOD) beneficiary designation.

Sometimes titling business ownership units to a revocable trust can cause confusion with respect to operation of the business's governing documents or buy-sell agreement. For example, if buy-sell provisions are triggered by the death of an owner, do they also apply at the death of a grantor of a living trust that holds title to ownership units? Therefore, if ownership units will be held in a living trust, the governing documents and buy-sell agreements should state clearly how and when living trust units should be treated as though they are held by the grantor of the living trust, and the trustee of the living trust (often the grantor) should agree that the trustee and successor trustees will be bound by the terms of the buy-sell agreement.

A TOD beneficiary designation is a simple way to avoid the confusion and other complications that can be caused by titling ownership units to a living trust during the grantor's lifetime. Most states allow securities to be titled with a TOD designation that can be given effect without probate at the death of the owner. To fund the living trust at death using a TOD designation, the owner would direct the company to register his or her units on the books of the company in the owner's name, followed by language identifying the living trust as the at-death beneficiary, such as "[Name of Owner], TOD [or 'transfer on death'] to trustees under the [Name of Living Trust]." (If the units are certificated, the TOD beneficiary can be shown on the certificate.) The company is then empowered simply to retitle the units to the owner's living trust upon his or her death. The owner can revoke or change the TOD designation at any time.

If the owners decide to use TOD designations for their family business ownership units, it can be helpful to include in the company's governing documents an express recognition of TOD designations and a procedure for registering units as TOD and implementing the TOD at an owner's death. Also, if an owner's units will not be held in the living trust during his or her lifetime, then the owner's power of attorney for financial matters should specify who will have authority to vote the owner's units if he or she is mentally incapacitated.

Note that the benefits of avoiding probate can be undermined if an heir or other person challenges the terms of a living trust in court. To discourage such litigation, the owner can include a "penalty" ("*in terrorem*") clause in the living trust, which could cancel the trust benefits of any person who challenges the terms of the trust or the actions of the fiduciaries without probable cause to do so. The enforceability of such clauses will depend on the facts and applicable state law. Also, such provisions would not be effective against a person who does not have a beneficial interest in the trust.

8.2 Asset Allocation

When a business owner's estate plan is drafted without the foundation of a business succession plan, the dispositive provisions often do not specify which ownership interests are to be allocated to particular beneficiaries. Often, ownership disputes arise among the beneficiaries because a pro rata allocation of ownership units is inconsistent with the beneficiaries' expectations or the best interests of the business. Therefore, the business owner's estate plan should be updated to be specific about how to allocate ownership units among the beneficiaries and how to fund the shares of beneficiaries who will receive a lesser interest (or none at all) in ownership units or other business assets.

When reviewing the senior owner's estate plan, it is again helpful to consider the attitudes and objectives of potential beneficiaries with regard to the family business interests. Recall section 3.1, which discusses how successor owners prioritize the four reasons for owning family business interests: cash flow, wealth accumulation, occupation/career, and legacy. As at other times in the business succession planning process, understanding these priorities can guide decisions about asset allocation in the estate plan.

For each separate family business entity, the estate plan should specify the amount or percentage of ownership interest to be allocated to each beneficiary or ongoing trust. Presumably, the beneficiaries who will have the most involvement in operating the business will receive the greater share of ownership interest of the companies that are most central to business operations, while other beneficiaries will receive lesser amounts or will receive interests in nonessential business elements, such as real estate or other assets that are leased to the operating business.

If beneficiaries who are not going to be involved in business operations will nevertheless receive a percentage of ownership interest, it may be best to allocate to them exclusively nonvoting units, and to provide for those units to be held in trust and managed by a fiduciary until they are redeemed or purchased by other owners. If such beneficiaries receive more liquid assets to fund their share of the owner's estate, they may participate in some level of the legacy and appreciation of the family business, but they may be less dependent on its cash flow or continuing success for their own financial needs. Further, if the ownership units of nonvoting minority owners are held by an independent trustee, the trustee can help protect the beneficiary's rights as an owner but also provide an emotional buffer between the beneficiary and the family members who are operating the business. For example, it less likely that an independent trustee would bring a lawsuit against the other owners and the managers without a compelling legal basis, and it is more likely that the independent trustee would make efforts to resolve any such legal claims before commencing adversarial proceedings.

Similarly, if the owner's spouse is not a parent of the beneficiaries who will primarily operate the business after the owner's death, particularly if their relationship is not amicable, it may be prudent to fund the surviving spouse's share of the estate with assets that do not include equity in the business. Alternatively, the spouse's interest in the business can be held by an independent trustee who can act as a buffer between the spouse and the other beneficiaries.

It is often best to include the spouse in the process of planning how his or her share of the decedent's assets will be funded and administered (and the lawyer may have a duty to do so if he or she represents the owner and the spouse jointly). A spouse is less likely to challenge the plan if he or she has agreed to it (or at least had notice of it) in advance.

Finally, decisions about allocation of the right to vote ownership units should be made separate from decisions about allocation of beneficial ownership of units or their financial attributes, as discussed in chapter 6. The estate planning documents should carry out decisions that the owners have made with respect to governance succession; this includes provisions that would apply if one of the beneficiaries predeceases the owner.

8.3 Liquidity Planning

When a senior owner dies, it is likely that his or her estate will need to have assets other than the family business interests to satisfy its obligations or otherwise achieve the senior owner's estate planning objectives. In particular, the senior owner's estate may need liquidity to pay debts, to fund the shares of beneficiaries who will not be succeeding to ownership of family business interests (including charity or a surviving spouse), and to pay estate taxes.

The objective of planning for liquidity in a senior owner's estate is generally consistent with efforts to plan for his or her security in retirement after exiting business ownership, but, if the estate will be subject to estate taxes, planning for liquidity at death has an extra dimension. Usually the liquidity for these needs must come from the deceased owner's liquid assets, a post-mortem sale of the deceased owner's nonbusiness assets, proceeds from life insurance, or a sale of family business interests to beneficiaries consistent with the succession plan. With respect to estate taxes, there may be some additional strategies.

8.3.1 Selling Units to Beneficiaries

When the senior owner will not have sufficient nonbusiness assets to fully fund bequests to beneficiaries who will not receive family business ownership units—such as children who are not active in the business, a surviving spouse, or charity—the estate plan can authorize the estate fiduciaries to raise the needed funds by selling ownership units to the other beneficiaries, pro rata, consistent with the ownership succession plan.

Note that, in many cases, if a senior owner is survived by children in the business, the senior owner's death probably will not trigger a purchase option under the business's buy-sell agreement because all of the children or trusts for them are likely to be permitted transferees. Therefore, if the deceased owner wants to grant some of his or her beneficiaries a right to purchase ownership units from the estate, then the estate plan must grant them that right.

Similar to a buy-sell agreement, the estate plan should describe the purchase price (or how to determine it) and the payment terms. If the estate is subject to estate taxes, the purchase price might be based on the value of the ownership interest as finally determined for federal estate taxes, but the estate plan can authorize the estate fiduciaries to sell the ownership units to the beneficiaries at a discount (or at a premium).

Although it is best to require the buyers to pay cash for as much of the purchase price as possible, it is likely that the buyers will not be able to pay the full purchase price in cash and thus will have to pay the balance over time. In such cases, the estate plan should require appropriate security and perhaps incentives for prepayment, such as a rising interest rate. Recognize, however, that if the buyers will not control dividend policy, they might not be able to rely on the purchased units to provide the cash flow that they need to pay installments on the purchase price. It might be helpful, as part of succession planning, to arrange for the buyers to borrow some of the purchase price from the business or from a commercial lender, with the business as a guarantor.

8.3.2 Estate Taxes

Although the U.S. Congress provided substantial federal estate tax relief over the last few years, many senior owners will hold business ownership interests that exceed the federal estate tax exemption amount and thus will need to address estate tax liability in their estate plan.

The problem of federal estate taxes may apply to married as well as single owners. Theoretically, if an owner is married, he or she can defer estate taxes on the share of the estate left to the surviving spouse or a trust that qualifies for the estate tax marital deduction. If the senior owner, however, does not intend to leave ownership units to the surviving spouse (perhaps because the surviving spouse is not a parent of the owner's children), then his or her estate may have to pay estate taxes or authorize the estate fiduciaries to sell the ownership units to certain beneficiaries as described above (or both!). Either option is unsatisfactory if the ownership units constitute a disproportionate part of the value of the deceased owner's estate.

For example, using 2019 rules, if a senior owner holds $90 million of ownership units and $10 million of other assets, and if he or she wants to leave half of the estate value but none of the ownership units to the surviving spouse, then the options are limited and unattractive. Assuming that charitable giving is not an objective, the estate plan might produce the following result:

The deceased owner leaves the surviving spouse $10 million of nonbusiness assets and $40 million of ownership units, and leaves the other $50 million of ownership units to the children. This would require the children to purchase $40 million of ownership units from the spouse, and to pay an estate tax of about $15.4 million on the other $50 million of ownership units, which they received by bequest. Without life insurance proceeds or other assets in the estate to liquidate or use to fund the bequest to the surviving spouse, the children would be left with a $55.4 million financial obligation they might not be able to satisfy.

This example illustrates the importance of planning for estate liquidity, even if the spouse survives. A more conventional approach when there is a surviving spouse may be to pass all of the estate, except the amount that is exempt from estate taxes, to a trust for the surviving spouse to defer the estate taxes in full until the second death. In the example above, however, this would leave the surviving spouse as the sole beneficial owner of a large stake in the family business for the rest of his or her life. Such a result could be awkward for all of the beneficiaries and not particularly secure for the surviving spouse, especially if he or she has no voice in managing the business.

Fortunately, transfers of ownership units during the senior owner's lifetime can address and avoid some of the adverse effects of estate taxes when a spouse is surviving. (See chapter 10 for a discussion of strategies for addressing potential estate tax liability through lifetime transfers of ownership units.)

As to payment of estate taxes at the death of an owner, there are some strategies that may be more appropriate than others. Liquidity strategies mentioned above, such as life insurance or selling other assets, can be used to pay estate taxes. Further, the Internal Revenue Code offers some strategies, such as Section 303, which allows favorable tax treatment for a partial redemption of a decedent's ownership units if the proceeds are used to pay estate taxes, or Section 6166, which allows the estate tax liability to be paid in installments and deferred over a period as long as fifteen years. Also, a technique called a "Graegin" loan (not sanctioned by the Internal Revenue Code) may allow the estate to obtain a loan from the family business to pay estate taxes and take the projected interest expense as an estate tax deduction.

Although such means of addressing the estate tax are not as efficient or effective as lifetime transfers, they can be valuable additional tools if they are consistent with the deceased owner's estate planning.

8.4 Trusts and Fiduciaries

In the past twenty years, many states have updated their trust statutes in ways that are tremendously beneficial for business succession planning. As a result, trusts have not lost their traditional benefits and advantages in estate planning; now, however, trusts also are flexible vehicles that can be tailored to many uses in business succession planning. In particular, trusts now can be established with multiple fiduciary and non-fiduciary decision makers, each with distinct authority and responsibilities with respect to trust administration and management of trust assets, including family business interests.

8.4.1 Fiduciaries and Decision Makers

Under traditional trust law, a grantor conveys property to a trustee, who agrees to manage and use the property for the benefit of the beneficiaries. Under that paradigm, the trustee holds legal title to the property and exercises all decision-making authority regarding the property and how its value is enjoyed by the beneficiaries within parameters set forth in the trust agreement, except for the power the grantor may have given a beneficiary to require the trustee to make distributions under particular circumstances (i.e., a power of appointment).

Under most states' trust statutes, the bundle of fiduciary duties and decision-making responsibilities that used to be allocated entirely to the trustee can now be divided among various trust fiduciaries and decision makers, commonly referred to as trustees, directing parties (trust advisors), and trust protectors (trust enforcers). Trusts that utilize a directing party are referred to as "directed trusts" and are particularly well suited to hold family business interests.

8.4.1.a Trustee

A trustee can still be appointed to hold all fiduciary powers in a traditional trust, but in a directed trust, the discretion to make investment or distribution decisions (or both) is vested in one or more directing parties.

In a directed trust, the trustee holds legal title to the trust assets and has a fiduciary duty to account for all activity affecting such assets. The trustee holds custody of the trust assets, or they are held by a custodian under the trustee's control. The trustee has legal authority to bind the trust, sometimes acting on its own discretion and sometimes carrying out the directions of the directing party (or a trust protector).

While the trustee under a directed trust serves as a fiduciary and owes traditional fiduciary duties to the beneficiaries (including the duties of due care, good faith, and loyalty), the trustee generally cannot be held liable for carrying out the directions of a directing party. However, state law varies on whether such exculpation applies in all instances, even when the directing party (or trust protector) is breaching the terms of the trust.

One of the advantages of a directed trust is that it allows the family to use the services of a corporate trustee for trusts that hold family business interests but then assign voting or managing family business investments to someone more familiar with the business and better suited to exercise discretion. In fact, in the past, some corporate fiduciaries were reluctant to serve as trustees of trusts that held family business interests, particularly for smaller businesses, because of the risk involved in holding a concentrated position in an investment that was difficult to monitor. With a directed trust, however, a corporate fiduciary can serve as trustee and perform those fiduciary functions better than individual trustees, safeguard trust assets, and account for trust activity. Further, many corporate fiduciaries will serve as trustee of a directed trust at a substantially lower fee than the rates they would charge under a traditional trust structure.

8.4.1.b Directing Party

Under a directed trust, the grantor can appoint one or more directing parties to manage trust investments or make distribution decisions. The directing party usually serves as a fiduciary within parameters set forth in the trust agreement.

When a directed trust holds family business interests, the trust agreement can grant the directing party authority to exercise the right to vote family business interests and to make decisions about whether to continue to hold the interests or sell them, or purchase more family business interests. The directing party also may authorize the trust to make capital contributions to a family business or capitalize the start of a new family business, make loans to a family business, and guarantee the debt of a family business.

Although a directed trust might grant the trustee, rather than the directing party, authority to manage cash, marketable securities, and other trust assets that are not family business interests, the trust should specify whether the directing party can require the trustee to use such assets to fund or finance activity relating to a family business. For example, the directing party may be authorized to require the trustee to sell marketable securities and use the proceeds to purchase additional family business units or invest in a new business venture.

The directing party should be a person who is familiar with the family business and will be able to maintain knowledge of family business activity. If the directing party is a person who has an interest in the family business or serves as a fiduciary in the business, then the trust agreement should waive that conflict of interest. In most states, the trust agreement can exculpate the directing party from liability for good-faith actions or omissions, and in some cases the directing party can serve in a non-fiduciary capacity. The role of directing party also can be assigned to a group of individuals, like a board. Choosing a directing party may be influenced by whether the trust will hold voting units or nonvoting units and whether the directing party will have authority to make distribution decisions.

8.4.1.c Trust Protector

A trust protector can be utilized in a traditional trust or in a directed trust. The trust protector usually is granted powers that are only exercised from time to time, usually when a beneficiary or trustee asks the trust protector to act. The trust protector's duties can include removing and appointing trust fiduciaries, approving trust accountings or trust fiduciaries' activities on behalf of incompetent beneficiaries, terminating grantor trust powers, adding or removing classes of beneficiaries, changing trust situs, decanting trust assets, amending trust provisions that do not affect beneficial interests, providing consent on behalf of incompetent beneficiaries with respect to nonjudicial settlements that change trust terms, and terminating the trust.

The trust protector may be treated as a fiduciary, but the trust agreement may exculpate the trust protector from liability for good-faith acts or omissions. In some cases, the trust protector can serve in a nonfiduciary capacity.

8.4.1.d Beneficiary's Role

An individual can serve as a trustee, directing party, or trust protector (or any combination of these roles) for a trust under which he or she is a beneficiary, but if a beneficiary has too much authority under a trust agreement, such as discretion to make trust distributions or power to terminate the trust, such authority may have unintended tax consequences or property law consequences that undermine the trust's purposes.

8.4.1.e Successor Appointments

Given the importance of the authority that trust fiduciaries and decision makers possess, it is prudent to provide in the trust agreement the means of removing persons who may no longer be a fit for their role with the trust and for appointing successors when the position is vacant. This is especially true for trusts that are likely to continue for more than one generation.

The role of the trust protector provides a simple starting point. For example, the trust agreement can grant the trust protector the authority to appoint and remove trustees and directing parties, and it can grant another person, such as certain trust beneficiaries, the authority to appoint and remove trust protectors, or, if there are multiple trust protectors, the remaining trust protectors can be given authority to fill any vacancies.

The trust agreement should state:

- who is appointed to serve initially, and identify any specific successors;
- who can remove a person serving in each position and the grounds required for doing so (e.g., with or without cause); and
- who can appoint persons to fill vacancies in each position and any requirements or other qualifications for the person appointed to serve (e.g., it must be a corporate fiduciary to be a beneficiary).

8.4.2 Trust to Hold Family Business Interests

This section discusses trusts that can be incorporated into a senior owner's estate plan to become irrevocable upon his or her death and to be funded with at least some family business ownership units. (For the use of irrevocable trusts to be funded during the senior owner's lifetime, particularly the use of grantor trusts, see chapter 10.) Under current trust law in most states, trusts that will hold family business interests can be tailored in many ways, and existing trusts may be modified by judicial action or nonjudicial settlement. This section primarily focuses on three types of trusts: beneficiary asset protection trusts, business continuation trusts, and dynasty trusts.

8.4.2.a Beneficiary Asset Protection Trust

Sometimes the senior owner might suggest passing family business interests free of trust to an adult child who is working in the business and does not need assistance managing his or her ownership units or other investments. In such cases, however, the senior owner should consider whether a trust might provide the beneficiary with desirable asset-protection features with respect to family business interests that the beneficiary could not otherwise enjoy.

Under the laws of most states, assets of an irrevocable trust that is established and funded by a person other than the beneficiary are not available to satisfy claims against the beneficiary if he or she does not have authority to withdraw trust assets or terminate the trust. Similarly, the assets of such a trust generally are not subject to property division at divorce. Also, the trust can be drafted to prevent the assets from being included in the beneficiary's estate for estate tax purposes.

Although a beneficiary might otherwise feel too restricted by the idea of a third-party trustee holding the beneficiary's share of family business interests, the trust agreement can grant the beneficiary substantial control over the management of trust assets by appointing the beneficiary to serve as the directing party and giving him or her the authority to remove and replace the trustee and trust protector.

Under that structure, the beneficiary, as directing party, can vote family business units held in the trust and can make all other decisions regarding management of trust investments, whether or not such investments are family business interests. The trustee would have authority to pay or withhold distributions of trust income or principal, but the trust agreement could give the beneficiary considerable influence over the trustee by granting the beneficiary the power to remove the trustee without cause, as long as the beneficiary appoints an independent trustee as a successor. Similarly, the trust protector would have power to terminate the trust, but the trust agreement could give the beneficiary considerable influence over the trust protector by granting the beneficiary the power to remove the trust protector without cause, as long as the beneficiary appoints an independent trust protector as a successor.

Under such a structure, the beneficiary's family business interests could be protected against claims of creditors, division at divorce, and estate tax liability, but the beneficiary would have nearly all the same rights as he or she would have if he or she held the interests free of trust. The trust also could give the beneficiary the ability to allocate the trust assets among family members by power of appointment that would be given effect at the beneficiary's death.

8.4.2.b Business Continuation Trust

In some instances, the senior owner's primary objective for his or her estate plan is to arrange for the family business to continue to be owned by the family as long as any family member wishes to work in the business and continue the family legacy.

One way to pursue that vision would be to execute a buy-sell agreement under which only family members who were employed in the business would be allowed to hold ownership units, and if a family member separated from the business, his or her shares would be redeemed. That model, however, could be costly for the business, as it would have to secure cash or financing every time a family member terminated employment.

A better alternative might be to create a trust to hold ownership of the family business for as long as any of the senior owner's descendants may wish to work in the business. During the term of the trust, voting rights associated with the ownership units could be exercised by directing parties, and profits could be distributed among a wide class of family beneficiaries. Family members working for the business or serving on the board would receive compensation from the business, but would not have to have their shares redeemed if they left the business for other career opportunities.

Eventually, the business would be sold (to a buyer within or outside of the family) and the proceeds could be invested in other assets, or they could be distributed per stirpes among the senior owner's then-surviving descendants. (However, see the next section for a discussion of the generation-skipping transfer (GST) tax that might affect a business continuation trust that terminates.)

8.4.2.c Dynasty Trust

Many states have eliminated the rule against perpetuities, which means that trusts in those states theoretically could continue for many generations. In general, property that passes through a trust to a grandchild or more remote descendant (a "skip person") is subject to a federal GST tax,[1] currently at a rate of 40 percent, but the Internal Revenue Code provides a GST tax exemption (up to $11.4 million at this writing). For a trust, the exemption is measured and can be applied as of when an irrevocable trust is funded. If the GST exemption is applied to trust assets, they continue to be sheltered and exempt from GST taxes while they remain in trust and upon distribution to a "skip person" (but not thereafter). Assets held in a GST tax-exempt trust are also sheltered from estate taxes when beneficiaries die, which means that regardless of how much the trust assets

---

1. IRC § 2601 *et seq.*

appreciate in value, they can avoid estate taxes indefinitely. Such trusts are commonly referred to as "dynasty trusts."

A dynasty trust can be held in separate shares for individual beneficiaries, and thus could be used as an asset-protection trust, described above, in which the primary beneficiary could vote and otherwise manage family business ownership units, or it could be structured as a business continuation trust, also described above, in which all family business ownership units would be held by the trustees until family members ceased to work in the business.

8.4.3 Tax Considerations

Planning that involves ownership of business interests in trust can create tax opportunities and tax problems. The senior owner's tax advisor should be consulted about trust planning to identify these opportunities and avoid the problems.

For example, on the opportunity side, income on assets held in a trust in a state that does not have a state income tax might not be subject to any state income taxation. Similarly, GST tax-exempt assets will not be subject to estate taxes as long as they are held in trust.

However, on the problem side, some trusts are not qualified to hold S corporation stock or must be registered with the Internal Revenue Service as soon as such a trust becomes a shareholder. Similarly, if a beneficiary of a GST tax-exempt trust has a right to withdraw trust property or a broad right to direct how trust property should pass upon his or her death, such assets could be subjected to estate taxes when the beneficiary dies.

It is good to be creative when tailoring trusts for a business owner's estate plan, but the income tax and transfer tax ramifications should always be reviewed before the estate plan is finalized or implemented.

Chapter Nine:

Retirement and Exit Planning

This chapter discusses financial resources and security for the senior owners in retirement, considering (1) income and assets that are not dependent on the family business and (2) how a senior owner's exit from the family business may be structured to supplement his or her other financial resources.

Sometimes senior owners can be overzealous about transferring wealth to their successors, and they do not give sufficient consideration to their own needs after succession. Senior owners may be willing to sacrifice much of their own future comfort to benefit their children and to preserve the legacy of the family business. In most cases, however, the sacrifice is not required. With proper planning in advance of substantial wealth transfers to their successors, senior owners can remain secure in retirement without undermining the success of the family business.

9.1 Retirement Planning

Senior owners' financial services and investment advisors should be brought into the discussion of business succession planning to assist with retirement planning. They can help the senior owners better forecast and quantify what needs they will have in retirement, determine and quantify the financial resources that the senior owners already have for retirement, and identify additional resources for retirement that the senior owners could acquire or accrue outside the family business.

9.1.a Living Expenses and Other Financial Needs

A critical part of retirement planning and designing an exit strategy for senior owners is determining the appropriate amount of wealth, cash flow, and other economic or material resources they will need after they cease to receive compensation and profits from the family business. Accountants and financial services providers can help the senior owners estimate such amounts over a broad range of scenarios, taking into account risks of profound health care challenges and possible future economic crises.

Some senior owners may have more than enough resources for retirement and can proceed to engage in aggressive lifetime wealth transfers to their successors to reduce potential estate tax liability or address other succession objectives. Many senior owners, however, may fall within a gray area, in which they find that they would be vulnerable to financial compromise if they did not secure greater resources to meet their needs in retirement.

When senior owners have a better understanding of their financial needs and risks in retirement, their advisors can help them develop strategies to address those needs and risks using their current wealth and additional resources they may accrue before retiring.

9.1.b Separate Resources

The solution for retirement planning for senior owners likely will involve not just one resource but rather diverse sources of wealth, cash flow, and risk management resources. Often, it is best if the successor owners do not have to rely on receiving cash flow from the family business in retirement. Otherwise, they will be extracting capital that the business may need for operations or growth, and their security will be partially dependent on the performance of the business under successor management.

Separate resources that senior owners will have in retirement may include Social Security, Medicare, and pensions and retirement plans from employment outside the family business. In addition, senior owners should consider other potential resources, such as the following:

• **Marketable securities accounts.** An investment advisor can help clients design an investment portfolio that has an appropriate risk profile and can then help forecast how much return the owners can expect when they start drawing on the account for living expenses. An investment advisor also can help determine how much owners should be trying to add to their marketable securities holdings in advance of retirement. These comments also apply to tax-deferred investment accounts, such as IRAs and 401(k) accounts.

• **Rental properties.** Senior owners' rental properties may be a good source of income in retirement, assuming they can be managed cost effectively. Even if the property is rented to the family business, it is not necessarily dependent on the business's ongoing success if the property could be leased or sold to other parties if the business defaulted.

• **Illiquid, unproductive assets.** Illiquid, unproductive assets, such as residential or recreational real estate, could be sold if needed to raise cash or to invest in an asset that will produce an annual return. Note, however, that from a family wealth perspective, it may be counterproductive to sell low-basis assets during the owner's lifetime. If the owner holds a low-basis asset until death, (under current tax law) the asset will be assigned a new basis equal to date-of-death value, which may substantially reduce the capital gains tax cost when the asset is sold by the owner's estate or estate beneficiaries.

• **High-interest debt.** Senior owners may be able to improve their balance sheet by retiring high-interest debt or refinancing it at a lower interest rate. Also, they should try to get released from all personal guaranties of business debt.

• **Insurance.** Senior owners should work with a qualified insurance professional to review all of their insurance to make sure that they are efficiently covering their risks, but are not supporting coverage that they do not need. They should consider whether disability coverage is at sufficient levels, and whether their life insurance has appropriate face amounts and duration. They may determine that life insurance is not needed for estate tax planning, but it may be desirable for other purposes. In some cases, it may be desirable to surrender old life insurance policies in exchange for the cash surrender value, or it may be possible to sell an in-force policy through a broker for substantially more than the cash surrender value. Also, senior owners should consider whether long-term care insurance could be an effective additional risk management tool.

9.1.c Family Business Resources

After senior owners determine the range of resources they need in retirement to maintain their desired standard of living, and after they identify and quantify the resources they have outside the family business to meet those needs, they can consider whether the family business or successor owners should also contribute to their retirement resources. Owners should consider some of the following ongoing relationships or transactions with the family business:

• **Fees for services.** The business can agree to pay a senior owner reasonable fees for services that he or she provides to the business after retiring from full-time employment. For example, the business could pay the senior owner fees for board service or for consulting services. Also, if the business's lender does not immediately release the senior owner from his or her personal guaranty of the business's debt upon retirement, the business can pay the senior owner a guaranty fee to compensate for the ongoing risk. (Note that if the senior owner's exit from ownership is structured as a redemption, some of these ongoing relationships could create unintentional income tax consequences.)

• **Rental, leasing, licensing.** If the senior owner retains ownership of real estate, equipment, or intellectual property used by the business, the business can continue to pay the senior owner for its use of these assets. In the alternative, the business or successor owners could purchase such assets from the senior owner and provide cash flow in payment of the purchase price, but purchasing such assets generally would be less tax efficient than leasing them because it would trigger a capital gains tax, which could be avoided if the senior owner holds the assets until death (at which time they would receive a new tax basis equal to date-of-death value and thus avoid tax on past appreciation). Also, leasing the assets may be more tax-efficient for the business than purchasing because leasing would be a current expense, as contrasted with purchasing the assets and expensing or depreciating them over time.

• **Non-qualified deferred compensation.** A nonqualified deferred compensation plan is, in essence, a promise by a company to pay an employee a sum of compensation in the future, generally after retirement, for services provided during the term of employment. The advantage of a non-qualified deferred compensation plan is that the company can establish the plan for the senior owner without being required to include other employees (although it can include other key employees). Also, the company can offer this benefit to a senior owner based on prior service, so it can become part of the succession plan even if the senior owner is already nearing retirement. For the senior owner, the risk of a non-qualified deferred compensation plan is that either it is not funded or, if assets are set aside to fund the plan, such assets remain subject to claims of the company's creditors. The use of a non-qualified deferred compensation plan should be explored with the business's tax advisors. Also, the business's banking relationship, financial services provider, or insurance agent may have access to resources that can be used to model and construct an appropriate non-qualified deferred compensation or retirement plan.

• **Redemption or cross-purchase proceeds.** The senior owner's exit from ownership can be structured to provide cash flow to the senior owner in retirement or it can be structured as a virtually gratuitous transaction, or some of both.

9.2 Ownership Exit Strategy

This section discusses structuring the senior owner's exit from ownership in a way that will provide the senior owner with cash flow and cash resources in retirement. (For transfers of stock by gift or in ways that are effectively gratuitous transfers, see chapter 10.) If the senior owner intends to sell his or her ownership units to the successor owners, the transaction should be structured in a way that allocates voting rights and equity, respectively, consistent with the succession plan and protects, as well as it can, the senior owner's right to be paid in full under the terms of the transaction.

9.2.a Purchase Price

If the purchase price is intended to provide fair value to the senior owner, the parties should obtain a formal opinion of value from a qualified business valuation professional, unless that is inconsistent with methodology set forth in a buy-sell agreement that governs the transaction. One of the advantages of working with a valuation professional is that he or she can help identify market and business risks that might affect the senior owner's ability to be paid over time.

Also, if the senior owner intends to sell his or her units in stages or to allocate the voting units separate from the nonvoting units, the valuation professional can help model those transactions, including premiums or discounts that might apply and how the units are likely to appreciate (or the risk that they will decline in value) between each stage of an exit that involves multiple transfers over a period of years.

Finally, sometimes it may be appropriate to incorporate adjustments to the purchase price, such as an earn-out or claw-back provisions, to account for superior performance by the business after the unit transfer, or to allow the senior owner to benefit if the business is sold shortly after he or she exits from ownership. For example, when the senior owner sells his or her units to the company or successor owners, the purchase price could be set at a conservative amount, but with the understanding that if the company subsequently performs better than expected or is sold for a higher price in the first few years after the senior owner's exit, then he or she will be paid additional sums based on a formula that has been written into the unit purchase agreement.

9.2.b Redemption or Cross-Purchase

The parties' accountants and tax advisors should participate in deciding whether to structure the senior owner's exit from ownership as a redemption or a cross-purchase, because it can involve important and nuanced tax issues for the senior owner, the company, and the remaining owners.

Usually the purchase of a senior owner's units may be best structured as a cross-purchase by specific successors, rather than a redemption by the company. This is true for several reasons.

First, a cross-purchase allows the owner to allocate voting and nonvoting units precisely as determined in the succession plan. In contrast, a redemption simply absorbs the voting and nonvoting units, accruing the benefit pro rata among the remaining owners, which, among other things, may have unintentional effects on the remaining owners' relative voting rights or economic rights.

Further, under many circumstances, a cross-purchase allows the senior owner to transfer his or her units in a series of transfers over time. In contrast, a partial redemption of stock of a family-owned corporation might cause the sales proceeds to be taxed as a dividend, which can create additional tax liability.

The tax problems associated with a partial redemption of corporation stock also can arise if the senior owner retains a role in the corporation, such as may be desired to provide additional retirement income or as part of the covenants used to protect the senior owner's rights as a creditor under an installment note issued in the redemption.

If, however, a redemption will not give rise to the problems discussed above, then a redemption, as opposed to a cross-purchase, of ownership units may have a greater tax advantage for the corporation and the remaining shareholders because of the increase in tax basis that may accrue to the company. (For an LLC taxed as a partnership, the benefit of increased basis for the company can be achieved in a cross-purchase, as well as a redemption, although the benefit will only accrue, pro rata, to the owners who participate.)

Another advantage of a redemption over a cross-purchase is that the company may have a greater ability to fund the purchase price than the remaining owners have. This is particularly important for a C corporation because of the tax inefficiencies involved in giving shareholders access to the corporation's cash resources. If a C corporation has cash resources or cash flow that the shareholders may need to fund a cross-purchase, the shareholders will incur income taxes on cash that the corporation pays them as a dividend. In the alternative, the C corporation could make a loan to the shareholders or, if they are employees, pay them bonus compensation, within reason, to pay for the cross-purchase, but these methods are cumbersome and limited.

9.2.c Staged Transfers

In some cases, the senior owner may wish to begin the process of ownership succession by allowing the successor owners to purchase some portion of the senior owner's ownership units before he or she is ready to retire or relinquish voting control. The parties can informally agree to execute a series of transactions under which the successors acquire a greater percentage of equity in each transaction. (In most cases involving a corporation (for the reasons described above regarding partial redemptions of corporation stock), it is likely that these transactions would have to be structured as a series of cross-purchases, rather than redemptions.)

For example, the senior owner could sell the successors equal amounts of his or her nonvoting stock in consecutive transactions, with each of the later transactions closing after the successor owners have fully paid the purchase price under the prior transaction. In that example, the senior owner would likely also sell his or her voting units in the final transaction of the series.

By transferring the units in a series of transactions, the senior owner can bring the successors into ownership gradually to test the succession process, incentivize the successor owners, and, with respect to successor owners who are active in the business, to focus their efforts and energy by giving them an economic stake in the business's performance.

Note that when the senior owner sells units to the successors, he or she will incur a capital gains tax on the transaction. Therefore, if the senior owner is the sole owner or is one of a small group of owners, it may be desirable to defer capital gains taxes on the first of the series of transactions by allowing the successors to purchase ownership units from the company. This will not result in the same cash flow to the senior owner, but it could help accomplish other objectives of using a series of transactions to transfer ownership more gradually. (There are other means of avoiding or deferring capital gains taxes on ownership transfers, but they generally involve a gift element. See, e.g., section 10.2.c.)

9.2.d Allocation of Voting Rights and Equity

Transfer of the senior owner's ownership units should be structured consistent with the desired result for allocation of the successors' voting rights and relative amounts of owner equity under the business succession plan. Often, greater amounts of equity will be allocated to successors who are active in the business. As discussed above in section 6.2.1, the significance of voting rights can vary, based on the terms of a company's governing documents, and voting rights can be delegated to fiduciaries or otherwise separated from the allocation of owner equity. It is likely, however, that if individual successors are investing in equity of the company and are incurring debt to pay the senior owner for such equity, they will want to have influence on the company's governance that corresponds to the relative levels of obligation and risk they are incurring in purchasing ownership units. (That is a consideration that may be far more acute in this context than it would be in a gratuitous transfer of ownership units.)

9.2.e Cash at Closing

To reduce the risk to the senior owner that the successors may default on the installment payments of purchase price, the parties should explore means of maximizing the amount of purchase price paid at closing.

If the succession plan is developed long in advance of the unit transfer, the business or successors may be able to create a sort of sinking fund of cash and marketable securities to be available for a large down payment to the senior owner. Note that if the fund is in the business, it may be difficult for the successor owners to use it for a cross-purchase, except perhaps as a loan to the successor owners.

The parties also should consider a loan from a bank or other third-party lender for a down payment to the senior owner. It may be unlikely that the successors will be able to borrower the entire purchase price from a third-party lender, but a loan for even a portion of the purchase price will be able to divert some of the risk of default away from the senior owner. Likely, the senior owner will have to agree that any promissory note he or she may receive from the successor owners for the balance of the purchase price will be subordinate to their obligation to a third-party lender. As a result, the senior owner might not be as free to negotiate for the terms, security, and covenants he or she might want for the successors' obligation to pay the balance, at least until the obligation to the third-party lender is fully satisfied.

9.2.f Payment Terms, Security, Covenants

When the senior owner accepts an installment obligation from the company or the successor owners for his or her ownership units, unless the senior owner has a donative intent, then he or she should try to negotiate payment terms, security, guaranties, and other commitments from the buyers that will help reduce the risk of default or will provide adequate and affordable remedies in the event of default.

9.2.f.i Terms

The promissory note from the buyers (i.e., the company or the successor owners) should require periodic payments that the buyer can be expected to pay out of net cash flow from operations. Payment in full should be required within six to ten years so that the senior owner does not have to worry about default or attempt to exercise remedies late in life, long after he or she has separated from the business. If circumstance might suppress the buyers' cash flow during the early years of repayment and thus might not allow equal payments throughout the term of the note, it may be preferable for the senior owner to insist on a balloon payment at the end of a shorter note, rather than to allow a schedule of lower payments to stretch beyond a period of ten years. When the balloon comes due, the buyers should be able to obtain financing from a third party to pay off the obligation to the senior owner, unless business performance has suffered.

To avoid unintended gift tax and income tax treatment, the interest rate should be no less than the appropriate applicable federal rate published by the Internal Revenue Service under section 1274(d) of the Internal Revenue Code for the month of the transaction. The interest rate, however, can be set higher, based on market rates of interest considering the duration of the period for repayment and an assessment of the risk of default.

9.2.f.ii Security and Guaranties

To protect the senior owner's right to recover the purchase price in the event of default, the buyers' installment obligation can be secured and guaranteed. These measures can motivate the successors to work harder to avoid default, and they can protect the senior owner vis-à-vis the buyers' other creditors.

If the ownership units are purchased by successor owners, then the company or affiliates can guarantee the owners' obligation to pay the purchase price. If the ownership units are redeemed, then individual owners can guarantee the company's obligation to pay the purchase price. In the case of a redemption, if the successor owners manage the business, then requiring them to personally guarantee the company's obligation to pay the senior owner can provide them with greater incentive to cause the company to satisfy that obligation. If the successor owners guarantee payment in a redemption, the guaranty can be pro rata among the owners or joint and several. If some of the owners are not active in the business, it might be unfair to expect them to provide a joint and several, as opposed to a pro rata, guaranty, given their limited ability to affect whether the company can satisfy its payment obligation.

The installment obligation can be secured by a pledge of the purchased units. If the units are certificated, the certificates can be held in escrow until the purchase price is paid in full. If the units are not certificated, the escrow agent can hold a unit transfer power, executed in blank. In the event of default, unless the parties agree otherwise, the senior owner's rights with respect to the pledged units will be governed by the procedures set forth in the Uniform Commercial Code (UCC), but those procedures, which generally require the secured party to attempt to sell the pledged units to the highest bidder, are not particularly well suited to the family business context. The parties should consider drafting alternative procedures into the pledge instrument. For example, the senior owner could be allowed to reacquire the units, including the voting rights, based on a valuation of the units rather than a bidding process. Note, however, that if the unit purchase is in the form of a redemption and the company is a corporation, allowing the senior owner the right to reacquire the units could cause unintended income tax consequences.

The installment obligation also can be secured by other assets of the buyers or the guarantors, such as real estate or equipment. The company, as borrower or guarantor, can sign a general security agreement pledging its assets to the senior owner. In each instance, the senior owner should take measures to perfect his or her lien on the pledged assets, such as by holding possession of the asset or its title, making appropriate UCC filings, and recording liens on real estate with the register of deeds.

Some of the measures discussed above may not be available if they are not approved by the company's commercial lenders or if they are inconsistent with the terms of a third-party loan that was taken to provide the senior owner with more cash at closing.

9.2.f.iii Loan Covenants

To further protect the senior owner against the risk of default on the installment obligation, the senior owner can require the company and the successor owners, as the obligated parties or guarantors, to agree to various loan covenants or other post-transaction accommodations.

Loan covenants can be categorized as follows:

• **Negative covenants,** under which the obligated parties agree not to engage in particular activities, such as not to incur additional debt, not to increase dividends or compensation to owners above agreed-upon limitations, and not to make extraordinary capital expenditures.

• **Affirmative covenants,** under which the obligated parties agree to perform certain tasks, such as provide the creditor with periodic financial statements or give notice upon the occurrence of particular events.

• **Financial covenants,** under which the company is prohibited from failing to maintain certain metrics relating to its balance sheet (such as net worth) or cash flow (such as a leverage ratio measuring debt versus earnings).

The senior owner also can maintain a seat on the board until the purchase price is paid in full (but, as discussed above, in the case of a redemption, continuing board service could cause unintended tax consequences).

9.2.g Other Participants; Employee Stock Ownership Plan

If the senior owner cannot afford to seller-finance a redemption or a cross-purchase of his or her units, the buyers might seek out an equity partner. Sometimes a private equity fund, another family's family office, or a wealthy individual might be willing to purchase a minority position with cash at closing.

The least obtrusive and most tax-efficient equity partner in a corporation, however, may be an employee stock ownership plan (ESOP). An ESOP can borrow from a commercial lender, with a guaranty from the business, to pay the senior owner cash at closing.

If the company is taxed as a C corporation at the time of closing, the senior owner can defer capital gains taxes on the proceeds by reinvesting them in qualified assets, such as marketable securities. Further, an ESOP is a tax-exempt entity and therefore does not pay income taxes on corporate dividends or, if the company is taxed as an S corporation, an ESOP does not pay taxes on its share of S income. Also, the company receives a current income tax deduction for annual contributions to the ESOP. These tax features of an ESOP make it easier for the ESOP to repay the funds that it borrows to purchase the senior owner's units. An ESOP is also a way of providing incentive to all employees of the business, because they ultimately will benefit from the company's appreciation.

Chapter Ten:

Lifetime Wealth Transfers

This chapter discusses means of transferring family business interests to potential successors in advance of a senior owner's exit. Sometimes it is desirable to transfer a minority percentage of ownership units to potential successors well in advance of the senior owners' exits. This can motivate potential successors to work for the business and take a more personal interest in its performance. Often, however, the transfer of ownership units to potential successors is motivated by a need to mitigate future estate tax liability.

This chapter describes how these pre-succession transfers of ownership units can be structured to be consistent with the succession plan but also flexible enough to adapt to changes in the plan that might occur by the time the senior owners fully exit the business.

10.1 Transfers for Successor Incentive and Involvement

Senior owners may wish to motivate potential successor owners by allowing them to acquire an ownership interest in the family business long before the senior owners plan to retire. If the owners have fully designed a succession plan, including plans for business governance after their exit, then transfers of ownership interests should be consistent with the business succession plan. If there is uncertainty in the succession plan, however, then transfers of ownership interests to potential successors should be controlled so that they do not limit changes to the plan as senior owners get closer to exiting ownership and management.

If the business succession plan, including post-succession governance, has been determined with a fair amount of certainty, then it is possible to allow designated successors to acquire ownership interests consistent with the roles they will assume as owners and, if applicable, managers under the succession plan.

Successor owners who will not be involved in management or governance might acquire a small amount of nonvoting units, in trust or free of trust, to allow them to begin participating in the legacy of family ownership and to better appreciate the business's mission and performance. If the owners have a family council, these nonvoting owners might be encouraged to participate on the family council to receive occasional updates on the state of the family business and provide limited input.

Successors who will be involved in governance might be given the opportunity to acquire a small number of voting units, in addition to nonvoting equity, to allow them to attend shareholder (or member) meetings, even if they cannot affect the results of a vote.

Further, it might be effective training and incentive to allow the most qualified potential leaders among them to attend board meetings as observers or junior board members.

The successor owners may acquire their units by gift from the senior owners or by purchase from the senior owners or the company, or, in some cases, as a bonus from the company if the successor is an employee. The form of the transaction should be determined based on the economic needs of the senior owners and the aggregate tax effect among the parties who participate in the transaction.

The successors' units should be held subject to a buy-sell agreement that will allow the company or other owners to reacquire the units for fair value if the succession plan changes, if a successor owner leaves employment with the business, or if a successor owner ceases to participate in ownership in a constructive manner. For example, the buy-sell agreement can provide that if an owner ceases to be an employee in the business, the company or other owners may purchase his or her units. If the company is an LLC, the operating agreement can give the company or the members the right to expel a member. In a corporation, the governing documents could grant the corporation the right to redeem shareholders whose ownership does not exceed a particular percentage of outstanding shares.

If the company is an S corporation, note that all of the shares of an S corporation must have the same economic rights; therefore, mechanisms allowing the corporation to reacquire a shareholder's stock should be structured to avoid the appearance of creating a second class of stock. For an S corporation, the corporation may be allowed to redeem a shareholder's stock upon a triggering event that would apply to any shareholders, but there may be greater flexibility in buy-sell agreements between shareholders that do not involve the company, and thus are less likely to be deemed to create a second class of stock.

Perhaps the easiest way to control unit ownership when the succession plan is uncertain, or with respect to successors owners who will not participate in management of the business, is to transfer the units in trust for the successor as a beneficial owner. The trust could be established so that the successor owner has nearly all the same rights of ownership as he or she would if the units were held free of trust, but the decision to continue to hold or sell the units could be assigned to a directing party or trust protector. For example, the ownership units of each successor owner who is not active in the business could be held in a trust, and the successor could serve as trustee of the trust, but if the directing party or trust protector determined that the successor's beneficial ownership of units had become disruptive or counterproductive, the directing party or trust protector could require the trust to sell the shares to the company or other owners for fair value.

10.2 Transfers to Manage Future Estate Tax Liability

For many family business owners, the family business is the largest single source of wealth and cash flow in the family. In such circumstances, if the death of a senior owner creates an estate tax liability, it is likely that the business will be adversely affected, because the successors may need to burden or invade the business to satisfy the estate tax liability. Although it may be possible, in some cases, to fund estate tax liability with life insurance or the proceeds of the sale of nonbusiness assets, many times the most effective means of managing future estate tax liability is the transfer of ownership units during the senior owner's lifetime.

The senior owner should not make transfers that are inconsistent with his or her plan for resources in retirement (see chapter 9), but he or she may need to make such transfers before the successor owners and managers have been finally identified.

10.2.a Transfer Taxes

Under tax law as of this printing, a federal estate tax of 40 percent is imposed on value of a decedent's estate in excess of $11.4 million (adjusted downward for certain taxable lifetime gifts). Property passing to a spouse or a qualified trust for a spouse is not subject to federal estate taxes. Roughly speaking, therefore, a married couple can exclude $22.8 million from federal estate taxes with proper planning. Current law is scheduled to sunset in 2025, and these exclusion amounts would be reduced by half.

The federal estate tax exclusion also can be applied to lifetime transfers to avoid federal gift taxes, which are assessed at a rate equal to 40 percent of the value of the taxable gift. A similar exclusion applies to transfers during lifetime or at death that otherwise would incur a federal tax on generation-skipping transfers (GST tax), also at a 40 percent rate. (A generation-skipping transfer is a transfer that has the effect of sheltering property from federal estate taxes, or otherwise skipping federal estate tax liability, for one or more generations, such as a gift to a grandchild (i.e., skipping the child) or a gift to a trust that continues beyond one generation.) Collectively, federal estate taxes, gift taxes, and GST taxes are often referred to as "transfer taxes."

Generally, lifetime transfers of family business units to a senior owner's children and grandchildren, or trusts for them, are an effective way to reduce future estate tax liability for the following reasons:

- Future income and appreciation of transferred units accrue to the transferee and thus are not included in the senior owner's taxable estate.
- Minority interests and nonvoting units transferred during lifetime can be valued at a discount for purposes of applying transfer tax exclusions, even if the senior owner is a controlling owner. The discount applies because the transferred interests or units do not carry the benefit of voting control (lack of control) and do not have a ready market for resale (lack of marketability). In contrast, if the senior owner dies while holding a controlling interest, none of his or her units will generally qualify for lack of control discounts for purposes of assessing the federal estate tax or applying the estate tax exclusion.
- A number of tax-efficient mechanisms for transfers of business ownership units are available during the senior owner's lifetime, but not at death. (See the next section.)

10.2.b Lifetime Transfer Techniques

Lifetime ownership transfers will almost always be more efficient, from a transfer tax perspective, than transfers at death, particularly if the senior owner holds a controlling interest, and if the return on the transferred interest exceeds the safe harbor interest rate for family loans and gifts to trusts involving retained or split interests. This section briefly recites some of the more common lifetime transfer techniques, and the next section discusses the use of grantor trusts in greater detail.

- **Gift to a successor.** If the senior owner makes a lifetime gift of a minority interest or nonvoting units to a successor, the gift should be valued at a discount for purposes of calculating the amount of transfer tax exclusion that must be applied to avoid a transfer tax. Further, all income and appreciation on the interest after the gift will accrue to the successor.

- **Installment sale to a successor.** If the senior owner sells a minority interest or nonvoting units to a successor, the units should be valued at a discount for purposes of calculating the amount of the purchase price that the successor must pay for the units to ensure that the transfer will not be treated as a taxable gift. The successor may pay the purchase price in the form of an installment note to the senior owner (i.e., the seller). The seller will likely incur capital gains tax on the purchase price, but the seller may elect to recognize the taxable gain over time as the installments are received. All income and appreciation on the units after the transfer will accrue to the successor, except to the extent that the successor uses income from the units to pay the installments.

- **Self-canceling installment note.** A senior owner can sell units to a successor in exchange for an installment note that will cancel the unpaid principal upon the senior owner's death. This is called a "self-canceling installment note," or "SCIN." Theoretically, the unpaid balance of the SCIN will not be subject to transfer taxes. To justify the self-canceling feature, however, the successor must pay a premium on the interest or purchase price based on the senior owner's life expectancy (with the premium being inversely proportionate to the life expectancy). If the senior owner outlives the term of the note, the successor will have paid a premium without a corresponding benefit, but if the senior owner dies before the note has been paid in full, the successor will experience a windfall through the self-canceling feature.

- **Grantor retained annuity trust.** A senior owner can gift units to a grantor retained annuity trust (GRAT), governed by section 2702 of the Internal Revenue Code. A GRAT is a trust that provides an annual payment to the trust grantor (in this case, the senior owner) for a term of years, and thereafter the trust terminates to, or continues for the benefit of, the successor. A gift to a GRAT provides the transfer tax benefits of a lifetime gift of stock, but with an additional valuation discount in recognition of the grantor's retained interest. GRATs are not flexible vehicles. For example, the GRAT must have a means of funding the annuity payments or the technique might fail. Also, the transfer tax benefit may not accrue if the grantor dies before the end of the annuity term, and for this reason, sometimes a series of short-term GRATS may be used, adding complexity to the technique.

- **Charitable lead trust.** A senior owner can gift units to a charitable lead trust (CLT), which distributes an annual sum to charities for a term of years and thereafter terminates to, or continues for the benefit of, the successor. The charitable interest in a CLT provides an additional valuation discount for transfer taxes because the charitable interest is not subject to transfer taxes. If the senior owner has charitable giving intentions, the CLT can provide a means to gift stock to the successor and make a charitable gift in a way that is more tax efficient together than such gifts would be separately.

- **Gift and sale to a grantor trust.** Perhaps the most flexible and tax-effective means of transferring ownership units is through a coordinated gift and sale to an intentionally defective grantor trust. (See the next section for a detailed discussion of this technique.)

10.2.c Transfers to an Intentionally Defective Grantor Trust

Transferring family business ownership units to an irrevocable grantor trust can be tax-efficient and can accomplish many objectives consistent with family business succession planning.

10.2.c.i Grantor Trusts

A "grantor trust" is a trust that is treated as though it is owned by the grantor for income tax purposes. An "intentionally defective" grantor trust is simply an irrevocable trust that the grantor creates for the benefit of someone else, usually his or her children and more remote issue, but purposely including trust provisions that cause the trust to be treated as the grantor's property for income tax purposes (but not estate tax purposes). For example, a provision allowing a benefit to the grantor's spouse, or allowing the grantor to swap property with the trust, or allowing the grantor to obtain unsecured loans from the trust could cause the trust to be treated as a grantor trust.

If the grantor's intention is to maximize the amount of wealth that he or she can transfer to children and other issue without incurring transfer taxes, the grantor trust has two special advantages. First, the grantor can sell property to a grantor trust without triggering a capital gains tax and without recognizing the interest on installment payments as taxable income. Second, and most important, the grantor can pay the income tax each year on income produced by the assets in the trust without treating that additional benefit to the trust as a taxable gift.

10.2.c.ii Unit Transfers to an Irrevocable Grantor Trust

Generally, the transfer of family business ownership units to an intentionally defective grantor trust proceeds as follows:

The senior owner establishes an irrevocable grantor trust for his or her intended successors. The trust can include the grantor's spouse as a beneficiary, and thus provide an economic safety net for the spouse in retirement. Under the laws of many states, the trust can essentially continue in perpetuity and thus shelter the trust assets from transfer taxes in future generations. The trust also can provide the senior owner with the power to terminate the grantor trust features in case payment of the trust's income taxes becomes an economic burden for the senior owner.

The senior owner then makes a gift of a minority interest or nonvoting units of the family business to the trust, not exceeding his or her transfer tax exclusions, but in an amount that will allow the trust to be a credible buyer in a subsequent unit purchase transaction with the grantor (often thought to be at least 10–11 percent of the value of the ownership units that the trust will purchase from the senior owner). The gifted units should be valued at a discount, and the gift should provide all the benefits of a gift of units described above.

Next, the senior owner sells additional units (also a minority interest or nonvoting units) to the trust in exchange for an installment note. Usually, the installment note runs for nine years, which is the maximum length of a note that can use the mid-term safe harbor interest rate for family transactions (i.e., the mid-term applicable federal rate pursuant to Section 1274(d) of the Internal Revenue Code). Although the interest paid by the grantor trust will not be recognized for income tax purposes, using a low safe harbor rate will help the trust more easily make the payments. Also, it may be possible to use an interest-only note or other payment schedule that includes a balloon at the end if cash flow from the trust cannot fund payments on a note that is fully amortized. Finally, in some cases, it may be advantageous to use an installment note with a self-canceling feature.

If the units are units of ownership in a flow-through entity, and if that entity distributes cash to owners to pay their share of income taxes on flow-through income, then the trust can use that cash flow to make the installment payments to the senior owner, because, as long as the trust is a grantor trust, it will not be taxed on its income—rather, the senior owner will be. Further, after the trust has paid off the installment note, it can accumulate and invest its cash flow from the units or it can purchase additional units from the senior owner. Cash flow from the units also can be used to pay premiums for insurance on the senior owner's life.

If the units are shares of stock in a C corporation, the units are not likely to produce cash flow sufficient to make the note payments on a fully amortized installment note. If this is the case, it may be helpful if the gift that the senior owner makes to originally fund the trust consists of income-producing assets, such as interests in a rental property—perhaps a property that is leased by the family business. (Note also that this is one of the reasons to consider conversion to an S corporation when the structure of the business is reviewed as described in chapter 5.)

10.2.d Serving Succession Objectives

Transfer of ownership units in trust can be particularly well tailored to meeting family business succession objectives, even if the transfers are motivated primarily for reasons of mitigating transfer taxes. This is because the trust instrument can appoint one or more fiduciaries to make decisions about the management and division of ownership units within segregated trust accounts for individual family members or family branches. These fiduciaries can be senior family members or independent parties, or a combination.

For example, if an individual family member holds ownership units in the family business, then regardless of his or her role in the business or the state of his or her relationship with the family, that individual family member will have all the rights and powers of an owner, perhaps including rights that are disruptive to the business and can be exercised in ignorance or bad faith, such as the right to demand accountings, the right to review books and records, and possibly the right to bring direct or derivative lawsuits against the directors, officers, and majority shareholder. It even may be difficult to negotiate a redemption with a unit holder who is determined to cause trouble. In contrast, if ownership units are held in a trust, then the trust fiduciaries hold the legal rights and powers of the owners and make all decisions about how those rights and powers will be exercised, including when to divest ownership in the units and on what terms.

Further, if the trust is funded with a variety of assets, the trustees may allocate family business ownership units to the segregated trust shares of family members who are most committed to the business and can allocate other assets to the segregated shares of family members who are not involved . With this kind of flexibility, the senior owners can make wealth transfers to mitigate transfer tax liability long before they make final decisions about the specifics of family business successor owners and leaders.

Conclusion

Family businesses are important to the U.S. economy and the states and local communities in which they operate. They provide quality goods and services, jobs, and unique workplaces. Family businesses are special because the owners are dependent on and identified with the quality of their business, and because they tend to emphasize long-term growth and sustainability over short-term gain.

For a lawyer, helping a family business ensure its long-term success is a rewarding project. The template laid out in this book can make that project more efficient, effective, and complete. It can be used to help a wide range of family businesses, and it can be used for multiple generations in the same business.

Although this template refers to family business succession planning as a project, it is a project that never really ends as long as the family continues. It is important for the lawyer to cover all elements of the template when he or she begins working with a family business with respect to the succession of ownership and leadership. Additionally, the lawyer also should review many of the template sections with the business and its owners from time to time. For example, issues relating to business structure and transfer tax planning may arise every time the business acquires a new asset or division, or the family invests in a new business venture. Issues relating to governance or ownership rights may arise every time a family member starts a career with the business or ceases employment with the business. Issues relating to senior owners' resources in retirement may need close, continuing attention. Further, the business's leadership contingency plan should be reviewed annually.

Over time, the family business lawyer will develop his or her own system of representing family businesses. In the meantime, this lawyer's template will serve as a useful guide.

Appendix A

[COMPANY NAME]
SUCCESSION PLANNING

The following is an outline of the projects that will create a coordinated succession plan for [Company Name] ("Company"), as ownership and leadership pass from the senior generation of the [Family Name] family ("G1 Owner" and "G1 Spouse") to their children (G2A, G2B, and G2C), who are currently involved in Company operations. The projects below are listed in sequential order:

1. Collecting Information. Before we begin to design a succession plan, the advisor team needs to review copies of current business governing documents, related-party contracts, and estate-planning documents that might affect governance, ownership, or succession of Company and the family real estate holdings. We also need to review the most recent statements or estimates of value for Company and the real estate, as well as a personal financial statement for G1 Owner and G1 Spouse. (We will not share or disclose any part of G1 Owner and G1 Spouse's estate planning or net worth information with any other family members except as they authorize us to do so.)

   In summary, we would like to review onsite or receive electronic copies of the documents listed on Schedule A to this outline.

2. Valuation. Proper succession planning requires a reliable valuation of Company stock, when planning commences and throughout the term of family ownership. **G1 Owner and G1 Spouse will look into obtaining a reliable valuation of Company** to assist us with succession planning and estate planning. The valuation professional can also help us draft valuation language in the shareholders' agreement that will control future transfers of Company stock. Thereafter, Company should obtain an updated opinion of value on a regular basis (such as every two years). The valuation process may have the added benefit of providing management with insight about which elements of Company's business or operations tend to increase value and which (if any) may be suppressing value, from a market perspective.

3. Business Continuation Plan. Currently, G1 Owner is the CEO of Company, chairman of the board, and the controlling shareholder. His sudden death or incapacity would be substantially disruptive to Company's operations, which could impair Company's profitability and value. Therefore, we will help Company install mechanisms that would be triggered by G1 Owner's death or incapacity, if it occurs before governance succession can be commenced in the normal course. We have discussed the utility of having a functioning board of

directors to govern Company in the event of a disruption of executive leadership (and this will be addressed in the paragraph on Governance, below). G1 Owner should clearly designate who should vote his stock if he is unable, and he should have a plan, under seal, about successor or interim executive leadership if Company loses his services temporarily or permanently. **We will provide a template for a Business Continuation Plan and assist in preparing any documents, such as powers of attorney, that may be needed to make it effective.**

4. Business Restructuring. After we review the existing business documents and obtain input regarding business valuation, we will work with Company's accountants to help determine whether the business should be restructured or reorganized. It may be that making changes to the legal structure or tax treatment of the components of the business will facilitate succession planning. For example, it may be easier to plan transitions of ownership if the primary source of cash flow is taxed as a partnership rather than a C corporation, or if the real estate assets are held in entities that are separate from primary operations. We will work with Company's accountants to make sure that any restructuring will be tax efficient (including income taxes and transfer taxes). We will take into account other advantages of restructuring, such as limitation of liability, operational efficiencies, and diversifying ownership opportunities for family members. We also will help make plans for how new ventures will be added to the structure in the future.

5. Current and Future Governance, Ownership, and Exit Mechanisms. Before we consider lifetime transfers of stock or update G1 Owner and G1 Spouse's estate plan with respect to the allocation of stock among their children, we need to determine how Company should be managed currently and in the next generation. This includes four topics, which can be addressed in Company's governing documents and an agreement among the shareholders:

   a. Share Voting—Power to appoint the board and approve major transactions. It may be desirable to create a class of nonvoting shares to make it easier to allocate voting rights among future owners.
      i. Now. For now, G1 Owner controls the voting stock. He needs to designate (consistent with the Business Continuation Plan, above) the person or persons having authority to vote his shares in the event of his death or incapacity.
      ii. Future. For succession planning, the family should consider how the voting shares should be allocated in the next generation. In some cases, voting shares can be held in trust, to be voted by a fiduciary or a committee of fiduciaries. Company's governing documents can enlarge or otherwise redefine shareholder voting powers.

   b. Board of Directors—Power to appoint and remove top executives and determine their compensation; power to issue dividends; and power to oversee budgets and long-range business planning, risk management, and strategic planning.
      i. Now. G1 Owner and G1 Spouse are the sole directors, but they have indicated an interest in establishing an independent presence on

Company's board. This could have many advantages, including benefits to current operations, opportunity for next generation leaders to learn from a formal board, and governance strength and continuity in the event of a sudden loss of G1 Owner's leadership services. **We can make several suggestions for appropriate candidates. Also, we will provide some examples of a Board Matrix, which will help Company to identify an appropriate mix of talents to be present on the board.**

    ii. <u>Future</u>. For succession planning, the family should consider how the board should be composed and elected after G1 Owner and G1 Spouse cease to be involved. For example, it may be desirable to "classify" the board so that each substantial shareholder can have one or two seats on the board. Company governing documents can enlarge, restrict, or otherwise redefine board authority.

  c. <u>Executive Authority</u>—Power and responsibility to run the day-to-day business, hire and terminate staff, and develop budgets and plans for approval by the board of directors; power to sign checks and contracts, including loan agreements (within limits set by the board).

    i. <u>Current</u>. It is anticipated that G1 Owner will continue to serve as CEO until he retires, phases out, or is unable to serve. Company continues to utilize the services of a non-family CFO and is working toward some redundancy or technical backup for that position. As long as G1 Owner is involved in company management, he can determine hiring, advancement, and compensation of family members. Any special relationships between Company and particular family members should be memorialized if they are to be continued/honored even after G1 Owner and G1 Spouse are no longer with Company (a point which is also addressed in the Business Continuation section, above). **We will prepare resolutions to formalize appointments of officers and executives to make sure that the Company record book is up to date.**

    ii. <u>Future</u>. For succession planning, the family should decide upon rules that apply to family member employment in Company. If Company's board of directors includes independent directors, then Company can rely on a committee of the independent directors to make decisions about family-member employment, advancement, and compensation, consistent with the rules that the family drafts and agrees upon while G1 Owner and G1 Spouse are able to assist and guide them. It would be impossible to make decisions now about which family members will be assigned to particular leadership posts in the future; instead, Company's governing documents should be updated to create systems for addressing family employment in an equitable manner.

  d. <u>Share Ownership</u>—Gives the owner the right to receive profits and appreciation from business operations. (Note: If the shareholders are also key employees, they may receive most of their annual economic return in the form of compensation.) The key questions are whether non-employee family members should own stock and whether stock should be held in trust (primarily to protect it from estate taxes, divorce of a shareholder, and claims of creditors).

    i. <u>Now</u>. G1 Owner owns all the stock. We can help Company split its stock into voting and nonvoting shares (1:99). G1 Owner and G1 Spouse are considering whether they should begin making gifts of nonvoting shares, primarily to give their children an even greater sense of engagement with the family business. (G1 Owner and G1 Spouse should consider making these gifts in trust, as discussed below in the section on "Lifetime Transfers.")

    ii. <u>Future</u>. For succession planning, the family should agree on a new shareholders' agreement that will restrict the ownership group and will provide mechanisms for owner exits that are fair to the exiting shareholder but are not disruptive to Company. It is our current understanding that G1 Owner and G1 Spouse would support a rule that requires owners to be active in the company, but only after each of their children has had a full opportunity to make a career choice after completing their advanced education and perhaps working outside Company for a period of years. One important element of the shareholders' agreement will be to establish a mechanism for determining purchase price when family members buy stock or Company redeems a shareholder.

We will review current Articles, Bylaws, and the Shareholders' Agreement to suggest immediate changes and to frame up the discussion for changes that may be desirable for the succession plan.

Although Company's governing documents can provide the legal rules by which Company is governed and operated, the family should draft a family constitution, mission statements, and other policies that will guide decision makers when they apply the legal rules. Company's legal documents cannot express the spirit and philosophy of the family as effectively as the principles that family members write in plain English and agree among one another to uphold. We can provide samples of such documents to assist with these important projects.

6. <u>Key Contracts</u>. We will help Company negotiate restatements of key contracts with third parties that should be (or must be) updated to be more consistent with business restructuring and anticipated changes of control or ownership. Such contracts include loan facilities and franchise/dealership agreements. The extent to which such contracts cannot be changed may affect decisions about how or when to implement other elements of the business succession plan.

The family should also consider whether written contracts for related-party transactions would make the succession plan more effective. Such contracts may include the following: leases between the operating business and family-owned entities that hold real estate or equipment used by the operating business; debt instruments for loans from owners to the business; reimbursement/contribution agreements among the business and the owners who have personally guaranteed business debt; and employment agreements for family members who work for the business.

7. <u>Update G1 Owner and G1 Spouse's Estate Plan</u>. After the family has reached consensus on future ownership and governance structures, we can update G1

Owner and G1 Spouse's estate plan to be consistent with such structures. In particular, we should consider whether Company stock should be held in trust for family members who own stock, to protect ownership and keep it in the family. Under recent changes to Wisconsin trust laws, it would be possible to hold each child's stock in trust, but allow the child to vote the stock as though he or she owned it outright.

8. Plan for G1 Owner and G1 Spouse's Resources in Retirement. Before we work on more substantial transfers of stock from G1 Owner and G1 Spouse to the children (or trusts for them), we should determine G1 Owner and G1 Spouse's needs in retirement and make sure that mechanisms are put in place to address those needs (preferably without regard to the success of Company after G1 Owner has retired or transferred his or her ownership to the next generation). This will require the assistance of G1 Owner and G1 Spouse's financial advisors.

9. Consider Lifetime Transfers to the Next Generation (by gift or sale). After we understand how Company would be owned and governed by the next generation and after we are sure that G1 Owner and G1 Spouse will be secure in their retirement, we can consider the possibility of more immediate transfers of stock to the next generation (by gift or sale), to reduce the potential estate tax burden that might otherwise be imposed on the value of the stock when G1 Owner and G1 Spouse die. In addition, each time a new investment or growth opportunity arises for Company or the family, such as development of real estate, we should consider whether the venture should be owned by the children to keep future income and appreciation out of G1 Owner and G1 Spouse's taxable estate.

SCHEDULE A
Request for Documents and Information
for Business Succession Panning.

Please provide us with access to or electronic copies of the following:

a. **Key Individuals and Entities.**
    i. Key advisors, with contact information, including accountants, investment advisors, insurance advisors, business valuation or asset appraisal professionals; and other important financial service providers, such as primary banking relationship, corporate trustees, or outsourced retirement plan administrator.
    ii. Family tree, showing the business owners and their offspring.
    iii. Organizational chart showing the entities that constitute the family business, including how each business is taxed (e.g., C corporation, S corporation, partnership).
    iv. Governing board members and key executives, such as general counsel, CFO, controller, and family member employees.

b. **Business Governing Documents.** For each business entity, the following documents (including amendments):
    i. Articles of Incorporation/Organization
    ii. Bylaws
    iii. Shareholders' Agreement/Operating Agreement
    iv. Voting Agreements or Voting Trusts
    v. Table of current ownership

c. **Related-Party Contracts.**
    i. Leases or other agreements between one family business entity and any other family business entity
    ii. Employment contracts with family members
    iii. Any deferred compensation or other nonqualified retirement benefit contract between the business and a family member
    iv. Any personal guaranties of business debt (and related business loan facilities)

d. **Estate-Planning Documents.** For the owners, the following documents:
    i. Wills
    ii. Revocable Trust or Trusts
    iii. Irrevocable Trust or Trusts (if any) (whether they are the grantors or the beneficiaries)
    iv. Marital Property Agreement (if any)
    v. Powers of Attorney for Health Care
    vi. Powers of Attorney for Financial Matters
    vii. Estate-Planning Flowchart (if any)
    viii. Most recent gift tax returns

e.   **Business/Asset Valuation.**
    i.   Most recent formal or informal valuation of the business or its component companies
    ii. Most recent indication of value of business or farm real estate (and statement of balance of any mortgage debt)
    iii. All loan facilities for substantial business debt and related security

f.   **Owner Financials.**
    i.   Statement of assets and liabilities (including face values of any life insurance)
    ii. Summaries of retirement plan assets and benefits, including social security, deferred comp, and any pensions for owners
    iii. All contracts of insurance on the lives of owners including policy owner, beneficiary designations, pledges or assignments, and in force illustrations

g.   **Family Governance Documents.**
    i.   Family Constitution, family mission statement, family employment policy, family council charter
    ii. Family (charitable) foundation documents, donor-advised fund account statements, or other collective charitable giving information

Appendix B

FAMILY BUSINESS
SUCCESSION PLANNING

CHECKLIST FOR TASKS AND DOCUMENTS
[DATE]

DEFINITIONS

Business Entities

[Identified and Defined]

Family

[Identified and Defined]

Trusts

[Identified and Defined]

Ref. No.	DOCUMENT	DOC. #	DRAFTER/ SOURCE	STATUS	REQUIRED SIGNATURES		EFF. DATE
A.	COMMENCE ENGAGEMENT						
1.							
2.							
3.							
4.							
5.							
B.	BUSINESS VALUE						
1.							
2.							
3.							
C.	BUSINESS CONTINUATION PLAN						
1.							
2.							
3.							
4.							
5.							
D.	BUSINESS RESTRUCTURING						
1.							
2.							
3.							
4.							
5.							
E.	BUSINESS GOVERNANCE AND OWNERSHIP						
1.							
2.							
3.							
4.							
5.							
F.	KEY CONTRACTS						
1.							
2.							
3.							
4.							
5.							

Ref. No.	DOCUMENT	DOC. #	DRAFTER/ SOURCE	STATUS	REQUIRED SIGNATURES	EFF. DATE
G.	SENIOR OWNER ESTATE PLANNING					
1.						
2.						
3.						
4.						
5.						
H.	SENIOR OWNER RETIREMENT AND EXIT PLANNING					
1.						
2.						
3.						
4.						
5.						
I.	LIFETIME WEALTH TRANSFERS					
1.						
2.						
3.						
4.						
5.						

Appendix C

BUSINESS CONTINUATION PLAN WORKSHEET
[DATE]

Many family businesses are run by a principal shareholder or member who is also the chief executive officer and chairman of the board of directors or the sole director or manager (the "Principal"). Upon the loss of the Principal, if the business does not have a comprehensive succession plan, the Principal's beneficiaries and the other shareholders may lose the value of their interests in the business while they try to establish new governance structures and ownership agreements.

A Business Continuation Plan can be a first step toward creation of a comprehensive succession plan and can help preserve business value if the Principal dies or becomes disabled before the business is ready for leadership and ownership transitions. A Business Continuation Plan can be implemented immediately upon the loss of the Principal, to enable the business to continue profitable operations with temporary management procedures until the owners settle on a more permanent succession arrangement.

The purpose of this Worksheet is to help develop a written Business Continuation Plan and guide the planning process.

1. THE PROBLEM

When a family business relies heavily on the leadership of one primary individual, the unplanned exit of that individual can be disruptive to the business, which can lead to a loss of value and discord among family members. These effects can exacerbate each other, with family frustrations mounting as business problems increase, and vice versa. Even the most well-intentioned family members may strongly disagree on how to proceed in such a crisis.

2. THE SOLUTION

A comprehensive Business Continuation Plan can help the business to continue profitable operations and maintain its value following the death or disability of the Principal until the family can agree upon a more permanent succession arrangement, whether that is a period of several months or several years.

In form, a Business Continuation Plan will consist of a master plan, with schedules and supplements that are updated from time to time. In addition, the Business Continuation Plan will require updates to the business's governing documents and the Principal's estate plan. The planning process might also identify contracts that should be changed or renegotiated to allow successful implementation of the Business Continuation Plan.

The process of creating a Business Continuation Plan also will identify many of the issues the family will need to discuss to create a comprehensive business succession plan.

3. CORPORATE/ENTITY STRUCTURE AND OWNERSHIP

To begin the process of business continuation planning, it is necessary to fully understand the current corporate/entity structure and ownership. Many businesses have a multi-tiered organizational structure involving a parent company and one or more subsidiaries and affiliates. Some parts of the business, such as real estate or distributorships, may be held by the same owners in an entity that is completely separate from principal business operations.

One key to business continuation planning is providing for the smooth and immediate transition of the business's voting control (see below). This cannot be done without a clear understanding of who has control of each entity in the business. Therefore, the Business Continuation Plan should begin with a description of the corporate/entity structure and ownership. If the structure is particularly complex, an illustration may be attached to the Business Continuation Plan as an exhibit.

4. VOTING CONTROL

Voting control of a company is primarily the authority to elect directors (or appoint managers, if the company is a manager-managed LLC), amend governing documents, and approve a sale, merger, or other disposition or restructuring of the business. If the Principal dies or is rendered mentally incapacitated (for purposes of this Worksheet, "disabled"), someone will need to vote the Principal's shares immediately to replace the Principal on the company's board of directors so that the board can act as may be necessary to replace the Principal in all of his/her other management positions within the business. If the business consists of multiple companies, voting control may be allocated differently at the different companies, so transition of voting control must be addressed separately for each company.

The Business Continuation Plan should identify who will succeed to the Principal's right to vote the controlling interests in each Company immediately after the Principal's death or disability and over the longer term, and how those voting rights will pass to such persons. For a business consisting of multiple companies, an illustration of who will succeed to voting control of each company may be attached to the Business Continuation Plan as an exhibit. The Principal's estate-planning documents may need to be amended to accomplish this element of the Business Continuation Plan.

(a) Upon Disability

Who has authority to vote the Principal's shares of company stock if the Principal is mentally incapacitated by reason of an accident or health event?

The Principal can execute a durable power of attorney (<u>POA</u>) that would grant an agent authority to vote the Principal's stock in the company if the Principal were to be disabled. The POA should name a primary and secondary agent and should be fairly easy to activate (or should be effective even without a determination of disability). In the alternative, if the stock is held in a revocable trust for estate-planning purposes, the successor trustees will be able to vote the stock in the event of the Principal's disability.

(b) Upon Death

1. Who has authority to vote the Principal's shares of company stock immediately after the Principal's death?

If the Principal holds the shares of stock in his/her own name, steps should be taken to ensure that someone will be able to vote the shares immediately upon the Principal's death. If the centerpiece of the Principal's estate plan is a revocable trust (which, in most cases, it should be), the shares can be titled to the revocable trust so that the successor trustee can vote them immediately upon the Principal's death. If the stock cannot be titled to the revocable trust during the Principal's lifetime—for example, due to transfer restrictions in a buy-sell agreement—then perhaps the revocable trust can be named as the TOD (transfer-on-death) beneficiary, which allows assets like stock to pass at death by operation of law and free of probate.[1] The revocable trust agreement can provide special instructions regarding which trustees are allowed to vote the stock and how the stock is to be voted in the immediate aftermath of the Principal's death (e.g., who should be elected to replace the Principal on the board).

2. Who should eventually succeed to voting control of the company after the Principal's death?

It is possible to separate voting rights from the beneficial or economic ownership of a company's stock, such as through a voting trust or by splitting the company's stock into voting and nonvoting shares. Therefore, it is possible to give voting control to the person or persons best suited to exercise that control without compromising the Principal's wishes about who should receive the economic benefit of owning the business. (See the section on "Beneficial Ownership" below.)

5.   BOARD OF DIRECTORS/MANAGERS

In some cases, a company's board of directors may continue to function effectively after the loss of the Principal. Many companies' bylaws allow the remaining directors to appoint another director to replace the Principal on the board. In some cases, however, the Principal may be the only director, or the loss of the Principal may create a schism on the board or even a deadlock. The Business Continuation Plan should identify who will replace the Principal as a director and how that will be accomplished immediately after the Principal's death or disability. If the Principal is the only director, the Business Continuation Plan should provide for election of a full board immediately upon the death or disability of the Principal. The Business Continuation Plan should contain analogous provisions for companies that are LLCs.

---

1. *See, e.g.,* WIS. STAT. § 705.21–30.

(a) Corporations

1. How should the company's board currently be constituted? Should the company have outside directors or an advisory board?

A board may function effectively without outside directors as long as the Principal is involved, but outside directors can be essential to successful business continuation after the Principal's death or disability. Outside directors bring knowledge and experience about business or the industry that the Principal's beneficiaries may not possess; they can provide valuable business contacts or credibility for the company in the business community; and they can be neutral parties who can resolve disputes involving the company among the Principal's beneficiaries. The question is whether to appoint outside directors to the company's board before the death or disability of the Principal or provide for outside directors to assume their roles only after the loss of the Principal.

Outside directors will function best in the aftermath of the Principal's death or disability if they become familiar with the business while the Principal is still involved. However, outside directors will have fiduciary duties to the company and the shareholders, including minority shareholders, which may put them at odds with the Principal or expose them to liability if they defer to the Principal too much. Further, outside directors may require the company to purchase D&O liability insurance to protect them from personal liability for their decisions. For these reasons, the Principal may find that the presence of outside directors on the company's board may be too restrictive on the Principal's leadership style and entrepreneurial instincts.

An alternative to appointing outside directors to the board while the Principal is managing the business is to establish an advisory board. Members of an advisory board will not have the liability exposure that directors would have and will not have authority to obstruct the Principal's activity. However, they will be in a position to learn about the business in advance so that they will be prepared to assume the role of director immediately upon the Principal's death or disability. In the meantime, they can benefit the Principal and the company with their knowledge and experience and their business contacts and credibility.

2. How should the board be constituted immediately after the death or disability of the Principal? How will the new directors be appointed or elected?

If the only vacancy on the board after the loss of the Principal will be the Principal's seat, the bylaws should allow the other directors to fill the vacancy, and the board should agree in advance who will be appointed to that seat. If a whole set of outside directors or a whole board will need to be appointed or elected, the Business Continuation Plan should identify the new directors and how they will assume their roles. For example, there may be a mechanism by which the advisory board members become directors immediately upon confirmation of the Principal's death or disability. The bylaws should be amended accordingly.

3. Who should serve as chairperson of the board if the Principal ceases to serve?

The Business Continuation Plan should designate the successor chairperson so that the board has leadership immediately upon the loss of the Principal. Some boards operate with a "vice chair" who will always lead the board when the chairperson is unavailable and will succeed to the position of chairperson if the board loses its chairperson unexpectedly.

4. How does the board make a determination that the Principal has been mentally incapacitated?

What is the standard of disability? "Disability" should be defined consistently across a company's governing instruments and contracts.

Who makes the decision that the Principal is disabled? It may be necessary for the Principal to give one or more of the other directors (or advisory board members) a limited HIPAA release for the purpose of determining whether the Principal is mentally incapacitated after an accident or serious health event.

5. What special rules will apply to board procedure immediately after the loss of the Principal?

Who can call an emergency meeting of the board? What notice rules apply? Is there a lesser requirement for quorum or board action? (See also the section on "Leadership Crisis Plan" below.) The Business Continuation Plan should set forth these rules, and emergency bylaws or procedures should be adopted.

(b) LLCs

1. How should management be constituted currently?

Most likely, the Principal serves as sole manager of any LLCs involved in the business. It is possible, however, to replicate *corporate* governance structure in an LLC by installing a board of managers that serves the function of a board of directors and appoints officers to run the day-to-day operations of the company. In the alternative (as discussed in the section on "Corporations" above), the company may have a board of advisors while the Principal is serving as manager.

2. How should management be constituted after the Principal's death or disability?

Should the company have a board of managers after the loss of the principal? If the company is one of a family of companies, it may be most efficient to have the parent company or the operating company serve as manager of all the subsidiaries and affiliates. This would allow the board of the company serving as manager to have effective, unified control of all the companies. If the various companies do not have identical ownership, it may be helpful to work out the terms of a management agreement between the managing company and the affiliated companies in advance of the loss of the Principal.

The Business Continuation Plan should identify the successor managers or members of the board of managers and provide the means for them to assume their roles immediately upon the loss of the Principal. The company's operating agreement should be amended as needed to accommodate the plans for management succession.

6.   OFFICERS/EXECUTIVES

If the Principal is serving as chief executive officer or president, the Business Continuation Plan should provide for the immediate appointment of a successor upon the loss of the Principal. (See the section on "Leadership Crisis Plan" below.) The Business Continuation Plan should also provide guidance for retention of other key executives.

(a) CEO/President

1. If the Principal dies or is disabled, who should succeed him/her as CEO/president, and how should his/her successor be appointed?

When a company loses its chief executive, almost any delay in appointing a successor can harm the company. Empirical research demonstrates a clear correlation between the length of time it takes to appoint a successor and the amount of the resulting decline in the company's profitability and value.[2] It typically takes companies a couple of years to recover,[3] but sometimes the damage can be irreparable, such as when the chief executive is the company's founder or has unique expertise, or when the loss occurs during a key transaction or leads to acceleration of debt.

The Business Continuation Plan should identify the successor chief executive of every company in the business and the means of appointing the successor immediately upon the loss of the Principal.

2. What will the successor's compensation be?

It is likely that the Principal is not compensated at a market rate for his/her services as chief executive (because of the value the Principal realizes through ownership), and therefore it should not be presumed that his/her successor will be willing to serve for the same compensation. Further, if the successor owners intend to sell the business, the successor chief executive may be concerned about the short-term nature of the position and may wish to take a more permanent opportunity elsewhere. In the event of the death or disability of the Principal, business operations cannot be suspended for several weeks while the new board investigates the market and then tries to negotiate an acceptable compensation package with a successor chief executive. The Business Continuation Plan should provide guidance as to compensation for the successor chief executive and stay incentives/deal bonuses that may be needed to appoint the designated successor and retain him/her through the sale of the business. (See also the section on "Cash Needs" below.) During the planning process, it may be helpful to consult with an executive search firm or a compensation consultant.

---

2. Bruce K. Behn, David D. Dawley, Richard Riley & Ya-wen Yang, *Deaths of CEOs: Are Delays in Naming Successors and Insider/Outsider Succession Associated with Subsequent Firm Performance?*, 18 J. Managerial Issues 32 (Spring 2006).

  3. *Id.*

(b) Other Executives

What other executives need to be retained upon the loss of the Principal, and what stay incentives may be appropriate?

Upon the loss of the Principal, other key executives may view their positions as insecure and may begin to seek other opportunities. The Business Continuation Plan should identify those executives who are the most important to retain and provide guidance as to stay incentives and deal bonuses for a successful sale of the business. (See also the section on "Cash Needs" below.) During the planning process, it may be helpful to consult with an executive search firm or a compensation consultant. Noncompetition agreements signed by executives while the Principal is managing the business also may make it easier to retain them after the Principal's death or disability.

7.   CONTRACTS/OPEN TRANSACTIONS

The loss of the Principal may have adverse consequences for the business under express or implied terms of loan facilities and other contracts. The Business Continuation Plan should identify those contracts and provide guidance as to how the adverse consequences can be avoided or mitigated. Whenever practical, such contract terms should be renegotiated to allow a transition of leadership or change of control.

(a) Contracts/Transactions with Third Parties

1. Would the Principal's death or disability cause acceleration of any debt obligations or complications arising out of personal guarantees?

Loan facilities should be reviewed to determine the effect, if any, that the Principal's death or disability would have on the terms of loans and lines of credit. Does the Principal's death or disability violate loan covenants, or could a decline in profitability after the Principal's death violate loan covenants? Has the Principal personally guaranteed any debt of the business, and what is the effect of the Principal's death with regard to that personal guaranty? Could lenders refuse to allow the business to draw on lines of credit if the Principal is no longer available to personally guarantee them? The answers to these questions may affect the liquidity needed upon the Principal's death or disability or may call for renegotiation of loan agreements. (See also the section on "Cash Needs" below.) The business may discover that it would be unable to access credit lines upon the loss of the Principal, when the additional liquidity will be especially important. The Business Continuation Plan should identify such issues and provide guidance as to how to address them if they cannot be resolved before the loss of the Principal.

2. Would the Principal's death or disability affect other contracts as a "material adverse condition" or constitute a triggering event as a "change of control"?

Other contracts with third parties should be reviewed to determine the effect of the Principal's death or disability. Some effects may be obvious from the express terms of the contract. Others may depend on the construction of contract terms, such as "material adverse condition" or "change of control." Some contracts may not terminate due to the loss of the Principal but may be harder to renew or extend if the Principal is no longer managing the business. The Business Continuation Plan should identify such issues and provide guidance on how to address them if they cannot be resolved before the loss of the Principal.

3. Would the Principal's death or disability adversely affect pending negotiations/transactions?

Parties negotiating with the business for joint ventures, supply or distribution contracts, exclusive rights to intellectual property, acquisitions on credit, and similar transactions may consider the loss of the Principal to be a material adverse condition that would terminate the negotiations. The existence of a Business Continuation Plan and a system for the effective transition of leadership upon the loss of the Principal may allow such transactions to proceed on the terms originally contemplated.

(b) Intercompany or Insider Contracts/Transactions

Should insider transactions or relationships between affiliated companies be formalized in written contracts to avoid disputes after the loss of the Principal?

While the Principal is managing the business, transactions between family members and the business or between related companies in the business are often handled informally because the Principal acts as the final arbiter of what is fair or appropriate. However, after the Principal's death or disability, such informal arrangements may become sources of conflict or dispute among the beneficiaries. During the process of developing a Business Continuation Plan, such informal arrangements should be reviewed and formalized in written contracts so that they can be continued after the loss of the Principal.

8. NOTICE

The loss of the Principal may cause concern among parties who have an economic relationship with the business, such as employees, investors, creditors, vendors, and customers. Such constituents are less likely to act on their concerns to the detriment of the business if the business promptly notifies them of the loss and assures them that there is an effective plan in place for leadership transition. (See the section on "Leadership Crisis Plan" below.)

1. Who should receive prompt notice of the Principal's death or disability and the resulting change in leadership?

The business should keep a current list of all parties who should receive prompt notice of the loss of the Principal. The Business Continuation Plan should include guidance as to the content of that notice and how it should be delivered, including press releases.

2. Who should be responsible for controlling communications about the Principal's death or disability?

The notice procedure set forth in the Business Continuation Plan should identify one person or a small team of individuals to control communications regarding the Principal's death or disability and the corresponding transition of leadership. These "communications coordinators" should control the content of all such communications. All inquiries regarding the Principal's death or disability or the transition of leadership should be referred to the communications coordinators.

9. CASH NEEDS

The Principal's death or disability might give rise to immediate liquidity needs for the business or for the Principal's family or estate. The Business Continuation Plan should identify those needs and provide the means to address them.

(a) Business

1. What cash needs would the business have upon the Principal's death or disability?

Would the Principal's death or disability cause an impairment of contracts that would give rise to cash needs, such as accelerations of debt or reductions of credit lines? (See the section on "Contracts/Open Transactions" above.) Would the business's expenses increase because of, for example, increases in fees for professional advice or compensation for the Principal's replacement as chief executive? Does the business need to be in a position to pay bonuses or stay incentives to key employees (see the section on "Officers/Executives" above) or to pay down amounts due to vendors who are reluctant to ship? Could revenues drop enough to create liquidity problems? Would the business need cash to pay a Principal disability or retirement benefits or to help the Principal's family pay estate taxes, such as through dividends or partial redemptions? The Business Continuation Plan should include a schedule of all such additional cash needs.

2. How can the business obtain the needed cash upon the Principal's death or disability?

Does the business have appropriate levels of life or disability insurance on the Principal? Does the business have sufficient lines of credit to cover increased cash needs in the immediate aftermath of the Principal's death or disability? Does the business have any assets that could be sold to generate cash? Should the Principal's fiduciaries and beneficiaries be advised to (or not to) contribute or loan funds to the business? The Business Continuation Plan should identify the sources of liquidity that will be available to meet the business's additional cash needs upon the loss of the Principal. If those sources of liquidity are insufficient, the business will need to make additional arrangements.

(b) Principal's Family/Estate

1. What cash needs would the Principal have upon his or her disability, or what cash needs would the Principal's family or estate have upon his or her death, and how would those cash needs affect the business?

Would the business have to increase dividends to meet the Principal's cash needs if he or she were disabled or to meet the Principal's family's cash needs if he or she died? Would the Principal or his/her family need to find a replacement for the Principal's earned income? Does the Principal have appropriate levels of disability insurance or life insurance? Are there assets that the Principal or his or her family could liquidate to replace income lost by reason of the Principal's death or disability? If the Principal or his or her family would need to draw cash out of the business as a result of the Principal's death or disability, the Business Continuation Plan should take that into account and should try to identify alternative sources of cash.

2. Would the business need to contribute toward payment of estate taxes upon the Principal's death?

Federal estate taxes will be due within nine months after the Principal's death, unless the Principal leaves a surviving spouse (and thus defers estate taxes until after the spouse's death). The amount of the estate taxes will be roughly 40 percent of the value of the Principal's net worth in excess of the first $5.45 million. The Principal's family almost certainly will require assistance from the business to timely pay the estate taxes. The Business Continuation Plan should identify the amount of assistance the family would need for payment of estate taxes and what form that assistance would take.

Would the business have to increase dividends or redeem some of the Principal's stock to pay estate taxes? Would the business have to lend money to the estate or allow the family to use its stock or assets as security for a loan from a third party? Would estate taxes on the value of the business qualify for deferred payment under Internal Revenue Code Section 6166 (i.e., interest only for the first five years, and then payment of the tax in ten annual installments), which could result in a tax lien on the business? Are there assets that could be sold to the business to generate cash?

The Principal should be encouraged to engage in active estate tax planning and to establish means of paying the estate tax that are less reliant on the business. For example, is there sufficient life insurance on the Principal to contribute toward payment of estate taxes? Are there assets other than the business that the Principal's fiduciaries could liquidate to generate cash for payment of estate taxes? Are there ways of transferring wealth from the Principal to his or her beneficiaries during lifetime that will not be subject to transfer taxes?

10. LEADERSHIP CRISIS PLAN

The business should have a coordinated, written "Leadership Crisis Plan" that instructs employees, officers, the boards, and the fiduciaries voting the Principal's stock how to promptly implement the initial stages of the Business Continuation Plan. The contents of the Leadership Crisis Plan will cover many of the issues raised in this Worksheet. Portions of the Leadership Crisis Plan will be incorporated into other documents of the business, such as bylaws, employment contracts, and policies and procedures manuals.

11. BENEFICIAL OWNERSHIP

Transfer of the beneficial ownership of the business can be separated from transfer of the voting rights. (See the section on "Voting Control," above.) Transfer of the beneficial ownership of the business will be controlled by the Principal's estate plan.

(a) Allocation

Who should receive beneficial ownership of the business after the Principal has died?

The Business Continuation Plan should be consistent with the Principal's estate plan.

(b) Long-Term Ownership Rights

What ownership rights and restrictions should apply to ownership of the business after the Principal's death?

The business will operate more smoothly if management and ownership after the Principal's death are controlled by shareholders' agreements, buy-sell agreements, and operating agreements that are established while the Principal is alive. For example, transfer restrictions can ensure that the business stays in the family until it can be sold, and drag-along provisions can ensure that a minority owner cannot veto the sale of the business. Other questions that can be addressed by such agreements are: Should the beneficiaries have an exit strategy that does not require sale of the entire business? How will the rights of employee-owners differ from those of owners who are not involved in the business? Who can decide when to sell the business? The Business Continuation Plan should identify those ownership rights and restrictions that apply to the owners of the business after the Principal's death, and the governing documents of the business should be amended accordingly.

12. SALE OF THE BUSINESS

It is possible that the Principal's beneficiaries will want to sell the business sometime after Principal's death if they can get the right purchase price and appropriate terms of sale (e.g., minimal seller financing). The Business Continuation Plan should make sure that the business is positioned to pursue the beneficiaries' most likely exit strategies.

(a) Existing Markets

1. What is the most likely market for the business?

The Principal should keep a list of potential buyers and provide written guidance regarding value of the business and prevailing market trends. The Principal should identify advisors and consultants who would best be able to help market the business and evaluate offers.

2. How can the business be best positioned for sale to the most likely buyers?

Are there measures that the business can implement during the Principal's lifetime that will better position it to be sold after the Principal's death?

(b) New Markets

Can the business create its own markets for purchase of the business?

Should the business be positioned to sell to inside markets, such as a management group or an ESOP? If yes, the Business Continuation Plan should include and facilitate implementation of a plan to successfully carry out such insider transactions.

13. CONCLUSION

After the issues set forth above have been thoroughly reviewed and considered, a Business Continuation Plan can be drafted and adopted to help ensure that the family business can continue profitable operations after the loss of the Principal until the family can agree on (and implement) a more permanent leadership and ownership succession plan.

Index

About the Author

Gregory Monday is a shareholder with law firm of Reinhart Boerner Van Deuren s.c., in Madison, Wisconsin. His practice focuses on helping family businesses with respect to ownership, governance, and succession. He received his law degree in 1993 from the University of Wisconsin Law School, where he has also taught as an adjunct professor. He is a member of the State Bar of Wisconsin and the American Bar Association, and he is a fellow with the American College of Trust and Estate Counsel. His articles about family businesses have been published in periodicals including *Business Law Today*, *Corporate Secretary*, *Trusts & Estates*, *Estate Planning*, and *Family Business Magazine*. He also writes weekly posts for his blog, *Monday's Family Business Law* (www.mondaybusinesslaw.com). For more information about Mr. Monday or to correspond with him, please visit www.reinhartlaw.com/people/gregory-monday/.